W9-BYB-644

Hebrew
phrase book

Berlitz Publishing / APA Publications GmbH & Co.
Verlag KG, Singapore Branch, Singapore

Layout: Media Marketing, Inc.
Cover photo: ©Digital Vision/Getty images

Printed in Singapore

Contents

Pronunciation

This section is designed to familiarize you with the sounds of Hebrew, using our simplified phonetic transcription. The pronunciation of the Hebrew letters and sounds is explained below, together with their "imitated" equivalents. This system is used throughout the phrase book. When you see a word spelled phonetically, simply read the pronunciation as if it were English, noting any special rules.

The Hebrew language

Hebrew is the ancient language of the Old Testament, and is now spoken by the overwhelming majority of Israelis. Hebrew script is descended from Phoenician, which also gave rise to the Greek and ultimately the Roman and Cyrillic alphabets. With a lot of patience and persistence it is just possible to make out the similarities with English letters. Even the names of Hebrew letters derive from their original pictorial meanings: **alef** and **bet** (which gave us the word "alphabet," via Greek) are, respectively, a bull's head and a house. The Hebrew language developed throughout Biblical and early Medieval times but remained fixed thereafter until the late 19th century.

During the intervening period, Hebrew was used solely for ritual and scholarly purposes, and played no part in ordinary daily life. Hebrew is thus the only language of antiquity to have been truly resurrected after lying dormant for many centuries.

Modern Hebrew has uniform rules of grammar and pronunciation, though its vocabulary is eclectic and draws on the Bible, on the Medieval languages of the Mediterranean, and on modern international scientific terminology. There is relatively little in the way of regional dialect, but Hebrew speakers or their ancestors may have brought with them from other countries special words for cultural specialties, such as food, dress, and social customs.

Speakers of Hebrew from a Middle Eastern background tend to stress the guttural sound of some letters more than those of European descent. The Middle Eastern pronunciation is supposed to be the authentic ancient pronunciation.

The Hebrew alphabet is written from *right to left*. Below you will find the sounds of the Hebrew language explained. The *j* and *zh* sounds have been introduced to cope with words of foreign origin.

Consonants

Letter	Approximate pronunciation	Symbol	Example	Phonetics
ב	*b* as in *b*at,	b	בית	<u>ba</u>yit
	or *v* as is *v*alley	v	עבר	a<u>var</u>
ג	*g* as in *g*ate	g	גן	gan
ג׳	hard *j* as in *j*eans	j	ג׳ינס	jins
ד	*d* as in *d*oor	d	דלת	<u>del</u>et
ה	*h* as in *h*ave	h	הר	har
ו	*v* as in *v*alley	v	וריד	va<u>rid</u>
ז	*z* as in *z*ebra	z	זית	<u>zay</u>it
ז׳	soft *je* as in beige	zh	ז׳קט	zha<u>ket</u>
ח	*ch* as in Scottish lo*ch*	kh	חמש	kha<u>mesh</u>
ט	*t* as in *t*ea	t	טלפון	<u>te</u>lefon
י	*y* as in *y*et	y	יפה	<u>ya</u>fe
כ	*k* as in *k*ing,	k	כן	ken
	or *ch* as in Scottish lo*ch*	kh	יכול	ya<u>khol</u>
ל	*l* as in *l*ip	l	לא	lo
מ	*m* as in *m*other	m	מלון	ma<u>lon</u>
נ	*n* as in *n*ever	n	נייר	ne<u>yar</u>
ס	*s* as in *s*un	s	ספר	<u>se</u>fer
פ	*p* as in *p*ot,	p	פרח	<u>pe</u>rakh
	or *f* as in *f*an	f	ספל	<u>se</u>fel
צ	hard *ts* as in po*ts*	tz	צמיג	tza<u>mig</u>
ק	*k* as in *k*ing	k	קפה	<u>ka</u>fe
ר	*r* as in *r*ain	r	ראש	rosh
ש	*sh* as in *sh*ine,	sh	שמש	<u>she</u>mesh
	or *s* as in *s*un	s	שדה	<u>sa</u>de
ת	*t* as in *t*ea	t	תרמיל	tar<u>mil</u>

Vowels

Strictly speaking, there are no vowels in unpointed Hebrew script (without the dots), and this is the script you'll see in this book. So you will find many words that appear to be made up of nothing but consonants. Even those letters that are technically semi-vowels – **alef** (א), **ayin** (ע), **heh** (ה) – are usually meant to be pronounced, effectively as guttural consonants.

Nevertheless, these letters are often silent and/or serve as vowels, mostly at the beginning or the end of words. In addition, **vav** (ו) and **yod** (י) are proper consonants that are frequently used as vowels in order to aid pronunciation.

Hebrew vowels tend to be short and flat, and rather more uniform than in English.

Letter	Approximate pronunciation	Symbol	Example	Phonetics
א	*a* as in f*a*r,	a	ארון	ar<u>o</u>n
	or *e* as in g*e*t,	e	ארץ	<u>e</u>retz
	or *o* as in p*o*t	o	ראש	rosh
ה	*a* as in f*a*r,	a	גבינה	gv<u>i</u>na
	or *e* as in g*e*t	e	הרבה	harb<u>e</u>
ו	*o* as in h*o*t,	o	גדול	gad<u>o</u>l
	or *u* as in f*u*ll	u	זוג	zug
י	*i* as in t*i*n	i	שמיכה	smi<u>kha</u>
ע	*a* as in f*a*r,	a	מרובע	merub<u>a</u>
	or *e* as in g*e*t	e	ערך	<u>e</u>rekh

Stress

In Hebrew the stress tends to fall on syllables with long vowels, otherwise usually on the last syllable. Stressed syllables are underlined in the pronunciation.

The Hebrew alphabet and script

Hebrew is written from right to left (except numbers
➤ 216). The alphabet consists of letters, just like English,
which are meant to remain separate, even in handwriting
(though that's not always the case). Five letters take on a slightly
different form at the end of a word, four of them by having a long
downstroke. These are:

kaf (כ, ך)

mem (מ, ם)

nun (נ, ן)

pe (פ, ף)

tzadi (צ, ץ)

<u>a</u>lef	א		<u>la</u>med	ל
bet	ב		mem	מ
<u>gi</u>mel	ג		nun	נ
<u>da</u>let	ד		<u>sa</u>mekh	ס
heh	ה		<u>a</u>yin	ע
vav	ו		pe	פ
<u>za</u>yin	ז		<u>tza</u>di	צ
khet	ח		kof	ק
tet	ט		resh	ר
yod	י		shin	ש
kaf	כ		tav	ת

Note: There are no capital letters in Hebrew.

Basic Expressions

ESSENTIAL

Yes.	כן.	*ken*
No.	לא.	*lo*
Okay.	בסדר.	*beseder*
Please.	בבקשה.	*bevakasha*
Thank you.	תודה.	*toda*
Thank you very much.	תודה רבה.	*toda raba*

Greetings/Apologies ברכות/התנצלויות

Hello.	שלום.	*shalom*
Good morning.	בוקר טוב.	*boker tov*
Good evening.	ערב טוב.	*erev tov*
Good night.	לילה טוב.	*layla tov*
Good-bye.	להתראות.	*lehitra-ot*
Excuse me!	סליחה!	*slikha!*
Sorry!	סליחה!	*slikha!*
Don't mention it.	אין בעד מה.	*eyn be-ad ma*
Never mind.	אין דבר.	*eyn davar*

MAKING FRIENDS ➤ 118

Communication difficulties
בעיות תקשורת

Do you speak English?	?אתה מדבר [את מדברת] אנגלית *ata medaber [at medaberet] anglit*
I don't speak much Hebrew.	.אני לא מדבר [מדברת] הרבה עברית *ani lo medaber [medaberet] harbe ivrit*
Could you speak more slowly?	?תוכל [תוכלי] לדבר יותר לאט *tukhal [tukhli] ledaber yoter le-at*
Excuse me?/What was that?	?סליחה?/מה זה *slikha/ma ze*
Please write it down.	.בבקשה כתוב [כתבי] את זה *bevakasha ktov [kitvi] et ze*
Can you translate this for me?	?תוכל [תוכלי] לתרגם את זה בשבילי *tukhal [tukhli] letargem et ze bishvili*
What does this/that mean?	?מה זאת אומרת *ma zot omeret*
Please point to the phrase in the book.	בבקשה הראה [הראי] לי את הביטוי .בספר *bevakasha har-e [har-i] li et habituy basefer*
I understand.	.[אני מבין [מבינה *ani mevin [mevina]*
I don't understand.	.[אני לא מבין [מבינה *ani lo mevin [mevina]*
Do you understand?	?[אתה [את] מבין [מבינה *ata [at] mevin [mevina]*

GRAMMAR

Hebrew has a masculine and a feminine form of "you," which means the sentence changes slightly depending on whether you are talking to a man or a woman. In the Basic Expressions section you will find the feminine form in brackets [ ] in the Hebrew column. In the rest of the book, however, only the masculine form is shown (➤ 169 for more details).

– *ze esrim shekel.* (That's twenty shekels.)
– *ani lo mevin [mevina].* (I don't understand.)
– *ze esrim shekel.* (That's twenty shekels.)
– *bevakasha ktov [kitvi] et ze. … aha esrim shekel … hine.* (Please write it down. … Ah, "Twenty shekels." … Here you are.)

Questions שאלות

GRAMMAR

Hebrew questions are simple to form. There are two types:
1. Questions to which the answer is "yes" (**ken**) or "no" (**lo**). These are formed either by simply raising the intonation at the end of a statement or by adding the question word **ha-im**:

shimkha daveed. Your name is David.
shimkha daveed?/ha-im shimkha david? Is your name David?

2. Other questions are formed by using the relevant question word (►12–17):

ma shimkha? What's your name?
matay niftakh hamuze-on? When does the museum open?

Where? איפה?

Where is it?	איפה זה?	eyfo ze
Where are you going?	?לאן אתה [את] הולך [הולכת]	le-an ata [at] holekh [holekhet]
across the road	מעבר לכביש	me-ever lakvish
around the town	מסביב לעיר	misaviv la-ir
at the meeting place [point]	בנקודת המפגש	binkudat hamifgash
far from here	רחוק מפה	rakhok mipo
from the U.S.	מארצות-הברית	me-artzot habrit
here (to here)	פה (לפה)	po (lepo)
in Israel	בישראל	be-israel
in the car	במכונית	bamkhonit
inside	בפנים	bifnim
near the bank	קרוב לבנק	karov labank
next to the post office	ליד הדואר	leyad hado-ar
opposite the market	מול השוק	mul hashuk
on the left/right	בצד שמאל/ימין	betzad smol/yamin
on the sidewalk [pavement]	על המדרכה	al hamidrakha
outside the café	מחוץ לבית הקפה	mikhutz lebeyt hakafe
there (to there)	שם (לשם)	sham (lesham)
to the hotel	למלון	lamalon
towards Jerusalem	לכיוון ירושלים	lekivun yerushalayim
up to the traffic light	עד לרמזור	ad laramzor

מתי? When?

When does the museum open?	מתי נפתח המוזאון? *matay niftakh hamuze-on*
When does the train arrive?	מתי מגיעה הרכבת? *matay magi-a harakevet*
10 minutes ago	לפני עשר דקות *lifney eser dakot*
after lunch	אחרי ארוחת צהריים *akharey arukhat tzohorayim*
always	תמיד *tamid*
around midnight	בערך בחצות *be-erekh bekhatzot*
at 7 o'clock	בשעה שבע *besha-a sheva*
before Friday	לפני יום ששי *lifney yom shishi*
by tomorrow	עד מחר *ad makhar*
every week	כל שבוע *kol shavu-a*
for 2 hours	למשך שעתיים *lemeshekh sha-atayim*
from 9 a.m. to 6 p.m.	מתשע בבוקר עד שש בערב *mitesha baboker ad shesh ba-erev*
in 20 minutes	בעוד עשרים דקות *be-od esrim dakot*
never	אף פעם לא *af pa-am lo*
not yet	עדיין לא *adayin lo*
now	עכשיו *akhshav*
often	לעתים קרובות *le-itim krovot*
on March 8	בשמיני למרץ *bashmini lemertz*
on weekdays	בימי חול *biymey khol*
sometimes	לפעמים *lif-amim*
soon	בקרוב *bekarov*
then	אז *az*
within 2 days	תוך יומיים *tokh yomayim*

What sort of ...? איזה סוג ...?

I'd like something ...	אבקש משהו ...	avakesh mashehu
It's ...	זה ...	ze
beautiful/ugly	יפה/מכוער	yafe/mekho-ar
better/worse	יותר טוב/יותר גרוע	yoter tov/yoter garu-a
big/small	גדול/קטן	gadol/katan
cheap/expensive	זול/יקר	zol/yakar
clean/dirty	נקי/מלוכלך	naki/melukhlakh
dark/light	כהה/בהיר	kehe/bahir
delicious/revolting	נפלא/מגעיל	nifla/mag-il
early/late	מוקדם/מאוחר	mukdam/me-ukhar
easy/difficult	קל/קשה	kal/kashe
empty/full	ריק/מלא	rek/male
good/bad	טוב/רע	tov/ra
heavy/light	כבד/קל	kaved/kal
hot/warm/cold	לוהט/חם/קר	lohet/kham/kar
next/last	הבא/האחרון	haba/ha-akharon
old/new	ישן/חדש	yashan/khadash
open/shut	פתוח/סגור	patu-akh/sagur
pleasant/unpleasant	נעים/לא נעים	na-im/lo na-im
quick/slow	מהיר/איטי	mahir/iti
quiet/noisy	שקט/רועש	shaket/ro-esh
tall/short	גבוה/נמוך	gavoha/namukh
vacant/occupied	פנוי/תפוס	panuy/tafus
young/old	צעיר/זקן	tza-ir/zaken

Why? מדוע?

Why's that?	מדוע זה?	madu-a ze
Why not?	מדוע לא?	madu-a lo
It's because of the weather.	זה בגלל מזג האוויר.	ze biglal mezeg ha-avir
It's because I'm in a hurry.	זה בגלל שאני ממהר [ממהרת].	ze biglal she-ani memaher [memaheret]
I don't know why.	אינני יודע [יודעת] מדוע.	eyneni yode-a [yoda-at] madu-a

14

Hebrew has two genders: masculine and feminine.

Most feminine nouns end with the sound **a** ("ah") or obviously refer to feminine people (**em** – mother; **bat** – girl/daughter, etc.).

ha, which is a prefix, means "the" and is used for both genders.

There is no equivalent of the English "a/an" or of the verb "to be" in the present ("is/am/are"). This means you can have many sentences and questions with no verb at all:

ani more.	I (am a) teacher.
eyfo habank?	Where (is) the bank?
kama ze?	How much (is) this?

Adjectives come after the noun. Those referring to feminine nouns also have to be feminine and are usuallyformed by adding **a**:

khum brown

sus khum (a) brown horse **susa khuma** (a) brown mare

Adjectives referring to plural nouns have to agree with both the number and the gender:

susim khumim brown horses **susot khumot** brown mares

How much/many? כמה?

How much is that?	כמה זה?	_ka_ma ze
How many are there?	כמה יש?	_ka_ma yesh
1/2/3	אחד/שניים/שלשה	_ekhad/shnayim/shlosha_
4/5	ארבעה/חמשה	arba-_a_/khami_sha_
There's none.	אין כלום.	eyn klum
about 100 shekels	בערך מאה שקל	be-_e_rekh me-_a_ _she_kel
a little	קצת	ktzat
a lot of traffic	הרבה תנועה	_har_be tnu-_a_
enough	מספיק	mas_pik_
few/a few of them	מעט/מעטים מהם	me-_at_/me-a_tim_ mehem
more than that	יותר מזה	yo_ter_ mi_ze_
less than that	פחות מזה	pa_khot_ mi_ze_
much more	הרבה יותר	_har_be yo_ter_
nothing else	שום דבר אחר לא	shum da_var_ a_kher_ lo
too much	יותר מדי	yo_ter_ mi_day_

מי?/איזה? Who?/Which?

Who is it for?	?בשביל מי זה	bishvil mi ze
for her/him	בשבילו/בשבילה	bishvilo/bishvila
for me	בשבילי	bishvili
for you	בשבילך	bishvilkha [bishvilekh]
for them	[בשבילם [בשבילן	bishvilam [bishvilan]
someone	מישהו	mishehu
no one	אף אחד לא	af ekhad lo
Which one do you want?	?[איזה אתה רוצה [את רוצה	eyze ata rotze [at rotza]
this one/that one	את זה/את ההוא	et ze/et hahu
not that one	לא את ההוא	lo et hahu
something	משהו	mashehu
nothing	שום דבר לא	shum davar lo

של מי? Whose?

Whose is that?	?של מי זה	shel mi ze
It's …	… זה	ze
mine/ours/yours (*sing.*)/ yours (*pl.*)	[שלי/שלנו/שלך/שלכם [שלכן	sheli/shelanu/shelkha [shelakh]/ shelakhem [shelakhen]
his/hers/theirs	[שלו/שלה/שלהם [שלהן	shelo/shela/shelahem [shelahen]

GRAMMAR

To express possession ("my/your/our," etc.) in Hebrew, you need to add a particular ending to the noun. For example:

khatul cat   **khatuli** my cat

Here is a table of the most important endings:

	ending	example
my	i	khatuli
your (masc. singular)	kha	khatulkha
your (fem. singular)	ekh	khatulekh
his	o	khatulo
her	a	khatula
our	enu	khatulenu
your (plural)	khem	khatulkhem
their	am	khatulam

You can also add the word **shel** (of) + an ending similar to the above:
ha-khatul shelo ("the cat of his") = his cat.

How? איך?

How would you like to pay?	איך תרצה [תרצי] לשלם?	eykh tirtze [tirtzi] leshalem
by cash	במזומן	bimzuman
by credit card	בכרטיס אשראי	bekartis ashray
How are you getting here?	איך תגיע [תגיעי] לשם?	eykh tagi-a [tagi-i] lesham
by car/bus/train	במכונית/באוטובוס/ברכבת	bimkhonit/be-otobus/berakevet
on foot	ברגל	baregel
quickly	מהר	maher
slowly	לאט	le-at
too fast	מהר מדי	maher miday
very	מאד	me-od
with a friend	עם ידיד [ידידה]	im yadid [yedida]
without a passport	בלי דרכון	bli darkon

Is it …? / Are there …? זה ...?/יש ?...

Is it free of charge?	זה בחינם?	ze bekhinam
It isn't ready.	זה לא מוכן.	ze lo mukhan
Is there a shower in the room?	יש מקלחת בחדר?	yesh miklakhat bakheder
Is there a bus into town?	יש אוטובוס העירה?	yesh otobus ha-ira
There it is/they are.	הנה הוא/הם.	hine hu/hem
Are there buses into town?	יש אוטובוסים העירה?	yesh otobusim ha-ira
There aren't any towels in my room.	אין מגבות בחדר שלי.	eyn magavot bakheder sheli

יכול? Can/May?

Can I ...?	אני יכול [יכולה] ...? *ani yakhol [yekhola]*
May we ...?	נוכל ...? *nukhal*
Can you show me ...?	תוכל [תוכלי] להראות לי ...? *tukhal [tukhli] lehar-ot li*
Can you tell me ...?	תוכל [תוכלי] לומר לי ...? *tukhal [tukhli] lomar li*
May I help you?	אוכל לעזור לך? *ukhal la-azor lekha [lakh]*
Can you direct me to ...?	תוכל [תוכלי] להדריך אותי ל...? *tukhal [tukhli] lehadrikh oti le*
I can't.	אני לא יכול [יכולה]. *ani lo yakhol [yekhola]*

מה אתה רוצה? What do you want?

I'd like ...	אבקש ... *avakesh*
Could I have ...?	אפשר לקבל ...? *efshar lekabel*
We'd like ...	נבקש ... *nevakesh*
Give me ...	תן [תני] לי ... *ten [tni] li*
I'm looking for ...	אני מחפש [מחפשת] ... *ani mekhapes [mekhapeset]*
I need to ...	אני צריך [צריכה] ... *ani tzarikh [tzrikha]*
go ...	ללכת ... *lalekhet*
find ...	למצוא ... *limtzo*
see ...	לראות ... *lir-ot*
speak to ...	לדבר עם ... *ledaber im*

– slikha. (Excuse me.)
– ken? (Yes?)
– efshar la-azor lekha [lakh]. (Can I help you?)
– efshar ledaber im mar sason?
  (Can I speak to Mr. Sasson?)
– rak rega, bevakasha. (Just a moment, please.)

Other useful words
מלים שימושיות אחרות

fortunately	למרבה המזל
	lemarbe hamazal
hopefully	יש לקוות
	yesh lekavot
of course	כמובן *kamuvan*
perhaps	אולי *ulay*
unfortunately	למרבה הצער
	lemarbe hatza-ar
also/but	גם/אבל *gam/aval*
and/or	ו-/או *ve/o-*

Exclamations מילות קריאה

At last!	סוף סוף! *sof sof*
Go on.	תמשיך [תמשיכי].
	tamshikh [tamshikhi]
Nonsense!	שטויות! *shtuyot*
That's true.	זה נכון. *ze nakhon*
No way!	בשום אופן לא!
	beshum ofen lo
How are things?	איך העניינים?
	eykh ha-inyanim
great/terrific	מצוין/נהדר
	metzuyan/nehedar
very good	טוב מאד
	tov me-od
fine	טוב *tov*
not bad	לא רע *lo ra*
okay	אוקיי *okey*
not good	לא טוב *lo tov*
fairly bad	די רע *day ra*
terrible	נורא *nora*

19

Accommodations

Israel has been a destination for pilgrims and visitors for centuries. It offers a wide range of accommodations, from Western-style hotels to youth hostels and campsites. It is advisable to reserve in advance, particularly during High Holidays (Passover/Easter and around the Jewish New Year). Check whether the management expects you to observe any religious customs, such as dietary laws or not driving on the Sabbath.

מלון ma*lon*
Hotel. These vary from five-star hotels, comparable to those in Europe and the U.S. and offering similar facilities and cuisine (as well as local food), to small local hotels. Tourist information bureaus often have lists with details and price ranges.

מלון דירות ma*lon* di*rot*
Apartment hotel. Hotels with kitchenettes, although the price often includes breakfast.

פנסיון pensi*yon*
Guest house. Usually family-run and often occupying part of the owner's house. Prices can be lower than hotels, but bathrooms are often shared.

צימר *tzimmer*
Rented room, similar to guest houses but often have their own bathrooms.

אכסניית נוער akhsani*yat* no-ar
Youth hostel. These can be found in many popular tourist locations in Israel. You may need an international YHA card to use these.

בית הארחה beyt ha-ara*kha*
Kibbutz guest house. Many are located in peaceful, out-of-the-way places, but may still have quite luxurious facilities, including swimming pools.

הוספיס *hospis*
Religious hospice. Some of these accept non-practicing Christians. Originally designed for pilgrims, many are spartan.

Reservations הזמנות

In advance מראש

Can you recommend a
hotel in …?

תוכל להמליץ על מלון ב...?
tukhal lehamlitz al malon be

Is it near the center of town?

זה קרוב למרכז העיר?
ze karov lemerkaz ha-ir

How much is it per night?

כמה זה ללילה? *kama ze lelayla*

Do you have a cheaper room?

יש לכם חדר יותר זול?
yesh lakhem kheder yoter zol

Could you reserve me a
room there, please?

תוכל להזמין לי חדר שם, בבקשה?
tukhal lehazmin li kheder sham bevakasha

How do I get there?

איך מגיעים לשם? *eykh magi-im lesham*

At the hotel במלון

Do you have a room?

יש לכם חדר? *yesh lakhem kheder*

I'm sorry. We're full.

מצטער. אנחנו מלאים.
mitzta-er. anakhnu mele-im.

Is there another hotel nearby?

יש מלון אחר בסביבה?
yesh malon akher basviva

I'd like a single/double room.

הייתי רוצה חדר ליחיד/לזוג.
hayiti rotze kheder leyakhid/lezug

Can I see the room, please?

אפשר לראות את החדר, בבקשה?
efshar lir-ot et hakheder bevakasha

I'd like a room with …

הייתי רוצה חדר עם ...
hayiti rotze kheder im

twin beds

מיטות נפרדות *mitot nifradot*

a double bed

מיטה זוגית *mita zugit*

a bath/shower

אמבטיה/מקלחת *ambatya/miklakhat*

– yesh lakhem kheder? (Do you have a room?)
– mitzta-er. anakhnu mele-im. (I'm sorry. We're full.)
– oh. yesh malon akher basviva?
(Oh. Is there another hotel nearby?)
– ken gvirti/adoni. malon ambasador karov me-od.
(Yes, madam/sir. The Ambassador Hotel is very near.)

קבלה Reception

I have a reservation.	יש לי הזמנה. *yesh li hazmana*
My name is …	שמי … *shmi*
We've reserved a double and a single room.	הזמנו חדר לזוג וחדר ליחיד. *hizmanu kheder lezug vekheder leyakhid*
I've reserved a room for two nights.	הזמנתי חדר לשני לילות. *hizmanti kheder lishney leylot*
I confirmed my reservation by mail.	אשרתי את הזמנתי בדואר. *isharti et hazmanati bado-ar*
Could we have adjoining rooms?	נוכל לקבל חדרים צמודים? *nukhal lekabel khadarim tzmudim*

Amenities and facilities תנאים ומתקנים

Is there (a/an) … in the room?	יש … בחדר? *yesh … bakheder*
air conditioning	מיזוג אויר *mizug avir*
TV/telephone	טלויזיה/טלפון *televizya/telefon*
Does the hotel have (a/an) …?	יש במלון …? *yesh bamalon*
fax	פקס *faks*
laundry service	שרות כביסה *sherut kvisa*
satellite/cable TV	טלויזיית לויין/כבלים *televizyat lavyan/kvalim*
sauna	סאונה *sauna*
swimming pool	בריכת שחייה *brekhat skhiya*
Could you put … in the room?	תוכלו לשים … בחדר? *tukhlu lasim … bakheder*
an extra bed	מיטה נוספת *mita nosefet*
a crib [child's cot]	עריסה *arisa*
Do you have facilities for children/the disabled?	יש לכם אמצעים לילדים/לנכים? *yesh lakhem emtza-im liyladim/lenekhim*

כמה זמן ...? How long ...?

We'll be staying ...	נשאר ... nisha-er
overnight only	רק ללילה אחד rak lelayla ekhad
a few days	כמה ימים kama yamim
a week (at least)	שבוע (לפחות) shavu-a (lefakhot)
I'd like to stay an extra night.	אבקש להשאר עוד לילה. avakesh lehisha-er od layla

---

–shalom. yesh li hazmana. shmi john nyuton.
(Hello. I have a reservation. My name's John Newton.)

– shalom mar nyuton. (Hello, Mr. Newton.)

– hizmanti kheder lishney leylot.
(I've reserved a room for two nights.)

–ze beseder. ana male tofes (harshama) ze.
(Very good. Please fill out this (registration) form.)

אפשר לראות את הדרכון, בבקשה?	May I see your passport, please?
בבקשה למלא טופס זה/לחתום פה.	Please fill out this form/sign here.
מה מספר המכונית שלך?	What is your license plate number?

חדר בלבד: ... שקל	room only: ... shekel
כולל ארוחת בוקר	breakfast included
ארוחות מוגשות	meals available
שם משפחה/שם פרטי	last name/first name
כתובת הבית/רחוב/מספר	home address/street/number
אזרחות/מקצוע	nationality/profession
תאריך/מקום לידה	date/place of birth
מספר דרכון	passport number
מספר המכונית	license plate number
מקום/תאריך (החתימה)	place/date (of signature)
חתימה	signature

Price מחיר

How much is it …?	כמה זה ...? _kama ze_
per night / week	ללילה/לשבוע _lelayla/leshavu-a_
for bed and breakfast	ללינה וארוחת בוקר _lelina ve-arukhat boker_

excluding meals	לא כולל ארוחות _lo kolel arukhot_
for full board (American Plan [A.P.])	לפנסיון מלא _lepensiyon male_
for half board (Modified American Plan [M.A.P.])	לחצי פנסיון _lekhatzi pensiyon_
Does the price include …?	האם המחיר כולל ...? _ha-im hamekhir kolel_
breakfast	ארוחת בוקר _arukhat boker_
VAT	מע"מ _ma-am_
Do I have to pay a deposit?	צריך להשאיר פקדון? _tzarikh lehash-ir pikadon_
Is there a discount for children?	יש הנחה לילדים? _yesh hanakha liyladim_

Decisions החלטה

May I see the room?	אפשר לראות את החדר? _efshar lir-ot et hakheder_
That's fine. I'll take it.	זה בסדר. אקח אותו. _ze beseder. ekakh oto_
It's too …	... זה יותר מדי ... _ze yoter miday_
dark / small	חשוך/קטן _khashukh/katan_
noisy	רועש _ro-esh_
Do you have anything …?	... יש לכם משהו ...? _yesh lakhem mashehu_
bigger / cheaper	יותר גדול/יותר זול _yoter gadol/yoter zol_
quieter / warmer / cooler	יותר שקט/יותר חם/יותר קריר _yoter shaket/yoter kham/yoter karir_
No, I won't take it.	לא, לא אקח אותו. _lo lo ekakh oto_

Problems and complaints
בעיות ותלונות

The ... doesn't work.	ה... לא פועל.
	ha... lo po-el
air conditioning	מיזוג אויר mizug avir
fan	מאוורר me-avrer
heating	הסקה hasaka
light	אור or
I can't turn the heat [heating] on/off.	אי אפשר להדליק/לכבות את ההסקה.
	i efshar lehadlik/lekhabot et hahasaka
There is no hot water / toilet paper.	אין מים חמים/נייר טואלט.
	eyn mayim khamim/neyar to-alet
The faucet [tap] is dripping.	הברז דולף. haberez dolef
The sink / toilet is blocked.	הכיור/בית השימוש סתום.
	hakiyor/beyt hashimush satum
The window is jammed.	החלון תקוע. hakhalon taku-a
My room has not been made up.	לא סידרו את החדר שלי.
	lo sidru et hakheder sheli
The ... is/are broken.	ה... שבור/שבורים.
	ha... shavur/shvurim
blinds / shutters	צילונים/תריסים tzelonim/trisim
lamp	מנורה menora
lock	מנעול man-ul
There are insects in our room.	יש חרקים בחדר שלנו.
	yesh kharakim bakheder shelanu

Action פעולה

Could you have that taken care of?	תוכל לדאוג שיטפלו בזה?
	tukhal lid-og sheyetaplu baze
I'd like to move to another room.	אני רוצה לעבור לחדר אחר.
	ani rotze la-avor lekheder akher
I'd like to speak to the manager.	אני רוצה לדבר עם המנהל.
	ani rotze ledaber im hamenahel

25

Requirements
דרישות כלליות

The current in Israel is the same as in continental Europe (220 volts). Sockets usually take three-pronged European plugs. Bring an adapter with you, as they are quite expensive to buy in Israel.

About the hotel לגבי המלון

Where's the …?	איפה ה...? _eyfo ha_
bar	בר _bar_
bathroom [toilet]	שרותים _sherutim_
dining room	חדר אוכל _khadar okhel_
elevator [lift]	מעלית _ma-alit_
parking lot [car park]	חנייה _khanaya_
shower room	חדר מקלחת _khadar miklakhat_
swimming pool	בריכת שחייה _brekhat skhiya_
tour operator's bulletin board	לוח ההודעות של חברת הנסיעות _lu-akh hahoda-ot shel khevrat hanesi-ot_
Does the hotel have a garage?	יש במלון מוסך? _yesh bamalon musakh_
Can I use this adapter here?	אפשר להשתמש פה במתאם הזה? _efshar lehishtamesh po bamat-em haze_

מכשירי גילוח בלבד	razors [shavers] only
יציאת חירום	emergency exit
דלת בטחון	fire door
נא לא להפריע	do not disturb
נא לחייג ... לקו חיצוני	dial … for an outside line
נא לחייג ... לדלפק הקבלה	dial … for reception
נא לא לקחת מגבות מהחדר	don't remove towels from the room

Personal needs דרישות אישיות

The key to room …, please.	המפתח לחדר ..., בבקשה.
	hamafte-akh lekheder … bevakasha
I've lost my key.	אבדתי את המפתח שלי.
	ibadeti et hamfte-akh sheli
I've locked myself out of my room.	סגרתי את עצמי מחוץ לחדר.
	sagarti et atzmi mikhutz lakheder
Could you wake me at …?	תוכלו להעיר אותי בשעה ...?
	tukhlu leha-ir oti besha-a
I'd like breakfast in my room.	אבקש ארוחת בוקר בחדר.
	avakesh arukhat boker bakheder
Can I leave this in the safe?	אפשר להשאיר את זה בכספת?
	efshar lehash-ir et ze bakasefet
Could I have my things from the safe?	אפשר לקחת את החפצים שלי מהכספת?
	efshar lakakhat et hakhafatzim sheli mehakasefet
Where can I find (a) …?	איפה אפשר למצוא ...?
	eyfo efshar limtzo
maid	חדרנית *khadranit*
our tour guide	את מדריך הטיולים שלנו
	et madrikh hatiyulim shelanu
May I have (an) extra …?	אפשר לקבל עוד ...? *efshar lekabel od*
bath towel	מגבת רחצה *magevet rakhatza*
blanket	שמיכה *smikha*
hangers	קולבים *kolavim*
pillow	כר *kar*
soap	סבון *sabon*
Is there any mail for me?	יש דואר בשבילי? *yesh do-ar bishvili*
Are there any messages for me?	יש הודעות בשבילי? *yesh hoda-ot bishvili*
Could you mail this for me?	תוכלו לשלוח את זה בדואר בשבילי?
	tukhlu lishlo-akh et ze bado-ar bishvili

BREAKFAST ➤ 43; CHANGING MONEY ➤ 138

Renting שכירות

We've reserved an apartment/cottage ...	... הזמנו דירה/קוטג'	hizmanu dira/kotej
in the name of ...	... על שם	al shem
Where do we pick up the keys?	?מאיפה נאסוף את המפתחות	me-eyfo ne-esof et hamaftekhot
Where is the ...?	...איפה ה	eyfo ha
electric meter	שעון חשמל	sha-on khashmal
fuse box	תיבת נתיכים	teyvat netikhim
valve [stopcock]	ברז ראשי	berez rashi
water heater	דוד הסקה	dud hasaka
Are there any spare ...?	?יש ... רזרביים	yesh ... rezerviyim
fuses	נתיכים	netikhim
gas bottles	מיכלי גז	meykhaley gaz
sheets	סדינים	sdinim
Which day does the maid come?	?באיזה יום באה החדרנית	be-eyze yom ba-a hakhadranit
Where do I put out the trash [rubbish]?	?איפה לשים את האשפה	eyfo lasim et ha-ashpa

Problems בעיות

How can I contact you?	?איך אפשר להתקשר אליך	eykh efshar lehitkasher eleykha
How does the stove [cooker]/ water heater work?	?איך פועל תנור הבישול/דוד ההסקה	eykh po-el tanur habishul/dud hahasaka
The ... is/are dirty.	.ה... מלוכלך/מלוכלכים	ha... melukhlakh/melukhlakhim
The ... has broken down.	.ה... מקולקל	ha... mekulkal
We accidentally broke/lost ...	... במקרה שברנו/איבדנו	bemikre shavarnu/ibadnu
That was already damaged when we arrived.	.זה כבר היה ניזוק כאשר הגענו	ze kvar haya nizok ka-asher higanu

HOUSEHOLD ARTICLES ➤ 148

Useful terms ביטויים שימושיים

boiler	דוד חימום	dud khimum
dishes [crockery]	כלי חרס	kley kheres
freezer	תא הקפאה	ta hakpa-a
frying pan	מחבת	makhavat
kettle	קומקום	kumkum
lamp	מנורה	menora
refrigerator	מקרר	mekarer
saucepan	סיר	sir
stove [cooker]	תנור בישול	tanur bishul
washing machine	מכונת כביסה	mekhonat kvisa
utensils [cutlery]	סכו״ם	sakum

Rooms חדרים

balcony	מרפסת	mirpeset
bathroom	חדר אמבטיה	khadar ambatya
bedroom	חדר שינה	khadar sheyna
dining room	חדר אוכל	khadar okhel
kitchen	מטבח	mitbakh
living room	חדר אורחים	khadar orkhim
toilet	שרותים	sherutim

Youth hostel אכסניית נוער

Do you have any places left for tonight?	יש לכם עוד מקומות להלילה? yesh lakhem od mekomot lehalayla
Do you rent out bedding?	אתם משכירים כלי מיטה? atem maskirim kley mita
What time are the doors locked?	מתי נועלים את הדלתות? matay no-alim et hadlatot
I have an International Student Card.	יש לי כרטיס סטודנט בינלאומי. yesh li kartis student beynle-umi

REQUIREMENTS ➤ 26; CAMPING ➤ 30

קמפינג Camping

Official campsites are found throughout Israel, offering amenities such as electricity, hot showers, stores and a café/restaurant. Reserve in advance during peak times. If camping elsewhere, you should notify the landowner/police in advance.

Reservations הזמנות

Is there a campsite near here?	יש בסביבה אתר קמפינג? yesh basviva atar kemping
Do you have space for a tent/trailer [caravan]?	יש לכם מקום לאוהל/לקרוון? yesh lakhem makom le-ohel/lekaravan
What is the charge …?	מה המחיר ...? ma hamekhir
per day/week	ליום/לשבוע leyom/leshavu-a
for a tent/car	לאוהל/למכונית le-ohel/limkhonit
for a trailer [caravan]	לקרוון lekaravan

Facilities מתקנים

Are there cooking facilities on site?	יש באתר מתקני בישול? yesh ba-atar mitkaney bishul
Are there any electrical outlets [power points]?	יש שקעי חשמל? yesh shik-ey khashmal
Where is/are the …?	איפה ה... eyfo ha…
drinking water	מי שתיה mey shtiya
trashcans [dustbins]	פחי אשפה pakhey ashpa
laundry facilities	מתקני כביסה mitkaney kvisa
showers	מקלחות miklakhot
Where can I get some butane gas?	איפה אפשר להשיג גז לבישול? eyfo efshar lehasig gaz lebishul

קמפינג אסור	no camping	
מי שתיה	drinking water	
אין להדליק אש	no fires	

תלונות Complaints

It's too sunny here.	יש פה יותר מדי שמש. yesh po yoter miday shemesh
It's too shady/crowded here.	יש פה יותר מדי צל/צפיפות. yesh po yoter miday tzel/tzfifut
The ground's too hard/uneven.	הקרקע יותר מדי קשה/לא ישרה. hakarka yoter miday kasha/lo yeshara
Do you have a more level spot?	יש לכם שטח יותר ישר? yesh lakhem shetakh yoter yashar
You can't camp here.	קמפינג אסור פה. kemping asur po

ציוד לקמפינג Camping equipment

butane gas	גז לבישול gaz lebishul
campbed	מיטת שדה mitat sade
charcoal	פחמים pekhamim
flashlight [torch]	פנס panas
groundcloth [groundsheet]	יריעת קרקע yeri-at karka
guy rope	חבל חיזוק khevel khizuk
hammer	פטיש patish
kerosene [primus] stove	תנור נפט tanur neft
knapsack	תרמיל גב tarmil gav
mallet	פטיש עץ patish etz
matches	גפרורים gafrurim
(air) mattress	מזרון (אוויר) mizron (avir)
paraffin	נפט neft
sleeping bag	שק שינה sak sheyna
tent	אוהל ohel
tent pegs	יתדות yetedot
tent pole	עמוד לאוהל amud le-ohel

יציאה Checking out

What time do we have to check out by?	עד איזו שעה צריך לצאת? ad _eyzo_ sha-a tzarikh latzet
Could we leave our baggage [luggage] here until … p.m.?	אפשר להשאיר את המזוודות כאן עד ... אחרי הצהריים? efshar lehash-ir et hamizva_dot_ po ad … akha_rey_ hatzoho_ra_yim
I'm leaving now.	אני עוזב עכשיו. ani _ozev_ akhshav
Could you order me a taxi, please?	אפשר להזמין לי מונית, בבקשה? efshar lehaz_min_ li mo_nit_ bevakasha
It's been a very enjoyable stay.	היה מאד נעים להיות פה. ha_ya_ na-_im_ me-_od_ li_hyot_ po

תשלום Paying

Tipping is not expected other than for special services. For example, there is no need to leave a tip if the restaurant has levied a 10–15% service charge. Tip room maids and bellhops according to the service rendered.

May I have my bill, please?	אפשר לקבל את החשבון, בבקשה? efshar lekabel et hakhesh_bon_ bevaka_sha_
How much is my telephone bill?	כמה חשבון הטלפון שלי? _kama_ khesh_bon_ hate_lefon_ she_li_
I think there's a mistake in this bill.	אני חושב שיש טעות בחשבון. ani kho_shev_ she_yesh_ ta-_ut_ bakhesh_bon_.
I've made … telephone calls.	היו לי ... שיחות טלפון. ha_yu_ li … si_khot_ telefon
I've taken … from the mini-bar.	לקחתי ... מהמיני-בר. laka_kh_ti … meha_mini_ bar.
Can I have an itemized bill?	אוכל לקבל חשבון מפורט? u_khal_ lekabel kheshbon mefo_rat_
Could I have a receipt, please?	אפשר לתת לי קבלה, בבקשה? efshar la_tet_ li kaba_la_ bevaka_sha_

Eating Out

Restaurants מסעדות

Israel is a meeting point of European, Asian, and North African cultures. For this reason there is a wide variety of Western and traditional restaurants, cafés, fast-food outlets, and stalls offering various snacks.

Although a few restaurants offer non-smoking areas, this is less common than in many Western countries. However, sometimes part of the seating is outside (either on the sidewalk or in a garden), and during much of the year this is an enjoyable alternative.

מסעדה mis-ada
Restaurant. Ranging from the very expensive to the budget end of the market. Often offering a mixture of Western and Middle Eastern dishes. Central and East European cuisine is also popular.

בית קפה beyt kafe
Café. This may be an upscale establishment with sophisticated desserts and drinks, or a place to grab a quick sandwich.

מזנון miznon
Fast-food bar. Anything from a falafel stall (➤ 40) to a burger restaurant. You will find the usual international fast-food chains.

Meal times זמני ארחות

Meals are generally served at the same times as in North America and Western Europe, though this may vary locally. In large cities you will usually find something open both very early and very late.

ארוחת בוקר *arukhat boker*
Breakfast is served between 7:00 and 9:00 a.m. in most hotels, later on Saturdays.

ארוחת צהריים *arukhat tzohorayim*
Lunch is usually eaten between 12.30 and 2.30 p.m., and can be either a lighter version of dinner or a snack such as a salad, particularly if a large breakfast was eaten.

ארוחת ערב *arukhat erev*
Dinner is usually the main meal of the day, eaten between 7:00 and 9:30 p.m.

Israeli cuisine המטבח הישראלי

Israeli cuisine is extremely eclectic. The country has gathered an enormous selection of types of food and restaurants from around the world, most obviously from areas in which Jews have settled: Central and Eastern Europe, the Levant, and North Africa. So-called "Oriental" cuisine is a Middle Eastern style of cooking embellished with many Arabic influences, and is widely available. If there is one thing which is typically Israeli, however, it is an emphasis on fruit, vegetables, and dairy products rather than meat – though fish and poultry are also popular.

Kosher כשרות

Kashrut, or the eating of kosher food, is the set of Jewish dietary laws. The one most obvious to visitors is the strict prohibition on mixing meat and dairy products (fish is not classified as meat). As a result, there are many dairy restaurants, serving soup, pasta, cheese pies, and salads, but no meat. Many restaurants get around the meat/dairy rule by serving non-dairy sauces, tea and coffee creamers, and even non-dairy ice cream. There are some restaurants where the rules are not observed, but as this deters a large number of potential Jewish customers, they are not always easy to find.

Another important set of rules governs the types of meat and fish that may be eaten. Briefly, those permitted are animals that have cloven hooves and chew the cud – hence beef, lamb, goat, and venison are kosher, with the most obvious exclusion being pork. Poultry is permitted, as is fish with scales and fins, such as carp and cod, but not shark or shellfish.

Leavened bread and cakes are prohibited at Pesach (Passover), in March/April. Instead, for one week Israelis eat **matzot**, a large, flat, stiff non-yeast bread. It can be ground up and the crumbs used, instead of flour, in a variety of cakes and pancakes.

Yom Kippur, in September or October, is a day of fasting. It is the holiest day in the Jewish calendar, and you will not find any restaurants or cafés open in Jewish areas.

A table for …, please.	שולחן ל..., בבקשה.
	shulkhan le… bevakasha
1/2/3/4	אחד/שניים/שלושה/ארבעה
	ekhad/shnayim/shlosha/arba-a
Thank you.	תודה. toda
The bill, please.	חשבון, בבקשה.
	kheshbon bevakasha

Finding a place to eat מציאת מקום לסעודה

Can you recommend a good restaurant?	תוכל להמליץ על מסעדה טובה?
	tukhal lehamlitz al mis-ada tova
Is there a(n) … restaurant near here?	יש מסעדה ... בסביבה?
	yesh mis-ada … basviva
dairy	חלבית khalavit
Middle Eastern	מזרחית mizrakhit
Chinese	סינית sinit
inexpensive	זולה zola
Italian	איטלקית italkit
vegetarian	צמחונית tzimkhonit
falafel restaurant	מסעדת פלאפל mis-adat falafel
fish restaurant	מסעדת דגים mis-adat dagim
Where can I find a(n) …?	איפה אפשר למצוא ...?
	eyfo efshar limtzo
burger stand	מזנון המבורגר miznon hamburger
café	בית קפה beyt kafe
restaurant	מסעדה mis-ada
with a terrace/garden	עם מרפסת/גינה im mirpeset/gina
fast-food restaurant	מזנון מהיר miznon mahir
ice-cream parlor	גלידריה glideriya
pizzeria	פיצריה pitzeriya
steak house	מסעדת סטייקים mis-adat stekim

DIRECTIONS ➤ 94

הזמנות Reserving a table

I'd like to reserve a table …	... אבקש להזמין שולחן avakesh lehazmin shulkhan
for two	לשניים lishnayim
for this evening/ tomorrow at …	...להערב/למחר ב leha-erev/lemakhar be
We'll come at 8:00.	נבוא בשמונה. navo bishmone
A table for two, please.	שולחן לשניים, בבקשה. shulkhan lishnayim bevakasha
We have a reservation.	עשינו הזמנה. asinu hazmana

לאיזו שעה?	For what time?
מה השם, בבקשה?	What's the name, please?
אני מצטער. אנחנו מאד עמוסים/מלאים.	I'm sorry. We're very busy/full.
יהיה לנו שולחן פנוי בעוד ... דקות.	We'll have a free table in … minutes.
אנא חזרו בעוד ... דקות.	Please come back in … minutes.

איפה לשבת Where to sit

Could we sit …?	...נוכל לשבת? nukhal lashevet
over there	שם? sham
outside	בחוץ bakhutz
in a non-smoking area	באיזור ללא עישון be-ezor lelo ishun
by the window	ליד החלון leyad hakhalon
Smoking or non-smoking?	מעשנים או לא מעשנים? me-ashnim o lo me-ashnim

– avakesh lehazmin shulkhan leha-erev.
(I'd like to reserve a table for this evening.)
– avur kama anashim? (For how many people?)
– le-arba-a. (For four.)
– le-eyzo sha-a? (For what time?)
– navo bishmone. (We'll come at eight.)
– uma hashem, bevakasha? (And what's the name, please?)
– roberts. (Roberts.)
– beseder gamur. lehitra-ot. (Very good. See you then.)

TIME ➤ 220; NUMBERS ➤ 216

Ordering הזמנת מאכלים

Waiter!/Waitress!	מלצר!/מלצרית!
	meltzar/meltzarit
May I see the wine list, please?	אוכל לראות את תפריט היינות, בבקשה?
	ukhal lir-ot et tafrit hayeynot bevakasha
Do you have a set menu?	יש לכם תפריט קבוע?
	yesh lakhem tafrit kavu-a
Can you recommend some typical local dishes?	תוכל להמליץ על מאכלים מקומיים אופייניים? tukhal lehamlitz al ma-akhalim mekomiyim ofyaniyim
Could you tell me what ... is?	תוכל לומר לי מה זה ...?
	tukhal lomar li ma ze
What's in it?	מה יש בזה? ma yesh baze
What kind of ... do you have?	איזה סוג של ... יש לכם?
	eyze sug shel ... yesh lakhem
I'd like ...	אבקש ... avakesh
I'll have ...	אקח ... ekakh
a bottle/glass/carafe of ...	בקבוק/כוס/קנקן של ...
	bakbuk/kos/kankan shel

מוכנים להזמין?	Are you ready to order?
מה תרצו?	What would you like?
תרצו להזמין קודם משקאות?	Would you like to order drinks first?
אני ממליץ על ...	I recommend ...
אין לנו ...	We don't have ...
זה יקח ... דקות.	That will take ... minutes.
תיהנו מהארוחה.	Enjoy your meal.

– mukhanim lehazmin? (Are you ready to order?)

– tukhal lehamlitz al ma-akhal mekomi ofyani?
(Can you recommend a typical local dish?)

ken. ani mamlitz al hadag ha-afuy.
(Yes. I recommend the baked fish.)

– beseder ekakh et ze, bevakasha. (OK, I'll have that, please.)

– beseder. uma tirtzu lishtot? (Certainly. And what would you like to drink?)

– kankan yayin adom, bevakasha. (A carafe of red wine, please.)

– beseder (Certainly.)

DRINKS ➤ 50; MENU READER ➤ 52

Accompaniments תוספות

Could I have … without the …?	?...אפשר לקבל ... בלי ה efshar lekabel … bli ha
With a side order of …	ועם ... בצד ve-im … batzad
Could I have a salad instead of vegetables, please?	אפשר לקבל סלט במקום ירקות, בבקשה? efshar lekabel salat bimkom yerakot bevakasha
Does the meal come with …?	?... הארוחה באה עם ha-arukha ba-a im
vegetables/potatoes	ירקות/תפודים yerakot/tapudim
rice/pasta	אורז/אטריות orez/itriyot
Do you have any …?	?...יש לכם yesh lakhem
ketchup/mayonnaise	קטשופ/מיונז ketchup/mayonez
I'd like … with that.	.אבקש ... עם זה avakesh … im ze
vegetables/salad	ירקות/סלט yerakot/salat
potatoes/French fries	תפודים/צ'יפס tapudim/chips
sauce	רוטב rotev
ice	קרח kerakh
May I have some …?	?... אפשר לקבל efshar lekabel
bread	לחם lekhem
butter	חמאה khem-a
lemon	לימון limon
mustard	חרדל khardal
pepper	פלפל pilpel
salt	מלח melakh
oil and vinegar	שמן וחומץ shemen vekhometz
sugar	סוכר sukar
artificial sweetener	ממתיק מלאכותי mamtik melakhuti
vinaigrette [French dressing]	רוטב חומץ rotev khometz

MENU READER ➤ 52

General requests בקשות כלליות

Could I/we have a(n) (clean) ..., please?	אוכל/נוכל לקבל ... (נקי), בבקשה? *ukhal/nukhal lek-abel ... (naki) bevakasha*
ashtray	מאפרה *ma-afera*
cup/glass	ספל/כוס *sefel/kos*
fork/knife	מזלג/סכין *mazleg/sakin*
plate/spoon	צלחת/כף *tzalakhat/kaf*
napkin	מפית *mapit*
I'd like some more ...	אבקש עוד ... *avakesh od ...*
That's all, thanks.	זה הכל, תודה. *ze hakol toda*
Where are the restrooms [toilets]?	איפה השרותים? *eyfo hasherutim*

Special requirements בקשות מיוחדות

I can't eat food containing ...	איני מסוגל לאכול מזון המכיל ... *eyneni mesugal le-ekhol mazon hamekhil*
salt/sugar	מלח/סוכר *melakh/sukar*
Do you have any dishes/drinks for diabetics?	יש לכם מאכלים/משקאות לחולי סכרת? *yesh lakhem ma-akhalim/mashka-ot lekholey sakeret*
Do you have vegetarian dishes?	יש לכם מאכלים צמחוניים? *yesh lakhem ma-akhalim tzimkhoniyim*

For the children לילדים

Do you have a children's menu?	יש לכם תפריט לילדים? *yesh lakhem tafrit liyladim*
Could you bring a child's seat, please?	תוכלו להביא כסא לילד, בבקשה? *tukhlu lehavi kise leyeled bevakasha*
Where can I change the baby?	איפה אפשר להחליף חיתולים? *eyfo efshar lehakhlif khitulim*
Where can I feed the baby?	איפה אפשר להניק את התינוק? *eyfo efshar lehanik et hatinok*

CHILDREN ➤ 113

מזנון/בית קפה Fast food/Café

משהו לשתות Something to drink

Fast food is very popular in Israel, with all sorts of stalls, cafés and small shops offering tasty and cheap meals. Pita filled with **falafel** (fried mashed chickpeas) is a common choice, as are **burekas** (pastry pockets filled with cheese, potatoes, or spinach) and a wide variety of salads and dairy dishes. In addition, most cities have a large number of American or American-style fast food outlets.

I'd like (a) …	… אבקש *avakesh*
beer	בירה *bira*
tea/coffee	תה/קפה *te/kafe*
black/with milk	שחור/בחלב *shakhor/bekhalav*
I'd like a … of red/white wine.	אבקש … יין אדום/לבן. *avakesh … yayin adom/lavan*
glass/carafe/bottle	כוס/קנקן/בקבוק *kos/kankan/bakbuk*
bottled/draft [draught]	בבקבוק/מהחבית *bebakbuk/mehakhavit*

ולאכול … And to eat …

A piece/slice of …, please.	חתיכת/פרוסת …, בבקשה. *khatikhat/prusat … bevakasha*
I'd like two of those.	אבקש שניים מאלה. *avakesh shnayim me-ele*
burger/fries	המבורגר/צ'יפס *hamburger/chips*
omelet/pizza	חביתה/פיצה *khavita/pitza*
sandwich/cake	כריך/עוגה *karikh/uga*
ice cream	גלידה *glida*
chocolate/strawberry/vanilla	שוקולד/תות שדה/וניל *shokolad/tut sade/vanil*
A … portion, please.	מנה …, בבקשה. *mana … bevakasha*
small	קטנה *ktana*
regular [medium]	בינונית *beynonit*
large	גדולה *gdola*
It's to go [take away].	זה לקחת איתי. *ze lakakhat iti*
That's all, thanks.	זה הכל, תודה. *ze hakol toda*

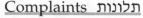

> – ma tirtze? (What would you like?)
> – pa-amayim kafe bevakasha. (Two coffees, please.)
> – shakhor o bekhalav? (Black or with milk?)
> – bekhalav, bevakasha. (With milk, please.)
> – mashehu le-ekhol? (Anything to eat?)
> – ze hakol, toda. (That's all, thanks.)

Complaints תלונות

I have no knife/fork/spoon.	אין לי סכין/מזלג/כף. eyn li sakin/mazleg/kaf
There must be some mistake.	בודאי נפלה טעות. bevaday nafla ta-ut
That's not what I ordered.	זה לא מה שהזמנתי. ze lo ma shehizmanti
I asked for …	ביקשתי … bikashti
I can't eat this.	איני מסוגל לאכול את זה. eyneni mesugal le-ekhol et ze
The meat is …	הבשר … habasar
overdone	מבושל יותר מדי mevushal yoter miday
underdone	מבושל פחות מדי mevushal pakhot miday
too tough	קשה מדי kashe miday
This is too …	זה יותר מדי … ze yoter miday
bitter/sour	מר/חמוץ mar/khamutz
The food is cold.	האוכל קר. ha-okhel kar
This isn't fresh.	זה לא טרי. ze lo tari
How much longer will our food be?	כמה זמן עוד נחכה לאוכל? kama zman od nekhake la-okhel
We can't wait any longer. We're leaving.	איננו יכולים לחכות יותר. אנחנו עוזבים. eynenu yekholim lekhakot yoter. anakhnu ozvim
This isn't clean.	זה לא נקי ze lo naki
I'd like to speak to the head waiter/manager.	הייתי רוצה לדבר עם המלצר הראשי/המנהל. hayiti rotze ledaber im hameltzar harashi/hamenahel

Paying תשלום

Tipping is not expected if – as is usual – a service charge has already been added. In smaller establishments you may want to leave about 10 percent for your waiter.

I'd like to pay.	אבקש לשלם.	avakesh leshalem
The bill, please.	חשבון, בבקשה.	kheshbon bevakasha
We'd like to pay separately.	אנחנו רוצים לשלם בנפרד. anakhnu rotzim leshalem benifrad	
It's all together, please.	הכל יחד, בבקשה. hakol yakhad bevakasha	
I think there's a mistake in this bill.	אני חושב שיש טעות בחשבון. ani khoshev sheyesh ta-ut bakheshbon	
What's this amount for?	עבור מה הסכום הזה? avur ma haskhum haze	
I didn't have that. I had …	לא קיבלתי את זה. קיבלתי … lo kibalti et ze. kibalti	
Is service included?	זה כולל שרות? ze kolel sherut	
Can I pay with this credit card?	אפשר לשלם עם כרטיס אשראי זה? efshar leshalem im kartis ashray ze	
I've forgotten my wallet.	שכחתי את הארנק שלי. shakhakhti et ha-arnak sheli	
I don't have enough cash.	אין עלי מספיק כסף מזומן. eyn alay maspik kesef mezuman	
Could I have a receipt, please?	אפשר לתת לי קבלה, בבקשה? efshar latet li kabala bevakasha	
That was a very good meal.	זו היתה ארוחה טובה מאד. zo hayta arukha tova me-od	

– meltzar! kheshbon, bevakasha. (Waiter! The bill, please.)

– beseder. hine. (Certainly. Here you are.)

– ze kolel sherut? (Is service included?)

– ken. ze kalul. (Yes, it is.)

– efshar leshalem im kartis ashray ze?
(Can I pay with this credit card?)

– ken kamuvan. (Yes, of course.)

– toda. zo hayta arukha tova me-od.
(Thank you. That was a very good meal.)

PAYING ➤ 32; NUMBERS ➤ 216

Course by course מנה אחרי מנה

Breakfast ארוחת בוקר

I'd like …	אבקש … *ava<u>kesh</u>*
bread	לחם *<u>lekhem</u>*
butter	חמאה *khem-<u>a</u>*
eggs	ביצים *bey<u>tzim</u>*
boiled/fried/scrambled	מבושלות/מטוגנות/מקושקשות *mevusha<u>lot</u>/metuga<u>not</u>/mekushka<u>shot</u>*
fruit juice	מיץ פירות *mitz pe<u>rot</u>*
grapefruit/orange	אשכוליות/תפוזים *eshkoli<u>yot</u>/tapu<u>zim</u>*
honey	דבש *dvash*
jam	ריבה *ri<u>ba</u>*
marmalade	ריבת תפוזים *ri<u>bat</u> tapu<u>zim</u>*
milk	חלב *kha<u>lav</u>*
rolls	לחמניות *lakhmani<u>yot</u>*
toast	טוסט *tost*

Appetizers/Starters מתאבנים/מנות ראשונות

It is usual to have an appetizer, even if it is just bread and olives. The most popular appetizer is **khumus** (chickpeas) with **tkhina** (tahini paste), flavored with garlic and cayenne pepper and sprinkled with olive oil and parsley. Lemon wedges are usually served on the side for you to use according to taste.

humus	חומוס *<u>khu</u>mus*
tahini	טחינה *t<u>khi</u>na*
salad	סלט *sa<u>lat</u>*
melon	מלון *me<u>lon</u>*
avocado	אבוקדו *avo<u>ka</u>do*
shakshuka ➤ 44	שקשוקה *shak<u>shu</u>ka*
blintzes ➤ 44	בלינצס *<u>blintzes</u>*
chopped liver	כבד קצוץ *ka<u>ved</u> kat<u>zutz</u>*

Soups מרקים

מרק עוף	marak of	chicken soup
מרק עגבניות	marak agvaniyot	tomato soup
מרק ירקות	marak yerakot	vegetable soup
מרק בשר	marak basar	beef soup
מרק דגים	marak dagim	fish soup
מרק בצל	marak batzal	onion soup
מרק תפוחי אדמה	marak tapukhey adama	potato soup
מרק אטריות	marak itriyot	noodle soup

בורשט borsht
Beetroot soup of East European origin. It can be eaten hot or cold, often with sour cream.

מרק עוף marak of
Chicken soup, usually eaten with dumplings or noodles.

מרק פירות marak perot
Cold fruit soup, eaten as a dessert.

Egg dishes מאכלי ביצים

חביתה	khavita	omelet
פנקייק	pankeyk	pancake
ביצים מקושקשות	beytzim mekushkashot	scrambled eggs

שקשוקה shakshuka
A very spicy dish of Tunisian origin, consisting of eggs scrambled with tomatoes and red peppers.

בלינצס blintzes
Thin pancakes, rolled and stuffed with meat, vegetables, fruit, or sweet cream cheese.

מלוואח melawakh
Yemeni pancakes.

Fish and seafood דגים ומאכלי ים

Fish is a traditional Jewish dish, but only fish with scales.
Shellfish, crustaceans, and fish without true scales, such as
shark or monkfish, are not kosher, but they can be found in
non-kosher restaurants. Carp is raised commercially and is
used to make **gefilte fish**.

בורי	_buri_	mullet
סול	_sol_	sole
אמנון	_amnun_	St. Peter's fish
בקלה	_bakala_	cod
דג מלוח	_dag malu-akh_	herring
טונה	_tuna_	tuna
קרפיון	_karpiyon_	carp
שפרוטים	_shprotim_	sprats (small herring)
שמך	_shemekh_	trout
אלתית	_iltit_	salmon
צדפות	_tzdafot_	mussels, clams, etc.
תמנון	_tamnun_	octopus
חסילונים	_khasilonim_	shrimp [prawns]

גפילטה פיש   ge_fi_lte fish
Finely chopped fish (usually carp, whitefish, or pike), mixed with matzo
meal, eggs, and seasonings, then shaped into ovals and cooked in a broth
and served chilled.

אמנון אפוי   amnun afuy
Baked St. Peter's fish from the Sea of Galilee, often served with a filling of
almonds and local herbs.

Meat and poultry בשר ועופות

Pork is forbidden to both Jews and Muslims and not generally available except in some Christian areas.

בקר	*bakar*	beef
עוף	*of*	chicken
ברווז	*barvaz*	duck
טלה	*tale*	lamb
פסיון	*pasyon*	pheasant
נקניק	*naknik*	sausages
סטיק	*stek*	steak
הודו	*hodu*	turkey
עגל	*egel*	veal
אווז	*avaz*	goose
חוגלה	*khogla*	partridge
שליו	*slav*	quail

Meat cuts נתחי בשר

כבד	*kaved*	liver
כליות	*klayot*	kidneys
צלעות	*tzla-ot*	ribs
רגל	*regel*	leg
אוכף	*ukaf*	saddle
קציצה	*ktzitza*	croquettes
סטיק (פילה/מותן/ אחוריים/עצם טי)	*stek (file/moten/ akhorayim/etzem ti)*	(fillet/sirloin/ rump/T-bone) steak

חמין **khamin**
A hearty stew of meat and beans; a traditional Jewish dish, prepared specially for the Sabbath.

קרפלך **kreplakh**
Dumplings filled with meat.

קבב **kabab**
Chunks of beef or lamb, grilled on a skewer.

ששליק **shishlik**
Spiced ground meat, grilled on a skewer.

Vegetables ‏ירקות‏

כרוב	*kruv*	cabbage
גזר	*gezer*	carrots
סלרי	*selery*	celery
קישואים	*kishu-im*	zucchini [courgettes]
מלפפון	*melafefon*	cucumber
חציל	*khatzil*	eggplant [aubergine]
שום	*shum*	garlic
שעועית ירוקה	*she-u-it yeruka*	green beans
חסה	*khasa*	lettuce
פטריות	*pitriyot*	mushrooms
בצלים	*betzalim*	onions
אפונה	*afuna*	peas
פלפל (אדום, ירוק)	*pilpel (adom, yarok)*	peppers (red, green)
תפודים	*tapudim*	potatoes
אורז	*orez*	rice
בצל ירוק	*batzal yarok*	shallots [spring onions]
לפת	*lefet*	rutabaga [swede]
עגבניות	*agvaniyot*	tomatoes
תרד	*tered*	spinach

Salad ‏סלט‏

סלט ירוק	*salat yarok*	green salad
סלט מעורב	*salat me-orav*	mixed salad
סלט תפודים	*salat tapudim*	potato salad
סלט יווני	*salat yevani*	Greek salad
סלט טורקי	*salat turki*	Turkish salad

Cheese גבינה

Cheese is popular in Israel, but as kosher law requires the separation of dairy products and meat, it is eaten mainly at breakfast. The most popular are **gvina kasha** – a hard cheese a little like a cross between cheddar and parmesan – and **gvina melukha** – a soft, salty white cheese.

גבינה רזה	gvina raza	low-fat curd cheese
גבינת שמנת	gvinat shamenet	cream cheese
גבינת עזים	gvinat izim	goat cheese
גבינה מלוחה	gvina melukha	salty cheese
גבינה קשה	gvina kasha	hard cheese
גבינה רכה	gvina raka	soft cheese

Dessert לקינוח

עוגת פרג	ugat pereg	poppy seed cake
עוגת גבינה	ugat gvina	cheesecake
שטרודל	shtrudel	apple strudel/ apple cake
קרם קרמל	krem karamel	crème caramel
פודינג שוקולד	puding shokolad	chocolate pudding
ליפתן	liftan	fruit compote
גלידה	glida	ice cream

בקלאווה baklawa
Shredded wheat with pistachios and hazelnuts, soaked in honey.

קרם בווריה krem bavariya
Cold custard pudding, with various flavorings such as vanilla, lemon, etc.

בלינצס blintzes
Thin pancakes stuffed with fruit, nuts, and/or sweet cream cheese.

פירות Fruit

תפוחים	tapu<u>khim</u>	apples
בננות	ba<u>na</u>not	bananas
דובדבנים	duvdeva<u>nim</u>	cherries
אשכולית	eshko<u>lit</u>	grapefruit
ענבים	ana<u>vim</u>	grapes
מלון	me<u>lon</u>	melon
תפוזים	tapu<u>zim</u>	oranges
אפרסקים	afar<u>sekim</u>	peaches
שזיפים	shezi<u>fim</u>	plums
רימונים	rimo<u>nim</u>	pomegranates
פטל	<u>pe</u>tel	raspberries
תות שדה	tut sa<u>de</u>	strawberries
אבטיח	ava<u>ti</u>-akh	watermelon
זיתים	zey<u>tim</u>	olives
תמרים	tma<u>rim</u>	dates
אבוקדו	avo<u>ka</u>do	avocado
אגסים	aga<u>sim</u>	pears
מישמשים	mishme<u>shim</u>	apricots
אפרסמון	afarse<u>mon</u>	persimmon
אוכמניות	ukhmani<u>yot</u>	blackberries
ענבי שועל	invey shu-<u>al</u>	blackcurrants
מנדרינות	manda<u>ri</u>not	mandarines
קלמנטינות	klemen<u>ti</u>not	tangerines
אננס	<u>a</u>nanas	pineapple
מנגו	<u>man</u>go	mango
תאנים	te-<u>enim</u>	figs

Drinks משקאות

Beer בירה

Most Israeli beer is similar to lager, and is usually drunk cold. Malt beer is dark and sweetish in taste, with a fairly low alcohol content. Licensing laws are minimal: beer is served at every kiosk, restaurant and café throughout the day.

Do you have … beer?	יש לכם בירה ...? yesh lakhem bira
bottled/draft [draught]	בבקבוק/מהחבית bebakbuk/mehakhavit

Wine יין

Israeli climate and geography are suitable for growing wine, and Mount Carmel has been known for its vineyards since Biblical times; in fact, the name means "God's Vineyard." Sweet red wines, and dry white wines similar to Hock, are available in most restaurants.

Can you recommend a … wine?	תוכל להמליץ על יין ...? tukhal lehamlitz al yayin
red/white/blush [rosé]	adom/lavan/roze אדום/לבן/רוזה
dry/sweet/sparkling	יבש/מתוק/נתזים yavesh/matok/netazim
I'd like the house wine, please.	אבקש את יין הבית. avakesh et yeyn habayit

Spirits and liqueurs משקאות חריפים

Israelis are not big consumers of spirits, though brandy, vodka, and a variety of liqueurs (mainly plum- and orange-flavored ones) are made locally. **Arak** is an aniseed-flavored brandy similar to the Greek *ouzo* or the French *pastis*. It turns a milky color when mixed with ice and water, and is mild and refreshing enough to be drunk with a meal.

straight [neat]	lo mahul לא מהול
on the rocks [with ice]	עם קרח im kerakh
with water/tonic water	עם מים/טוניק im mayim/tonik
I'd like a single/double …	אבקש ... רגיל/כפול avakesh … ragil/kaful
brandy/gin/whisky/vodka	ברנדי/ג'ין/ויסקי/וודקה brendi/jin/viski/vodka

Non-alcoholic drinks
משקאות לא-אלכוהוליים

Fruit juices (mainly citrus fruit, peach, and apple) are very
popular, either bottled or squeezed in front of you at the kiosk.
Gazoz is a drink made from a syrup with soda water added.
Soda water is also drunk on its own or with ice.

Coffee can be drunk either in the traditional Middle Eastern way – thick,
very strong, sweet, and black – or in any number of Western-style cafés
where espresso, capuccino and Viennese coffee with whipped cream are
served. Arabic (Turkish) coffee is flavored with **hel** (cardamon).

Tea is served in a glass, black with lemon, and/or **na'ana** (mint leaves).
Herb tea, for example, made from rose hips, is becoming more popular.

I'd like (a) …	אבקש … *ava*kesh
tea	תה *te*
(Turkish) coffee	קפה (טורקי) *kafe (turki)*
(hot) chocolate	שוקו (חם) *shoko (kham)*
cola/lemonade	קולה/לימונדה *kola/limonada*
fruit juice	מיץ פירות *mitz perot*
orange/grapefruit/ pineapple/tomato	תפוזים/אשכוליות/אננס/עגבניות *tapuzim/eshkoliyot/ananas/agvaniyot*
milk shake	מילקשייק *milksheyk*
mineral water	מים מינרליים *mayim mineraliyim*
carbonated/ non-carbonated [still]	תוסס/לא תוסס *toses/lo toses*

Menu Reader

This Menu Reader gives listings under main food headings. You will see that the Hebrew words are shown in large type with the aim of helping you to identify, from a menu that has no English, at least the basic ingredients making up a dish.

Meat and poultry

בשר	ba<u>sar</u>	meat (general)
בקר	ba<u>kar</u>	beef
טלה/כבש	tale/<u>ke</u>ves	lamb/mutton
עוף	of	chicken
אווז	a<u>vaz</u>	goose
הודו	<u>ho</u>du	turkey
כבד	ka<u>ved</u>	liver
סטייק	stek	steak
כליות	kla<u>yot</u>	kidneys
צלעות	tzla-<u>ot</u>	ribs
קציצות	ktzitz<u>ot</u>	croquettes
נקניק	nak<u>nik</u>	sausages

Fish and seafood

דגים	_dagim_	fish (general)
בורי	_buri_	mullet
סול	_sol_	sole
טונה	_tuna_	tuna
אמנון	_amnun_	St. Peter's fish
בקלה	_bakala_	cod
אוקונוס	_okunos_	bass
אלתית	_iltit_	salmon
שמך	_shemekh_	trout
קרפיון	_karpiyon_	carp
גפילטה פיש	_gefilte fish_	gefilte fish
כריש	_karish_	shark
צדפות	_tzdafot_	mussels, clams, etc.
תמנון	_tamnun_	octopus
חסילונים	_khasilonim_	shrimp [prawns]
סרטן	_sartan_	crab and lobster

Vegetables

ירקות	_yerakot_	vegetable(s) (general)
שעועית ירוקה	she-u-_it_ yeru_ka_	green beans
תרד	_tered_	spinach
תפודים	tapu_dim_	potatoes
עגבניות	agvani_yot_	tomatoes
חסה	_khasa_	lettuce
מלפפון	melafe_fon_	cucumber
קישוא	ki_shu_	zucchini [courgettes]
גזר	_gezer_	carrots
בצל	_batzal_	onions
שום	shum	garlic
תירס	_tiras_	corn
זיתים	zey_tim_	olives
סלט	sa_lat_	salad (general)

Fruit

פירות	*perot*	fruit (general)
תפוחים	*tapukhim*	apples
תפוזים	*tapuzim*	oranges
בננות	*bananot*	bananas
מלונים	*melonim*	melons
אגסים	*agasim*	pears
שזיפים	*shezifim*	plums
תותי שדה	*tutey sade*	strawberries
תמרים	*tmarim*	dates
אננס	*ananas*	pineapple
תאנים	*te-enim*	figs
מנגו	*mango*	mango
מישמש	*mishmesh*	apricot
אבוקדו	*avokado*	avocado
אבטיח	*avati-akh*	watermelon
פטל	*petel*	raspberries

Staples: bread, rice, pasta, etc.

לחם	_lekhem_	bread
אורז	_orez_	rice
חיטה מפוצחת	khi_ta_ mefut_za_khat	cracked wheat
פסטה	_pasta_	pasta
עדשים	ada_shim_	lentils
שעועית	she-u-_it_	beans [pulses]
חימצה	khim_tza_	chickpeas

Condiments

מלח	_me_lakh	salt
פלפל	pil_pel_	pepper
חומץ	_kho_metz	vinegar
שמן זית	_she_men _za_yit	olive oil

Herbs and spices

צ׳ילי	_chili_	chili
פטרוסיליה	_petrosiliya_	parsley
קורנית	_koranit_	thyme
כרפס	_karpas_	celery
הל	_hel_	cardamon
כמון	_kamon_	cumin
ציפורן	_tziporen_	cloves
כורכום	_kurkum_	saffron
חרדל	_khardal_	mustard
נענע	_na-na_	mint
שום	_shum_	garlic
כוסבר	_kusbar_	coriander
צלף	_tzalaf_	capers
טרי	_tari_	fresh
מיובש	_meyubash_	dried

בגריל	*bigril*	grilled
מטוגן	*metugan*	fried
מעושן	*me-ushan*	smoked
מבושל	*mevushal*	boiled
כבוש	*kavush*	marinated
אפוי	*afuy*	baked
מוקרם	*mukram*	creamed
חתוך לקוביות	*khatukh lekubiyot*	diced
מוחמץ	*mukhmatz*	pickled
נא	*na*	raw
ממולא	*memula*	stuffed
שלוק	*shaluk*	poached
מאוייד	*me-uyad*	steamed

Classic dishes

חומוס	_khu_mus	humus mashed chickpeas, mixed with tahini, olive oil, lemon juice, and spices
פלאפל	_fa_la_fel	falafel fried chickpea balls served in a pita with salad, tahini, pickled gherkins, and spices
בורקס	bu_re_kas	bourekas thin pastry parcels with cheese, potato, or spinach filling
קבב	ka_bab_	kebab grilled or roasted lamb or mutton
ששליק	_shish_lik	shashlik-kebab skewered grilled meat and vegetables
שוורמה	sha_war_ma	doner-kebab lamb grilled on a spit
צ'ולנט	_cho_lent	cholent hearty meat and bean stew
שניצל	shni_tzel	escalope breaded veal, chicken, or turkey, baked or fried
לטקס	_lat_kes	latkes fried potato pancakes
חצילים בטחינה	khatzi_lim_ bitkhi_na	eggplant [aubergine] and tahina salad
עלי-גפן ממולאים	_aley gefen memula-im_	grape leaves stuffed with lamb, rice, and herbs

Drinks

משקאות	*mashka-ot*	drinks (general)
מים	*mayim*	water
חלב	*khalav*	milk
תה	*te*	tea
תה צמחים	*te tzmakhim*	herb tea
קפה	*kafe*	coffee
שוקו	*shoko*	chocolate milk
קקאו	*kakao*	cocoa
בירה	*bira*	beer
יין	*yayin*	wine
ויסקי	*viski*	whisky
ג'ין	*jin*	gin
וודקה	*vodka*	vodka

Drinks

ברנדי	_brendi_	brandy
עראק	_arak_	arak
מיץ (פירות)	_mitz (perot)_	(fruit) juice
מיץ תפוזים	_mitz tapuzim_	orange juice
מיץ אשכוליות	_mitz eshkoliyot_	grapefruit juice
לימונדה	_limonada_	lemonade
קולה	_kola_	cola
סוון אפ	_seven ap_	Seven-up®
סודה	_soda_	soda water
מים מינרליים	_mayim mineraliyim_	mineral water
טוניק	_tonik_	tonic water
מילקשייק	_milksheyk_	milk shake

Snacks

צ׳יפס	chips	French fries [chips]
המבורגר	_hamburger_	burger
ביסקויטים	biskvitim	cookies [biscuits]
עוגה	uga	cake
כריך	karikh	sandwich
פריכי תפודים	prikhey tapudim	potato chips [crisps]
בוטנים	botnim	peanuts
פלאפל	falafel	falafel ➤ 59
חומוס	khumus	humus ➤ 59
בורקס	burekas	bourekas ➤ 59
לטקס	latkes	latkes ➤ 59

Dairy products

גבינה	*gvina*	cheese
גבינת שמנת	*gvinat shamenet*	cream cheese
גבינת קוטג׳	*gvinat kotej*	cottage cheese
יוגורט	*yogurt*	yogurt
שמנת	*shamenet*	cream
שמנת חמוצה	*shamenet khamutza*	sour cream
חמאה	*khem-a*	butter
חלב	*khalav*	milk
לבן	*leben*	low-fat curdled milk
מרגרינה	*margarina*	margarine
ביצים	*beytzim*	eggs

Desserts

גלידה	_glida_	ice cream
סלט פירות	_salat perot_	fruit salad
קרם קרמל	_krem karamel_	crème caramel
עוגה	_uga_	cake
קרם בווריה	_krem bavariya_	crème Bavarois _cold custard, flavored with vanilla, etc._
פשטידה	_pashtida_	pie
ליפתן	_liftan_	fruit compote
בלינצס	_blintzes_	blintzes _thin pancakes stuffed with fruit and/or sweet cream cheese_
עוגת פרג	_ugat pereg_	poppyseed cake
עוגת שיש	_ugat shayish_	marble cake
מיקצפת	_miktzefet_	meringue pie

Travel

ESSENTIAL

1 ticket to …	כרטיס אחד ל... kartis ekhad le
2/3 tickets to …	שני/שלושה כרטיסים ל... shney/shlosha kartisim le
To …, please.	ל..., בבקשה le… bevakasha
one-way [single]	בכיוון אחד bekivun ekhad
round-trip [return]	הלוך ושוב halokh vashov
How much …?	כמה ...? kama

Safety בטיחות

Would you accompany me to the bus stop?	תוכל ללוות אותי לתחנת האוטובוס? tukhal lelavot oti letakhanat ha-otobus
I don't want to … on my own.	אינני רוצה ... לבדי. eyneni rotze … levadi
stay here	להישאר פה lehisha-er po
walk home	ללכת הביתה lalekhet habayta
I don't feel safe here.	אינני מרגיש בטוח פה. eyneni margish batu-akh po

POLICE ➤ 159; EMERGENCY ➤ 224

Arrival באים

Tourists from West European and North American countries do not normally need visas to enter Israel, but you should check with your travel agent or with the nearest Israeli consulate a few weeks before your departure. If a visa is required, it is always best to obtain it in your own country prior to travel.

You may experience difficulties in getting a visa to many Arab countries if you have evidence of a visit to Israel on your passport: on arrival, you could ask the passport control clerk to stamp a separate form and insert it loosely into your travel document.

The usual system of red channel/green channel operates for goods passing through customs. It is best to avoid bringing in expensive electronic goods or alcohol, unless they are clearly intended for your own personal use.

Passport control ביקורת דרכונים

We have a joint passport.	יש לנו דרכון משותף. yesh _lanu_ darkon meshu_taf_
The children are on this passport.	הילדים רשומים בדרכון הזה. hayla_dim_ reshu_mim_ badar_kon_ haze
I'm here on vacation [holiday]/business.	באתי לחופשה/לעסקים. _bati_ lekhuf_sha_/le-asa_kim_
I'm just passing through.	אני רק במעבר. a_ni_ rak bema-_avar_
I'm going to …	אני נוסע ל... a_ni_ nose-a le...
I'm on my own.	אני לבדי. a_ni_ leva_di_
I'm with my family.	אני עם משפחתי. a_ni_ im mishpakh_ti_
I'm with a group.	אני עם קבוצה. a_ni_ im kvut_za_

WHO ARE YOU WITH? ➤ 120

Customs מכס

I have only the normal allowances.	יש לי רק המיכסות הרגילות. yesh li rak hamikhsot haregilot
It's a gift.	זו מתנה. zo matana
It's for my personal use.	זה לשימושי האישי. ze leshimushi ha-ishi

יש לך משהו להצהיר?	Do you have anything to declare?
צריך לשלם מכס על זה.	You must pay duty on this.
איפה קנית את זה?	Where did you buy this?
נא לפתוח את התיק הזה.	Please open this bag.
יש לך עוד מזוודות?	Do you have any more luggage?

I would like to declare …	אני רוצה להצהיר ... ani rotze lehatzhir
I don't understand.	אני לא מבין. ani lo mevin
Does anyone here speak English?	מישהו פה מדבר אנגלית? mishehu po medaber anglit

ביקורת דרכונים	passport control
מעבר גבול	border crossing
מכס	customs
אין טובין להצהיר	nothing to declare
טובין להצהיר	goods to declare
טובין פטורים ממכס	duty-free goods

Duty-free shopping קניות פטורות ממכס

What currency is this in?	באיזה מטבע זה? be-eyze matbe-a ze
Can I pay in …	אפשר לשלם ב... efshar leshalem be
dollars	דולרים dolarim
shekels	שקלים shkalim
pounds	לירות שטרלינג lirot sterling

מטוס Plane

Because of the short distances involved, internal flights in Israel are not particularly plentiful nor cheap. The domestic airline Arkia operates efficient and reliable services between the main cities, and to several tourist destinations. Flying to Eilat does save a long (and sometimes hot) overland journey.

Tickets and reservations כרטיסים והזמנות

When is the ... flight to New York?	מתי הטיסה ... לניו יורק? matay hatisa ... linyu york
first/next/last	הראשונה/הבאה/האחרונה harishona/haba-a/ha-akharona
I'd like two ... tickets to New York.	אבקש שני כרטיסים ... לניו יורק. avakesh shney kartisim ... linyu york
one-way [single]	בכיוון אחד bekivun ekhad
round-trip [return]	הלוך ושוב halokh vashov
first class	מחלקה ראשונה makhlaka rishona
business class	מחלקת עסקים makhleket asakim
economy class	מחלקת תיירים makhleket tayarim
How much is a flight to ...?	כמה עולה טיסה ל...? kama ola tisa le
Are there any supplements/ reductions?	יש היטלים/הנחות? yesh hetelim/hanakhot
I'd like to ... my reservation for flight number 154.	אבקש ... את הזמנתי לטיסה מספר 154. avakesh ... et hazmanati letisa mispar 154
cancel	לבטל levatel
change	לשנות leshanot
confirm	לאשר le-asher

Inquiries about the flight בירורים על הטיסה

How long is the flight?	מה משך הטיסה? ma meshekh hatisa
What time does the plane leave?	באיזו שעה יוצא המטוס? be-eyzo sha-a yotze hamatos
What time will we arrive?	באיזו שעה נגיע? be-eyzo sha-a nagi-a
What time do I have to check in?	באיזו שעה עלי להירשם לטיסה? be-eyzo sha-a alay leherashem latisa

Checking in הרשמה לטיסה

Where is the check-in desk for flight …?	איפה ההרשמה לטיסה ...?
	eyfo haharshama letisa
I have …	... יש לי
	yesh li
three cases to check in	שלוש מזוודות לשלוח
	shalosh mizvadot lishlo-akh
two pieces of hand luggage	שני פריטי מטען יד
	shney pritey mit-an yad
How much hand luggage is allowed free?	כמה מטען יד מותר לקחת ללא תשלום?
	kama mit-an yad mutar lakakhat lelo tashlum

כרטיס/דרכון, בבקשה.	Your passport, please.
אתה רוצה מושב ליד החלון או במעבר?	Would you like a window or an aisle seat?
מעשנים או לא מעשנים?	Smoking or non-smoking?
אנא התקדם לאולם היוצאים.	Please go through to the departure lounge.
כמה מזוודות יש לך?	How many pieces of baggage do you have?
יש לך מטען עודף.	You have excess baggage.
עליך לשלם היטל של ... שקל.	You'll have to pay a supplement of … shekels.
זה יותר מדי כבד/גדול למטען יד.	That's too heavy/large for hand baggage.
האם ארזת את המזוודות האלה בעצמך?	Did you pack these bags yourself?
האם הן מכילות פריטים חדים או אלקטרוניים?	Do they contain any sharp or electronic items?

באים	arrivals
יוצאים	departures
בדיקה בטחונית	security check
אין להשאיר חפצים ללא השגחה	do not leave bags unattended

BAGGAGE ➤ 71

Information מודיעין

Is there any delay on flight …?	...יש עיכוב בטיסה ? yesh i-_kuv_ beti_sa_
How late will it be?	מה יהיה האיחור? _ma yihiye ha-ikhur_
Has the flight from … landed?	האם הטיסה מ... נחתה? ha-_im_ hatisa mi… nakha_ta_
Which gate does flight … leave from?	...מאיזה שער יוצאת טיסה ? me-_eyze sha-ar yotzet_ tisa

Boarding/In-flight עליה למטוס/בטיסה

Your boarding pass, please.	כרטיס עליה למטוס, בבקשה. kar_tis_ aliya lama_tos_ bevaka_sha_
Could I have a drink/ something to eat?	אפשר לקבל שתיה/משהו לאכול? ef_shar_ leka_bel shtiya/mashehu le-ekhol_
Please wake me for the meal.	בבקשה להעיר אותי לארוחה. bevaka_sha_ leha-_ir oti_ la-arukha
What time will we arrive?	באיזו שעה נגיע? be-_eyzo sha-a_ nagi-_a_
An airsickness bag, please.	שקית למחלת אויר, בבקשה. sa_kit_ lemakha_lat avir_ bevaka_sha_

Arrival באים

Where is/are the …?	...איפה ה _eyfo ha_
buses	אוטובוסים _otobusim_
car rental	שכירת מכוניות _skhirat_ mekhoniyot
currency exchange	החלפת מטבע _hakhlafat_ matbe-a
exit	יציאה _yetzi-a_
taxis	מוניות _moniyot_
Is there a bus to Tel Aviv?	יש אוטובוס לתל-אביב? yesh _otobus_ letel a_viv_
How do I get to the … hotel?	...איך מגיעים למלון ? eykh magi-_im_ lemalon

Baggage מזודות

Porters at airports and train stations usually expect a tip.

Porter! Excuse me!	סבל! סליחה! _sabal slikha_
Could you take my luggage to …?	תוכל לקחת את המזודות שלי ל… _tukhal lakakhat et hamizvadot sheli le_
a taxi/bus	מונית/אוטובוס _monit/otobus_
Where is/are the …?	…איפה ה _eyfo ha_
luggage carts [trolleys]	עגלות מטען _agalot mit-an_
baggage check [left-luggage office]	שמירת חפצים _shmirat khafatzim_
baggage claim	קבלת מזודות מהטיסה _kabalat mizvadot mehatisa_
Where is the luggage from flight …?	…איפה המזודות מטיסה? _eyfo hamizvadot mitisa_

Loss, damage, and theft אבדן, נזק וגניבה

I've lost my baggage.	אבדתי את המטען שלי. _ibadeti et hamit-an sheli_
My baggage has been stolen.	המטען שלי נגנב _hamit-an sheli nignav_
My suitcase was damaged.	המזודה שלי ניזוקה. _hamizvada sheli nizoka_
Our baggage has not arrived.	המטען שלנו לא הגיע. _hamit-an shelanu lo higi-a_

איך המטען שלך נראה?	What does your baggage look like?
יש לך תווית קבלה?	Do you have the claim check [reclaim tag]?
… המטען שלך	Your luggage …
…אולי נשלח ל	may have been sent to …
אולי יגיע יותר מאוחר היום	may arrive later today
אנא חזור מחר.	Please come back tomorrow.
צלצל למספר זה כדי לברר האם המטען שלך הגיע.	Call this number to check if your baggage has arrived.

POLICE ➤ 159; _COLOR_ ➤ 143

רכבת Train

Train travel in Israel is scenic and cheap. However, some provincial stations are outside town centers, trains run infrequently, and the network is fairly limited: Jerusalem to Tel Aviv (recommended for the mountain views if you are not in a hurry), along the entire Mediterranean coast, and via Beer Sheva to the northeastern Negev. Seats may be reserved, and there is only one class.

Student discounts are available for holders of an International Student Card.

To the station לתחנה

How do I get to the train station?	איך מגיעים לתחנת הרכבת? *eykh magi-im letakhanat harakevet*
Do trains to Haifa leave from … station?	האם רכבות לחיפה יוצאות מתחנת ...? *ha-im rakavot lekheyfa yotz-ot mitakhanat*
How far is it to there?	מה המרחק לשם? *ma hamerkhak lesham*
Can I leave my car there?	אפשר להשאיר שם את המכונית? *efshar lehash-ir sham et hamekhonit*

At the station בתחנה

Where is/are the …?	איפה ה... *eyfo ha*
baggage check [left-luggage office]	שמירת חפצים *shmirat khafatzim*
currency exchange	החלפת מטבע *hakhlafat matbe-a*
information desk	מודיעין *modi-in*
lost and found [lost property office]	משרד אבדות ומציאות *misrad avedot umtzi-ot*
platforms	רציפים *retzifim*
snack bar	מזנון *miznon*
ticket office	קופה *kupa*
waiting room	חדר המתנה *khadar hamtana*

כניסה	entrance
יציאה	exit
לרציפים	to the platforms
מודיעין	information
מקומות שמורים	reservations
מגיעים	arrivals
יוצאים	departures

Tickets and reservations

כרטיסים והזמנות

Be sure to check out the timetable and the ticket prices in advance at the station of departure. Buying the correct tickets could take some time if language difficulties are encountered – and you don't want to do it five minutes before the train is due to leave!

I'd like a … ticket to Haifa.	אבקש כרטיס ... לחיפה. *avakesh kartis … lekheyfa*
one-way [single]	בכיוון אחד *bekivun ekhad*
round-trip [return]	הלוך ושוב *halokh vashov*
discounts [concessionary]	במחיר הנחה *bimkhir hanakha*
I'd like to reserve a(n) … seat.	אבקש להזמין מקום ... *avakesh lehazmin makom*
aisle	במעבר *bama-avar*
window	ליד החלון *leyad hakhalon*

DIRECTIONS ➤ *94*

מחיר Price

The train is the cheapest means of transportation in Israel. Reductions are available for children, pensioners, and groups. Soldiers travel very cheaply (or sometimes for free), and partly as a result of that it is best to avoid Sunday mornings, Fridays, and the evening before festivals.

How much is that?	כמה זה? _kama ze_
Is there a reduction for …?	יש הנחה ל... _yesh hanakha le_
children/families	ילדים/משפחות _yeladim/mishpakhot_
senior citizens	קשישים _kshishim_
students	סטודנטים _studentim_

Queries בירורים

Do I have to change trains?	אני צריך להחליף רכבת? _ani tzarikh lehakhlif rakevet_
Is it a direct train?	זו רכבת ישירה? _zo rakevet yeshira_
You have to change at …	צריך להחליף ב... _tzarikh lehakhlif be_
How long is this ticket valid for?	לכמה זמן הכרטיס הזה בתוקף? _lekama zman hakartis haze betokef_
Can I take my bicycle onto the train?	אפשר לקחת את האופניים שלי ברכבת? _efshar lakakhat et ha-ofanayim sheli barakevet_
Can I return on the same ticket?	אני יכול לחזור באותו כרטיס? _ani yakhol lakhazor be-oto kartis_
In which car [coach] is my seat?	באיזה קרון המושב שלי? _be-eyze karon hamoshav sheli_
Is there a dining car on the train?	יש מזנון ברכבת? _yesh miznon barakevet_

– ava<u>kesh</u> kar<u>tis</u> lenaha<u>ri</u>ya.
(I'd like a ticket to Naharia.)
– beki<u>vun</u> e<u>khad</u> o ha<u>lokh</u> va<u>shov</u>?
(One-way or round-trip?)
– ha<u>lokh</u> va<u>shov</u>, bevaka<u>sha</u>. (Round-trip, please.)
– ze me-a <u>she</u>kel. (That's 100 shekels.)
– a<u>ni</u> tza<u>rikh</u> lehakh<u>lif</u> ra<u>ke</u>vet?
(Do I have to change trains?)
– ken. a<u>ta</u> tza<u>rikh</u> lehakh<u>lif</u> be<u>khey</u>fa.
(Yes. You have to change at Haifa.)
– to<u>da</u>. sha<u>lom</u>. (Thank you. Good-bye.)

Train times זמני רכבות

Could I have a timetable, please?	אפשר לקבל לוח זמנים, בבקשה? ef<u>shar</u> leka<u>bel</u> <u>lu</u>-akh zma<u>nim</u> bevaka<u>sha</u>
When is the … train to Jerusalem?	מתי הרכבת ה... לירושלים? ma<u>tay</u> hara<u>ke</u>vet ha… lirusha<u>la</u>yim
first/next/last	ראשונה/באה/אחרונה risho<u>na</u>/ba-<u>a</u>/akharo<u>na</u>
How frequent are the trains to …?	מה תדירות הרכבות ל...? ma tadi<u>rut</u> haraka<u>vot</u> le
once/twice a day	פעם/פעמיים ביום <u>pa</u>-am/pa-a<u>ma</u>yim be<u>yom</u>
five times a day	חמש פעמים ביום kha<u>mesh</u> pe-a<u>mim</u> be<u>yom</u>
every hour	כל שעה kol sha-<u>a</u>
What time do they leave?	באיזו שעה הן יוצאות? be-<u>ey</u>zo sha-<u>a</u> hen yotz-<u>ot</u>
on the hour	על השעה al hasha-<u>a</u>
20 minutes past the hour	עשרים דקות אחרי כל שעה es<u>rim</u> da<u>kot</u> akha<u>rey</u> kol sha-<u>a</u>
What time does the train arrive in …?	באיזו שעה מגיעה הרכבת ל...? be-<u>ey</u>zo sha-<u>a</u> magi-<u>a</u> hara<u>ke</u>vet le
How long is the trip [journey]?	מה משך הנסיעה? ma <u>me</u>shekh hanesi-<u>a</u>
Is the train on time?	הרכבת עומדת בלוח הזמנים? hara<u>ke</u>vet o<u>me</u>det be<u>lu</u>-akh hazma<u>nim</u>

Departures יוצאים

Which platform does the train to … leave from?	?...מאיזה רציף יוצאת הרכבת ל	me-*eyze* ratzif yotzet harakevet le
Where is platform 4?	?איפה רציף ארבע	*eyfo* ratzif *arba*
over there	שם	sham
on the left/right	משמאל/מימין	mismol/miyamin
Where do I change for …?	?...איפה מחליפים רכבת ל	*eyfo* makhlifim rakevet le
How long will I have to wait for a connection?	כמה זמן אצטרך לחכות לרכבת ?הממשיכה	kama zman etztarekh lekhakot larakevet hamamshikha

Boarding עליה לרכבת

Is this the right platform for …?	?...זה הרציף הנכון ל	ze haratzif hanakhon le
Is this the train to …?	?...זו הרכבת ל	zo harakevet le
Is this seat taken?	?המקום הזה תפוס	hamakom haze tafus
That's my seat.	.זה המקום שלי	ze hamakom sheli
Here's my ticket reservation.	.הנה כרטיס ההזמנה	hine kartis hahazmana
Are there any seats available?	?יש מקומות פנויים	yesh mekomot pnuyim
Do you mind if …?	?...אכפת לך אם	ikhpat lekha im
I sit here	אשב פה	eshev po
I open/close the window	אפתח/אסגור את החלון	eftakh/esgor et hakhalon

TIME ➤ 220; DIRECTIONS ➤ 94

On the journey בנסיעה

How long are we stopping here for?
כמה זמן אנחנו עוצרים פה?
kama zman anakhnu otzrim po

When do we get to ...?
מתי נגיע ל...?
matay nagi-a le

Have we passed ...?
עברנו את ...?
avarnu et

Where is the dining car?
איפה המזנון?
eyfo hamiznon

I've lost my ticket.
איבדתי את הכרטיס שלי.
ibadeti et hakartis sheli

מעצור חירום	emergency brake	
אזעקה	alarm	
דלתות אוטומטיות	automatic doors	

Long-distance bus [Coach]
אוטובוס בינעירוני

Long-distance buses are an excellent means of travel in Israel, reaching practically every village in the country. They are cheap, frequent, reliable, and usually clean and comfortable, but can be crowded on Sunday mornings and on Fridays. It is possible to reserve a ticket in advance, though you can usually obtain one from the driver (or from the bus station ticket office).

Where's the bus [coach] station?
איפה התחנה המרכזית?
eyfo hatakhana hamerkazit

When's the next bus [coach] to ...?
מתי האוטובוס הבא ל...?
matay ha-otobus haba le

Where does it leave from?
מאיפה הוא יוצא?
me-eyfo hu yotze

Where are the bus stops [coach bays]?
איפה עומדים האוטובוסים?
eyfo omdim ha-otobusim

Does the bus [coach] stop at ...?
האם האוטובוס עוצר ב...?
ha-im ha-otobus otzer be

How long does the trip [journey] take?
כמה זמן נמשכת הנסיעה?
kama zman nimshekhet hanesi-a

Are there ... on board?
יש ... באוטובוס?
yesh ... ba-otobus

refreshments
אוכל ושתיה
okhel ushtiya

toilets
שרותים
sherutim

TIME ➤ 220

Shared taxi שרות

Another popular means of long-distance travel is the shared taxi or microbus (**sherut**: literally "service"), which is the middle ground between long-distance buses and private taxis. These run between towns from known starting points, charge a fixed fare, and usually seat seven to ten people. Each **sherut** will wait until full and then depart, though at Tel Aviv airport it may occasionally leave short of full and will usually drop you off at your hotel or another destination. You can also reserve one to pick you up.

From where does the shared taxi to … leave?	?...מאיפה יוצא השרות ל me-_eyfo_ yotze hashe_rut_ le
How much is the fare to …?	?...מה המחיר ל ma hame_khir_ le

Bus אוטובוס

Buses are a cheap way to travel around cities, but avoid them during the crowded rush hours. You will find the bus number in Western figures, but the destination (if shown) may be written only in Hebrew characters, so you'll need to ask around to find the correct bus. You will usually pay the driver, so have small change ready.

Where is the bus stop?	?איפה תחנת האוטובוס _eyfo_ takha_nat_ ha-_otobus_
Where can I get a bus to …?	?...איפה יש אוטובוס ל _eyfo_ yesh _otobus_ le
What time is the … bus to Jaffa?	?מתי האוטובוס ... ליפו ma_tay_ ha-_otobus_ … le-_yafo_
first/next/last	הראשון/הבא/האחרון hari_shon_/ha_ba_/ha-akh_aron_

.אתה צריך את התחנה שם	You need that stop over there.
... אתה צריך אוטובוס מספר	You need bus number …
...אתה צריך להחליף אוטובוס ב	You must change buses at …

תחנת אוטובוס	bus stop
אסור לעשן	no smoking
יציאה/יציאת חירום	exit/emergency exit

Buying tickets קניית כרטיסים

Where can I buy tickets?	איפה אפשר לקנות כרטיסים? *eyfo efshar liknot kartisim*
A … ticket to Tiberias, please.	כרטיס ... לטבריה, בבקשה. *kartis … litverya bevakasha*
one-way [single]	בכיוון אחד *bekivun ekhad*
round-trip [return]	הלוך ושוב *halokh vashov*
A booklet of tickets, please.	כרטיסיה, בבקשה. *kartisiya bevakasha*
How much is the fare to …?	כמה זה ל...? *kama ze le*

Traveling בנסיעה

Is this the right bus to …?	זה האוטובוס הנכון ל...? *ze ha-otobus hanakhon le*
Could you tell me when to get off?	תוכל לומר לי מתי לרדת? *tukhal lomar li matay laredet*
Do I have to change buses?	אני צריך להחליף אוטובוס? *ani tzarikh lehakhlif otobus*
How many stops are there to …?	כמה תחנות יש עד ...? *kama takhanot yesh ad*
Next stop, please!	התחנה הבאה, בבקשה! *hatakhana haba-a bevakasha*

קופה ticket office

– *slikha* ze ha-otobus hanakhon la-iriya?
(Excuse me. Is this the right bus for the town hall?)
– *ken mispar shmone. (Yes, number eight.)*
– *ekhad* la-iriya, bevakasha.
(One for the town hall, please.)
– *ze arba-a shekel. (That's four shekels.)*
– *tukhal lomar li matay laredet?*
(Could you tell me when to get off?)
– *ze arba takhanot mipo. (It's four stops from here.)*

NUMBERS ➤ 216; DIRECTIONS ➤ 94

Subway [Metro] רכבת תחתית

A subway system is planned for Tel Aviv, but so far the only established line is the Karmelit in Haifa, an underground mountain railway from downtown to the top of Mount Carmel.

General enquiries בירורים כלליים

Where's the nearest Karmelit station?	איפה תחנת הכרמלית הקרובה؟ *eyfo* takha*nat* hakarme*lit* hakro*va*
Where can I buy a ticket?	איפה אפשר לקנות כרטיס؟ *eyfo* ef*shar* lik*not* kartis
Could I have a map of the routes?	אפשר לקבל מפת קווים؟ ef*shar* leka*bel* ma*pat* ka*vim*

Traveling נסיעה

Is this the Karmelit station?	זו תחנת הכרמלית؟ zo takha*nat* hakarme*lit*
Which stop is this?	איזו תחנת זו؟ *eyzo* takha*na* zo
How many stops is it to …?	כמה תחנות יש עוד ל...؟ *kama* takha*not* yesh od le
Is the next stop …?	האם התחנה הבאה היא ...؟ ha-*im* hatakha*na* haba-*a* hi
Where are we?	איפה אנחנו؟ *eyfo* a*nakh*nu
When is the first/next train?	מתי הרכבת הראשונה/הבאה؟ ma*tay* hara*ke*vet risho*na*/haba-*a*
When is the last train to …?	מתי הרכבת האחרונה ל...؟ ma*tay* hara*ke*vet ha-akhro*na* le

---

לרכבות   to the trains

NUMBERS ➤ 216; BUYING TICKETS ➤ 73, 79

Ships שייט

Cruises are available along some parts of the Mediterranean and Red Sea coasts and on the Sea of Galilee (**yam kineret**). These are more likely to be tourist excursions than any kind of scheduled passenger service. Haifa is Israel's main passenger port. There are regular sailings and cruises between Haifa and Cyprus, Greece, Italy, and other Mediterranean countries.

Is there a ferry/boat to …?	יש מעבורת/ספינה ל...?
	yesh ma-aboret/sfina le
When's the first/next/last sailing to …?	מתי ההפלגה הראשונה/הבאה/ האחרונה ל...?
	matay hahaflaga harishona/haba-a/ha-akhrona le
A round-trip [return] ticket for …	כרטיס הלוך ושוב ל...
	kartis halokh vashov le
one car and one trailer [caravan]	מכונית אחת וקרוון אחד
	mekhonit akhat vekaravan ekhad
two adults and three children	שני מבוגרים ושלושה ילדים
	shney mevugarim ushlosha yeladim
I'd like to reserve a single/ double cabin.	אבקש להזמין תא ליחיד/לזוג.
	avakesh lehazmin ta leyakhid/lezug

חגורת הצלה	life preserver [life belt]
סירת הצלה	lifeboat
נקודת איסוף	muster station
אין מעבר	no access

Boat trips טיולים בספינה

Is there a …?	יש ...? *yesh*
boat trip/river cruise	טיול בספינה/שייט בנהר
	tiyul bisfina/shayit banahar
What time does it leave?	באיזו שעה מפליגים?
	be-eyzo sha-a mafligim
What time does it return?	באיזו שעה חוזרים?
	be-eyzo sha-a khozrim
Where can we buy tickets?	איפה אפשר לקנות כרטיסים?
	eyfo efshar liknot kartisim

TIME ➤ 220; BUYING TICKETS ➤ 73, 79

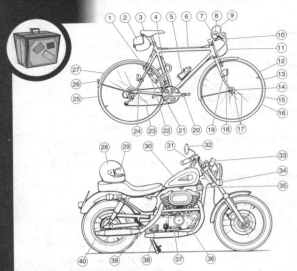

1 brake pad רפידת בלמים _refidat blamim_
2 bicycle bag תיק אופניים _tik ofanayim_
3 saddle אוכף _ukaf_
4 pump משאבה _mash-eva_
5 water bottle בקבוק מים
   bakbuk mayim
6 frame מסגרת _misgeret_
7 handlebars כידון _kidon_
8 bell פעמון _pa-amon_
9 brake cable כבל מעצור
   kevel ma-atzor
10 gear shift [lever] ידית הילוכים
   yadit hilukhim
11 gear control cable כבל הילוכים
   kevel hilukhim
12 inner tube צמיג פנימי _tzamig pnimi_
13 front/back wheel גלגל קדמי/אחורי
   galgal kidmi/akhori
14 axle ציר _tzir_
15 tire [tyre] צמיג _tzamig_
16 wheel גלגל _galgal_
17 spokes חישורים _khishurim_
18 bulb נורה _nura_
19 headlamp פנס קדמי _panas kidmi_
20 pedal דוושה _davsha_

21 lock מנעול _man-ul_
22 generator [dynamo] דינמו _dinamo_
23 chain שרשרת _sharsheret_
24 rear light פנס אחורי _panas akhori_
25 rim חישוק _khishuk_
26 reflectors רפלקטורים _reflektorim_
27 fender [mudguard] כנף _kanaf_
28 helmet קסדה _kasda_
29 visor מגן פנים _magen panim_
30 fuel tank מיכל דלק _mekhal delek_
31 clutch lever ידית מצמד _yadit matzmed_
32 mirror ראי _re-i_
33 ignition switch מתג הצתה
   meteg hatzata
34 turn signal [indicator] מתג איתות
   meteg itut
35 horn צופר _tzofar_
36 engine מנוע _mano-a_
37 gear shift [lever] ידית הילוכים
   yadit hilukhim
38 kick stand [main stand] משענת ראשית
   mish-enet rashit
39 exhaust pipe צינור פליטה _tzinor plita_
40 chain guard מגן שרשרת
   magen sharsheret

REPAIRS ➤ 89

Bicycle/Motorbike אופניים/אופנוע

Bicycles can be rented in some tourist resorts, and are a cheap and fun alternative to taxis. Nahariya in the north has been Israel's bicycle capital for many years.

I'd like to rent a …	... הייתי רוצה לשכור *hayiti rotze liskor*
3-/10-speed bicycle	אופניים עם שלושה/עשרה הילוכים *ofanayim im shlosha/asara hilukhim*
moped	אופניים עם מנוע *ofanayim im mano-a*
motorbike	אופנוע *ofno-a*
How much does it cost per day/week?	כמה זה עולה ליום/לשבוע? *kama ze ole leyom/leshavu-a*
Do you require a deposit?	אתם דורשים פקדון? *atem dorshim pikadon*
The brakes don't work.	הבלמים אינם פועלים. *hablamim eynam po-alim*
There are no lights.	אין פנסים. *eyn panasim*
The front/rear tire [tyre] has a flat [puncture].	יש תקר בצמיג הקדמי/האחורי. *yesh teker batzamig hakidmi/ha-akhori*

Hitchhiking טרמפים

Hitchhiking has always been popular in Israel, with the usual precautions advisable for women on their own. However, the main problem is the competition from soldiers traveling between home and their base, who enjoy priority at many well-known road junctions.

Where are you heading?	לאיזה כיוון אתה נוסע? *le-eyze kivun ata nose-a*
I'm heading for …	... אני נוסע לכיוון *ani nose-a lekivun*
Is that on the way to …?	...זה בדרך ל? *ze baderekh le*
Could you drop me off …?	...תוכל להוריד אותי? *tukhal lehorid oti*
here/at …	...כאן/ב *kan/be*
at the … exit	...ביציאה ל *bayetzi-a le*
downtown	במרכז העיר *bemerkaz ha-ir*
Thanks for giving me a lift.	תודה על הטרמפ. *toda al hatremp*

DIRECTIONS ➤ 94; NUMBERS ➤ 216

מונית Taxi

Taxis can be hired by phoning the nearest company (ask at your hotel), finding a taxi stand or flagging one down. You may agree to a fixed price or insist on the driver using his meter which he is required to do by law if you request him to.

Where can I get a taxi?	איפה אוכל להשיג מונית? *eyfo ukhal lehasig monit*
Do you have the number for a taxi?	יש לך מספר טלפון למוניות? *yesh lekha mispar telefon lemoniyot*
I'd like a taxi …	הייתי רוצה מונית ... *hayiti rotze monit*
now	עכשיו *akhshav*
in an hour	בעוד שעה *be-od sha-a*
for tomorrow at 9:00	למחר בתשע בבוקר *lemakhar betesha baboker*
The address is …	הכתובת היא ... *haktovet hi …*
I'm going to …	אני נוסע ל... *ani nose-a le…*

◎ פנוי for hire ◎

Please take me to (the) …	קח אותי בבקשה ל... *kakh oti bevakasha le*
airport	נמל התעופה *nemal hate-ufa*
station	תחנה *takhana*
this address	כתובת זו *ktovet zo*
How much will it cost?	כמה זה יעלה? *kama ze ya-ale*
Please turn on the meter.	הפעל את המונה, בבקשה. *haf-el et hamone bevakasha*
How much is that?	כמה זה? *kama ze*
Keep the change.	העודף בשבילך. *ha-odef bishvilkha*

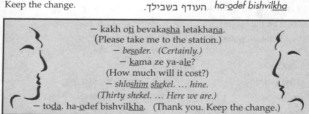

— kakh oti bevakasha letakhana.
(Please take me to the station.)
— beseder. (Certainly.)
— kama ze ya-ale?
(How much will it cost?)
— shloshim shekel. … hine.
(Thirty shekel. … Here we are.)
— toda. ha-odef bishvilkha. (Thank you. Keep the change.)

NUMBERS ➤ 216; DIRECTIONS ➤ 94

Car/Automobile מכונית

Having your own car can be an advantage if you are planning a tour not covered by direct bus routes or organized trips.

You'll need an international driver's license. Seat belts are required at all times for drivers and passengers. Driving is on the right, passing is on the left.

Israelis tend to drive fast and aggressively, and you should not assume that the right of way is given automatically. The horn is used much more freely than in Western countries, and can mean anything from a warning to a remonstration.

Conversion chart

Distances and speeds are always given in kilometers and kmph.

km	1	10	20	30	40	50	60	70	80	90	100	110	120	130
miles	0.62	6	12	19	25	31	37	44	50	56	62	68	74	81

Road network

Roads in Israel range from narrow, twisting, and bumpy to modern, well-maintained highways [motorways]. Town centers, particularly the older ones, have complicated one-way systems, with some zones reserved for pedestrians and others reserved for public and emergency vehicles only.

Car ownership is quite high, and even two-lane highways can be very congested at approaches to large towns and cities. There is a constant program of road modernization, and maps tend to get out of date fairly quickly.

Road signs are the internationally accepted ones, and you should have no trouble recognizing them. Major direction signs are in Hebrew, Arabic, and English, though the English spelling of place names is often arbitrary and inconsistent.

Car rental שכירת מכונית

Renting a car is easy in most large towns and cities, with local companies tending to be cheaper than international ones. You will usually have to be at least 21 and to have held a license for two years.

Where can I rent a car?	איפה אוכל לשכור מכונית? *eyfo ukhal liskor mekhonit*
I'd like to rent a(n) …	אבקש לשכור ... *avakesh liskor*
2-/4-door car	מכונית עם 4/2 דלתות *mekhonit im shtey/arba dlatot*
an automatic	מכונית עם הילוכים אוטומטיים *mekhonit im hilukhim otomatiyim*
car with 4-wheel drive	רכב שטח ארבע על ארבע *rekhev shetakh arba al arba*
car with air conditioning	מכונית עם מיזוג אוויר *mekhonit im mizug avir*
I'd like it for a day/week.	אני רוצה אותה ליום/לשבוע. *ani rotze ota leyom/leshavu-a*
How much does it cost per day/week?	כמה זה עולה ליום/לשבוע? *kama ze ole leyom/leshavu-a*
Is insurance included?	זה כולל ביטוח? *ze kolel bitu-akh*
Are there special weekend rates?	יש תעריף מיוחד לסוף-שבוע? *yesh ta-arif meyukhad lesof shavu-a*
Can I return the car at …?	אוכל להחזיר את המכונית ב...? *ukhal lehakhzir et hamekhonit be*
What sort of fuel does it take?	איזה סוג דלק היא צריכה? *eyze sug delek hi tzrikha*
Where is the high [full]/low [dipped] beam?	איפה האורות הגבוהים/הנמוכים? *eyfo ha-orot hagvohim/hanemukhim*
Could I have full insurance?	אפשר לעשות ביטוח מלא? *efshar la-asot bitu-akh male*

Gas [Petrol] station   תחנת דלק

Where's the next gas [petrol] station, please?	איפה תחנת הדלק הקרובה, בבקשה? *eyfo takhanat hadelek hakrova bevakasha*
Is it self-service?	זה שרות עצמי? *ze sherut atzmi*
Fill it up, please.	מלא, בבקשה. *male bevakasha*
… liters, please.	… ליטר, בבקשה. *… liter bevakasha*
premium [super]/regular	אוקטן גבוה/רגיל *oktan gavoha/ragil*
lead-free/diesel	נטול עופרת/דיזל *netul oferet/dizel*
I'm at pump number …	אני במשאבה מספר … *ani bemash-eva mispar*
Where is the air pump/water?	איפה משאבת האוויר/המים? *eyfo mash-evat ha-avir/hamayim*

מחיר לליטר   price per liter

Parking   חנייה

On-street parking is difficult in most town centers. Watch out for red-and-white curb markings, which indicate restrictions. There are parking meters in busy urban areas. Illegal parking may lead to fines or even booting [clamping]. Large hotels have their own underground parking, and there are parking lots [car parks] identified by a white-on-blue "P" in English and the equivalent in Hebrew and Arabic.

Is there a parking lot [car park] nearby?	יש מגרש חנייה בסביבה? *yesh migrash khanaya basviva*
What's the charge per hour/day?	מה המחיר לשעה/ליום? *ma hamekhir lesha-a/leyom*
Do you have some change for the parking meter?	יש לך כסף קטן למדחן? *yesh lekha kesef katan lamadkhan*
My car has been booted [clamped]. Who do I call?	שמו סנדל על המכונית שלי. למי צריך להתקשר? *samu sandal al hamekhonit sheli.* *lemi tzarikh lehitkasher*

NUMBERS ➤ 216; *DIRECTIONS* ➤ 94

קלקול Breakdown

If your rental car breaks down, follow the procedures in your rental agreement – which you should make sure you have a copy of before you set off.

Where's the nearest garage?	איפה המוסך הקרוב? *eyfo hamusakh hakarov*
My car broke down.	המכונית שלי התקלקלה. *hamekhonit sheli hitkalkela*
Can you send a mechanic/ tow [breakdown] truck?	תוכלו לשלוח מכונאי/רכב גורר? *tukhlu lishlo-akh mekhonay/rekhev gorer*
I'm a member of …	אני חבר ב... *ani khaver be*
My license plate [registration] number is …	מספר המכונית הוא ... *mispar hamekhonit hu*
The car is …	המכונית נמצאת ... *hamekhonit nimtzet*
on the highway [motorway]	על הכביש המהיר *al hakvish hamahir*
2 km from …	שני קילומטר מ... *shney kilometer mi*
How long will you be?	כמה זמן יקח לכם? *kama zman yikakh lakhem*

מה לא בסדר? What's wrong?

My car won't start.	המכונית לא מתניעה. *hamekhonit lo matni-a*
The battery is dead.	המצבר שובת. *hamatzber shovet*
I've run out of gas [petrol].	נגמר לי הדלק. *nigmar li hadelek*
I have a flat [puncture].	יש לי תקר. *yesh li teker*
There's something wrong with …	משהו לא בסדר עם ... *mashehu lo beseder im*
I've locked the keys in the car.	נעלתי את המפתחות בתוך המכונית. *na-alti et hamaftekhot betokh hamekhonit*

Repairs תיקונים

Do you do repairs?
אתם עושים תיקונים?
atem osim tikunim

Can you repair it?
אתם יכולים לתקן את זה?
atem yekholim letaken et ze

Please make only essential repairs.
עשו רק תיקונים הכרחיים, בבקשה.
asu rak tikunim hekhrekhiyim bevakasha

Can I wait for it?
אפשר לחכות לזה?
efshar lekhakot leze

Can you repair it today?
אתם יכולים לתקן את זה היום?
atem yekholim letaken et ze hayom

When will it be ready?
מתי זה יהיה מוכן?
matay ze yihye mukhan

How much will it cost?
כמה זה יעלה?
kama ze ya-ale

That's outrageous!
זה לא יתכן!
ze lo yitakhen

Can I have a receipt for my insurance?
אפשר לתת לי קבלה לביטוח?
efshar latet li kabala labitu-akh

ה... לא פועל.	The ... isn't working.
אין לי החלקים הנחוצים.	I don't have the necessary parts.
אצטרך להזמין את החלקים.	I will have to order the parts.
אני יכול לעשות רק תיקון זמני.	I can only repair it temporarily.
המכונית שלך אינה בת-תיקון.	Your car is beyond repair.
אי אפשר לתקן אותה.	It can't be repaired.
זה יהיה מוכן ...	It will be ready ...
יותר מאוחר היום	later today
מחר	tomorrow
בעוד ... ימים	in ... days

DAYS OF THE WEEK ➤ 218; NUMBERS ➤ 216

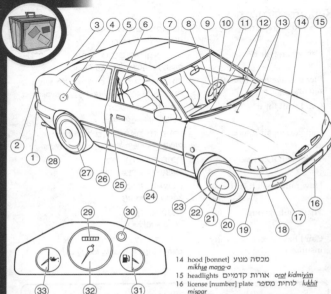

1 taillights [back lights] אורות אחוריים
  orot akhoriyim
2 brakelights אורות בלמים *orot blamim*
3 trunk [boot] תא מטען *ta mit-an*
4 gas cap [petrol cap] מכסה מילוי דלק
  mikhse miluy delek
5 window חלון *khalon*
6 seat belt חגורת בטיחות
  khagorat betikhut
7 sunroof גגון שמש *gagon shemesh*
8 steering wheel הגה *hege*
9 ignition key הצתה *hatzata*
10 ignition key מפתח הצתה
   mafte-akh hatzata
11 windshield [windscreen] שמשה קדמית
   shimsha kidmit
12 windshield [windscreen] wipers מגבים
   magavim
13 windshield [windscreen] washer
   שוטף שמשה קדמית
   shotef shimsha kidmit

14 hood [bonnet] מכסה מנוע
   mikhse mano-a
15 headlights אורות קדמיים *orot kidmiyim*
16 license [number] plate לוחית מספר *lukhit mispar*
17 fog lamp פנס ערפל *panas arafel*
18 turn signals [indicators] פנסי איתות
   panasey itut
19 bumper פגוש *pagosh*
20 tires [tyres] צמיגים *tzmigim*
21 hubcap צלחת גלגל
   tzalakhat galgal
22 valve שסתום *shastom*
23 wheels גלגלים *galgalim*
24 outside [wing] mirror ראי צד *re-i tzad*
25 automatic locks נעילה מרכזית
   ne-ila merkazit
26 lock מנעול *man-ul*
27 wheel rim שולי הגלגל
   shuley hagalgal
28 exhaust pipe צינור פליטה
   tzinor plita
29 odometer [milometer] מד מרחק
   mad merkhak
30 warning light נורת התראה
   nurat hatra-a
31 fuel gauge מד דלק *mad delek*

90

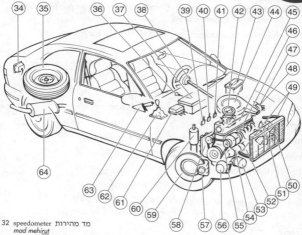

32 speedometer מד מהירות
   mad mehi_rut_

33 oil gauge מד שמן mad _shemen_

34 backup [reversing] light פנס נסיעה לאחור
   panas nesi-_g_a le-a_khor_

35 spare wheel גלגל רזרבי
   gal_gal rezervi_

36 choke משנק mash_nek_

37 heater חימום khimum

38 steering column עמוד הגה _amud hege_

39 accelerator גז דוושת dav_shat gaz_

40 brake pedal דוושת בלמים dav_shat blamim_

41 clutch מצמד matz_med_

42 carburetor מאייד me-a_yed_

43 battery מצבר matz_ber_

44 air filter מסנן אוויר masnen avir

45 camshaft גל פיקות gal _pikot_

46 alternator אלטרנטור alternator

47 distributor מפלג maf_leg_

48 points פלטינות plati_not_

49 radiator hose (top/bottom)
   צינור מקרן (עליון/תחתון)
   tzinor makren (_elyon/takhton_)

50 radiator מקרן makren

51 fan מאוורר me-avrer

52 engine מנוע mano-a

53 oil filter מסנן שמן masnen _shemen_

54 starter motor מנוע התנעה matne-a

55 fan belt רצועת מאוורר
   retzu-_at_ me-avrer

56 horn צופר tzofar

57 brake pads רפידות בלמים
   refi_dot_ blamim

58 transmission [gearbox] תיבת הילוכים
   tevat hilukhim

59 brakes בלמים blamim

60 shock absorbers בולמי זעזועים
   bolmey za-azu-_im_

61 fuses נתיכים netikhim

62 gear shift [lever] ידית הילוכים
   yadit hilukhim

63 handbrake יד מעצור
   ma-atzor yad

64 muffler [silencer] משתיק mash_tik_

REPAIRS ➤ 89

Accidents תאונות

If you have an accident, phone the police (☎ 100) and, if necessary, the paramedic ambulance service (Magen David Adom, ☎ 101). Report minor accidents at a police station. Try not to get into a dispute about blame at the accident scene, as it could easily escalate. If the car is rented, inform the rental company as soon as possible and ask for instructions.

There has been an accident.	קרתה תאונה.	karta te-una
It's …	זה …	ze
on the highway [motorway]	בכביש המהיר	bakvish hamahir
near …	ליד …	leyad
Where's the nearest telephone?	איפה הטלפון הקרוב?	eyfo hatelefon hakarov
Call …	קרא ל...	kra le
an ambulance	אמבולנס	ambulans
a doctor	רופא	rofe
the fire department [brigade]	כבאים	kaba-im
the police	משטרה	mishtara
Can you help me please?	תוכל לעזור לי בבקשה?	tukhal la-azor li bevakasha

Injuries פציעות

There are people injured.	יש פצועים.	yesh petzu-im
No one is hurt.	אין פצועים.	eyn petzu-im
He's seriously injured.	הוא נפצע קשה.	hu niftza kashe
She's unconscious.	היא ללא הכרה.	hi lelo hakara
He can't breathe.	הוא לא מסוגל לנשום.	hu lo mesugal linshom
He can't move.	הוא לא מסוגל לזוז.	hu lo mesugal lazuz
Don't move him.	אל תזיז אותו.	al taziz oto

Legal matters נושאים משפטיים

What's your insurance company?	?מה חברת הביטוח שלך *ma khevrat habitu-akh shelkha*
What's your name and address?	?מה שמך וכתובתך *ma shimkha uktovtekha*
The car ran into me.	.המכונית פגעה בי *hamekhonit pag-a bi*
The car was going too fast.	.המכונית נסעה מהר מדי *hamekhonit nas-a maher miday*
The car was driving too close.	.המכונית נסעה קרוב מדי *hamekhonit nas-a karov miday*
I had the right of way.	.היתה לי זכות קדימה *hayta li zkhut kdima*
I was (only) driving at … kmph.	נהגתי (רק) במהירות של ... קמ״ש. *nahagti (rak) bimhirut shel … kilometer lesha-a*
I'd like an interpreter.	.הייתי רוצה מתורגמן *hayiti rotze meturgeman*
I didn't see the sign.	לא ראיתי את השלט *lo ra-iti et hashelet*
This person saw it happen.	.האדם הזה ראה את המקרה *ha-adam haze ra-a et hamikre*
The license plate number was …	מספר הרכב היה ... *mispar harekhev haya*

?אפשר לראות את ... שלך, בבקשה	Can I see your …, please?
רשיון הנהיגה	driver's license
תעודת הביטוח	insurance card
ממסמכי הרישוי של הרכב	vehicle registration document
?באיזו שעה זה קרה	What time did it happen?
?איפה זה קרה	Where did it happen?
?האם עוד מישהו היה מעורב	Was anyone else involved?
?יש עדים למקרה	Are there any witnesses?
.נסעת במהירות מופרזת	You were speeding.
.האורות שלך אינם פועלים	Your lights aren't working.
.תצטרך לשלם קנס	You'll have to pay a fine.
.אתה צריך לתת הודעה בתחנה	You need to make a statement at the station.

TIME ➤ 220

Excuse me, please.	סליחה.	*slikha*
How do I get to …?	איך מגיעים ל...?	*eykh magi-im le*
Where is …?	איפה ...?	*eyfo*
Can you show me on the map where I am?	תוכל להראות לי על המפה איפה אני נמצא?	*tukhal lehar-ot li al hamapa eyfo ani nimtza*
I've lost my way.	תעיתי בדרך.	*ta-iti baderekh*
Can you repeat that, please?	תוכל לחזור על זה, בבקשה?	*tukhal lakhazor al ze bevakasha*
More slowly, please.	יותר לאט, בבקשה.	*yoter le-at bevakasha*
Thanks for your help.	תודה על העזרה.	*toda al ha-ezra*

Traveling by car נסיעה במכונית

Is this the right road for …?	זו הדרך הנכונה ל...?	*zo haderekh hanekhona le*
Is it far?	זה רחוק?	*ze rakhok*
How far is it to … ?	מה המרחק ל... מפה?	*ma hamerkhak le… mipo*
Where does this road lead?	לאן הדרך הזו מובילה?	*le-an haderekh hazo movila*
How do I get onto the highway [motorway]?	איך מגיעים לכביש המהיר?	*eykh magi-im lakvish hamahir*
What's the next town called?	איך נקרא הישוב הבא?	*eykh nikra hayishuv haba*
How long does it take by car?	כמה זמן זה לוקח במכונית?	*kama zman ze loke-akh bimkhonit*

– *slikha. eykh magi-im letakhanat harakevet?*
(Excuse me, please. How do I get to the train station?)
– *kakh et hapniya hashlishit yemina veze yashar kadima.*
(Take the third right and then go straight ahead.)
– *hapniya hashlishit yemina. ze rakhok?*
(The third right. Is it far?)
– *ze e-ser dakot baregel.* (It's ten minutes on foot.)
– *toda al ha-ezra.* (Thanks for your help.)
– *eyn be-ad ma.* (You're welcome.)

איתור Location

זה ...	It's ...
ישר קדימה	straight ahead
בצד שמאל	on the left
בצד ימין	on the right
בסוף הכביש	at the end of the street
בפינה	on the corner
מעבר לפינה	around the corner
בכיוון ...	in the direction of ...
מול .../מאחורי ...	opposite .../behind ...
ליד .../אחרי ...	next to .../after ...
לך אל ...	Go down the ...
רחוב הצדדי/רחוב הראשי	side street/main street
חצה את ...	Cross the ...
הכיכר/הגשר	square/bridge
קח את הפנייה השלישית ימינה.	Take the third right.
פנה שמאלה ...	Turn left ...
אחרי הרמזור הראשון	after the first traffic light
בהצטלבות השנייה	at the second intersection [crossroad]

במכונית By car

זה ... מכאן.	It's ... of here.
צפונה/דרומה	north/south
מזרחה/מערבה	east/west
סע לכיוון ...	Take the road for ...
אתה בדרך הלא-נכונה.	You're on the wrong road.
אתה צריך לחזור ל...	You'll have to go back to ...
סע לפי השילוט לכיוון ...	Follow the signs for ...

מה המרחק? How far?

זה ...	It's ...
קרוב/רחוק	close/a long way
חמש דקות ברגל	5 minutes on foot
עשר דקות במכונית	10 minutes by car
כמה מטר בהמשך הכביש	about 100 meters down the road
כעשרה קילומטר מכאן	about 10 kilometers away

TIME ➤ 220; NUMBERS ➤ 216

שילוט כבישים Road signs

מעקף	detour [diversion]
כביש חד-סטרי	one-way street
הכביש סגור	road closed
בית ספר לפניך	school zone [path]
עצור	stop
אין עקיפה	no passing [overtaking]
סע לאט	drive slowly
הדלק אורות	use headlights

מפות ערים Town plans

נמל תעופה	airport
בנק	bank
קו אוטובוס	bus route
תחנת אוטובוס	bus stop
כנסיה	church
חנות כלבו	department store
בית חולים	hospital
מודיעין	information office
רחוב ראשי	main [high] street
מסגד	mosque
קולנוע	movie theater [cinema]
גן	park
מגרש חניה	parking lot [car park]
מעבר להולכי-רגל	pedestrian crossing
מדרחוב	pedestrian zone [precinct]
תחנת משטרה	police station
דואר	post office
מגרש ספורט	playing field [sports ground]
בית ספר	school
אצטדיון	stadium
בית כנסת	synagogue
תחנת מוניות	taxi stand [rank]
תיאטרון	theater
תחנת רכבת	train station
אתה נמצא כאן	you are here

DICTIONARY ➤ 169; SIGHTSEEING ➤ 97

Sightseeing

Tourist information office מודיעין לתיירים

You will find tourist offices with information about local attractions, special events, etc. in most large towns and major tourist areas. You will also be able to find information about special tours – of Biblical sites or Crusader forts, for example – with English-speaking guides.

Where's the tourist information office?	איפה המודיעין לתיירים?
	eyfo hamodi-in letayarim
What are the main points of interest?	מהם האתרים המעניינים?
	mahem ha-atarim hame-anyenim
We're here for …	באנו ל... *banu le*
a few hours	כמה שעות *kama sha-ot*
a day	ליום אחד *leyom ekhad*
a week	לשבוע אחד
	leshavu-a ekhad
Can you recommend …?	תוכלו להמליץ על ...?
	tukhlu lehamlitz al
a sightseeing tour	סיור מאורגן
	siyur me-urgan
an excursion	טיול *tiyul*
a boat trip	טיול בספינה
	tiyul bisfina
Do you have any information on …?	יש לכם מידע על ...?
	yesh lakhem meyda al
Are there any trips to …?	יש טיולים ל...?
	yesh tiyulim le

DAYS OF THE WEEK ➤ 218; *DIRECTIONS* ➤ 94

טיולים Excursions

How much does the tour cost?	כמה עולה הטיול? *kama ole hatiyul*
Is lunch included?	זה כולל ארוחת צהריים? *ze kolel arukhat tzohorayim*
Where do we leave from?	מאיפה אנחנו יוצאים? *me-eyfo anakhnu yotz-im*
What time does the tour start?	באיזו שעה מתחיל הטיול? *be-eyzo sha-a matkhil hatiyul*
What time do we get back?	באיזו שעה נחזור? *be-eyzo sha-a nakhzor*
Do we have free time in …?	יהיה לנו זמן חפשי ב...? *yihiye lanu zman khofshi be*
Is there an English-speaking guide?	יש מדריך דובר אנגלית? *yesh madrikh dover anglit*

On tour בטיול

Are we going to see …?	האם נראה ...? *ha-im nir-e*
We'd like to have a look at the …	היינו רוצים להסתכל על ... *hayinu rotzim lehistakel al*
Can we stop here …?	נוכל לעצור כאן ...? *nukhal la-atzor kan*
to take photographs	כדי לצלם *kdey letzalem*
to buy souvenirs	כדי לקנות מזכרות *kdey liknot mazkarot*
to use the restrooms [toilets]	כדי ללכת לשרותים *kdey lalekhet lasherutim*
Would you take a photo of us, please?	תוכל לצלם אותנו, בבקשה? *tukhal letzalem otanu bevakasha*
How long do we have here/ in …?	כמה זמן יש לנו פה/ב...? *kama zman yesh lanu po/be*
Wait! … isn't back yet.	חכה! ... עוד לא חזר. *khake! … od lo khazar*

Where is the …?	איפה ...? _eyfo_
art gallery	גלריית האמנות _galeriyat ha-omanut_
battle site	שדה הקרב _sde ha-krav_
botanical garden	הגן הבוטני _ha-gan ha-botani_
castle	המצודה _ha-metzuda_
cathedral	הקתדרלה _ha-katedrala_
cemetery	בית הקברות _beyt ha-kvarot_
church	הכנסיה _ha-knesiya_
downtown area	מרכז העיר _merkaz ha-ir_
fountain	המזרקה _ha-mizraka_
historic site	האתר ההיסטורי _ha-atar ha-histori_
market	השוק _ha-shuk_
(war) memorial	האנדרטה (למלחמה) _ha-andarta (lamilkhama)_
monastery	המנזר _ha-minzar_
mosque	המסגד _ha-misgad_
museum	המוזאון _ha-muze-on_
old town	העיר העתיקה _ha-ir ha-atika_
opera house	בית האופרה _beyt ha-opera_
palace	הארמון _ha-armon_
park	הפארק _ha-park_
parliament building	הכנסת _ha-kneset_
ruins	החורבות _ha-khoravot_
shopping area	איזור הקניות _ezor ha-kniyot_
spring	המעיין _hama-ayan_
statue	הפסל _ha-pesel_
synagogue	בית הכנסת _beyt ha-kneset_
theater	התאטרון _ha-te-atron_
tomb	הקבר _ha-kever_
tower	המגדל _ha-migdal_
town hall	העיריה _ha-iriya_
tunnel	המנהרה _ha-minhara_
viewpoint	נקודת התצפית _nekudat ha-tatzpit_
well	הבאר _habe-er_
Can you show me on the map?	תוכל להראות לי על המפה? _tukhal lehar-ot li al hamapa_

Admission כניסה

Museums are usually closed on the High Holidays (➤ 219). Some may require you to buy a ticket in advance if visiting on Saturday (the Sabbath). Hours vary widely.

Is the … open to the public?	?האם ה... פתוח לציבור ha-**im** ha... pa**tu**-akh latzi**bur**
Can we look around?	?אפשר להסתכל efshar lehistakel
What are the opening hours?	?מה שעות הפתיחה ma she-**ot** hap**ti**kha
When does it close?	?מתי זה נסגר matay ze nisgar
Is … open on Fridays/ Saturdays/Sundays?	?האם ... פתוח בימי שישי/שבת/ראשון ha-**im** ... pa**tu**-akh bi**y**mey shishi/sha**bat**/rishon
When's the next guided tour?	?מתי הסיור המודרך הבא matay hasi**yur** hamud**rakh** haba
Do you have a guidebook (in English)?	?יש לכם חוברת הדרכה (באנגלית) yesh la**khem** kho**ver**et hadra**kha** (be-ang**lit**)
Can I take photos?	?מותר לצלם mu**tar** letza**lem**
Is there access for the disabled?	?יש גישה לנכים yesh gi**sha** lene**khim**
Is there an audioguide in English?	?יש הדרכה מוקלטת באנגלית yesh hadra**kha** muk**let**et be-ang**lit**

Paying/Tickets תשלום/כרטיסים

… tickets, please.	כרטיסים, בבקשה ... karti**sim** bevaka**sha**
How much is the entrance fee?	?מה דמי הכניסה ma dmey hakni**sa**
Are there any reductions for …?	?יש הנחות ל... yesh hana**khot** le
children	ילדים ye**ladim**
groups	קבוצות kvut**zot**
senior citizens	קשישים kshi**shim**
students	סטודנטים stu**dentim**
the disabled	נכים ne**khim**
One adult and two children, please.	.מבוגר אחד ושני ילדים, בבקשה mevu**gar** e**khad** ush**ney** yela**dim** bevaka**sha**
I've lost my ticket.	.איבדתי את הכרטיס שלי i**badeti** et hakar**tis** sheli

– khami<u>sha</u> kartisim bevakasha. yesh hana<u>kh</u>ot?
(Five tickets, please. Are there any discounts?)
– ken. yela<u>dim</u> vegimla-<u>im</u> ze khami<u>sha</u> shkalim.
(Yes. Children and senior citizens are five shekels.)
– shney mevuga<u>rim</u> ushlo<u>sha</u> yela<u>dim</u> bevakasha.
(Two adults and three children, please.)
– ze shlo<u>shim</u> vekhami<u>sha</u> shkalim bevaka<u>sha</u>.
(That's 35 shekels, please.)

הכניסה בחינם	free admission
סגור	closed
חנות מתנות	gift shop
כניסה אחרונה בחמש בערב	latest entry at 5 p.m.
הסיור הבא ב...	next tour at …
אין כניסה	no entry
אסור לצלם במבזק	no flash photography
אסור לצלם	no photography
פתוח	open
שעות הביקור	business hours

Impressions התרשמויות

It's …	ze זה ...
amazing	מפליא ma<u>fli</u>
beautiful	יפה ya<u>fe</u>
boring	משעמם mesha-a<u>mem</u>
incredible	לא יאומן lo ye-u<u>man</u>
interesting	מעניין me-an<u>yen</u>
magnificent	מפואר mefo-<u>ar</u>
romantic	רומנטי ro<u>man</u>ti
strange	מוזר mu<u>zar</u>
stunning	מדהים mad<u>him</u>
superb	נהדר nehe<u>dar</u>
terrible	נורא no<u>ra</u>
ugly	מכוער mekho-<u>ar</u>
I like it.	זה מוצא חן בעיניי. ze mo<u>tze</u> khen be-ey<u>nay</u>
I don't like it.	זה לא מוצא חן בעיניי. ze lo mo<u>tze</u> khen be-ey<u>nay</u>

Tourist glossary
<u>מילון לתייר</u>

מצודה	*metzu<u>da</u>*	castle
אתר היסטורי	*<u>a</u>t<u>ar</u> hist<u>o</u>ri*	historic site
ארמון	*ar<u>mon</u>*	palace
גן	*gan*	garden
קבר	*<u>ke</u>ver*	tomb
מוזאון	*muze-<u>on</u>*	museum
עיר עתיקה	*ir at<u>i</u>ka*	old city
כנסיה	*knesi<u>ya</u>*	church
מסגד	*mis<u>gad</u>*	mosque
בית כנסת	*beyt k<u>ne</u>set*	synagogue
פארק	*park*	park
חוף	*khof*	beach
מקדש	*mik<u>dash</u>*	temple

ארכאולוגיה	*arkhe-ologiya*	archeology
אדריכלות	*adrikhalut*	architecture
אמנות	*omanut*	art
קליגרפיה	*kaligrafiya*	calligraphy
קרמיקה/קדרות	*keramika/kadarut*	ceramics/pottery
עבודות יד	*avodot yad*	handicrafts
מוצרי לכה	*mutzrey laka*	lacquerware
ציור	*tziyur*	painting
עבודות נייר	*avodot neyar*	papercrafts
טקסטיל	*tekstil*	textiles
פסלות	*pasalut*	sculpture
עבודות עץ	*avodot etz*	woodcrafts

Who? / What? / When? מי/מה/מתי?

What's that building? מה הבניין ההוא? *ma habinyan hahu*

When was it built? מתי הוא נבנה? *matay hu nivna*

Who was the artist / architect? מי היה האמן/האדריכל? *mi haya ha-oman/ha-adrikhal*

What style is that? איזה סגנון זה? *eyze signon ze*

Some of the sightseeing highlights of a country rich in history and architecture:

Jerusalem
The Old City: Wailing Wall; Temple Mount; Church of the Holy Sepulchre; the **shuk** (or **suk** in Arabic – traditional market).
Mount of Olives: Tomb of the Prophets; Mary's Tomb; Garden of Gethsemane.
The Kirya: Israel Museum; the Knesset (parliament); Hebrew University.
Mount Herzl: Herzl's tomb; Yad Va'Shem Holocaust memorial museum.

Bethlehem
Church of the Nativity.

Tel Aviv
Tel Aviv museum; Shalom Tower; Dizengoff Street (cafés and galleries); Tel Aviv University; the beach.
Old Jaffa: the markets; artists' quarter.

Haifa
Mount Carmel; Baha'i shrine and gardens.

Tiberias and Sea of Galilee
Mount of Beatitudes; Hammat Gader Roman baths; hot springs.

Golan Heights
Banias: source of the Jordan river and waterfalls; Mount Hermon.

Jericho and the Dead Sea
Hisham's early Islamic palace; Monastery of the Temptation; Qumran caves; Ein Gedi gorge and hot springs; the fortress of Masada.

Eilat and the Red Sea
Coral beach nature preserve and scuba diving.

Religion / places of worship מקומות תפילה

Jews make up over 80% of the population, but Israel is also home to significant populations of Muslims, Samaritans, Christians (Protestants, Catholics, Armenian Orthodox, Eastern Orthodox, Copts), Druse, Baha'is and other denominations. You should always ask permission before entering a place of worship, and follow the rules regarding conduct and dress code.

Catholic/Protestant church	כנסיה קתולית/פרוטסטנטית
	knesiya katolit/protestantit
mosque	מסגד *misgad*
synagogue	בית כנסת *beyt kneset*
temple	מקדש *mikdash*
What time is …?	באיזו שעה ה...? *be-eyzo sha-a ha*
mass/the service	מיסה/תפילה *misa/tfila*

Rulers שליטים

What period is that?

מאיזו תקופה זה?
me-eyzo tkufa ze

Early and Israelite civilizations   5000 B.C. – 63 B.C.

Early humans lived in caves on Mount Carmel more than half a million years ago and Jericho is reputed to be the first city. What is now Israel was largely under Egyptian influence until around 1000 B.C. Kings Saul, David, and Solomon consolidated a Hebrew kingdom which had its capital in Jerusalem. Later it split into two rival kingdoms. From about 500 B.C. the region was ruled by the Persians, the Greeks, and finally by the Romans.

Roman (Byzantine) empire   63 B.C. – A.D. 700

The Roman empire, later the Eastern or Byzantine empire, dominated the Middle East.

Early Islam and the Middle Ages   610 – 1520

After Mohammed's death in 632, his followers conquered a huge area from Spain to India. The period was dominated by the Papal Crusades and the Mogul invasions of Genghis Khan. For nearly 300 years, beginning in 1250, much of the region was ruled by the Mamelukes, self-styled soldier monarchs.

Ottoman empire   1520 – 1914

In 1453, the Islamic Ottomans took Constantinople, ending a thousand years of Byzantine history. They expanded their empire to include most of the Middle East.

The Twentieth Century

During the period between the world wars, the British held a League of Nations mandate over Palestine, and this continued during the Second World War. In November 1947, the United Nations voted to partition the country, and Israel was founded in May 1948. Its recent history has been characterized by several wars with its Arab neighbors, culminating in peace treaties with Egypt and Jordan (some areas occupied during those wars are now under Palestinian self-rule), and by huge waves of Jewish immigration.

In the countryside מחוץ לעיר

I'd like a map of …	... הייתי רוצה מפה של hayiti rotze mapa shel
this region	האיזור הזה ha-ezor haze
walking routes	מסלולי הליכה masluley halikha
cycle routes	מסלולי אופניים masluley ofanayim
How far is it to …?	מה המרחק ל...? ma hamerkhak le
Is there a right of way?	יש אפשרות מעבר? yesh efsharut ma-avar
Is there a trail/scenic route to …?	יש שביל/דרך נופית ל...? yesh shvil/derekh nofit le
Can you show me on the map?	תוכל להראות לי על המפה? tukhal lehar-ot li al hamapa
I'm lost.	תעיתי בדרך. ta-iti baderekh

Organized walks טיול מאורגן ברגל

When does the guided walk start?	מתי מתחיל הטיול המודרך? matay matkhil hatiyul hamudrakh
When will we return?	באיזו שעה נחזור? be-eyzo sha-a nakhzor
Is it a hard course?	זה מסלול קשה? ze maslul kashe
gentle/medium/tough	קל/בינוני/מפרך kal/beynoni/mefarekh
I'm exhausted.	אני תשוש. ani tashush
How long are we resting here?	כמה זמן ננוח פה? kama zman nanu-akh po
What kind of … is that?	איזה סוג של ... זה? eyze sug shel … ze
animal/bird	חיה/ציפור khaya/tzipor
flower/tree	פרח/עץ perakh/etz

WALKING/HIKING GEAR ➤ 145

Geographic features מושגים גאוגרפיים

beach	חוף	khof
bridge	גשר	gesher
canal	תעלה	te-ala
cave	מערה	me-ara
cliff	צוק	tzuk
farm	חווה	khava
field	שדה	sade
footpath	שביל	shvil
forest	יער	ya-ar
hill	גבעה	giv-a
lake	אגם	agam
mountain	הר	har
mountain pass	מעבר הרים	ma-avar harim
mountain range	שרשרת הרים	sharsheret harim
nature preserve	שמורת טבע	shmurat teva
panorama	פנורמה	panorama
park	פארק	park
peak	פיסגה	pisga
picnic area	אתר פיקניק	atar piknik
pond	בריכה	brekha
rapids	אשדות	ashadot
river	נהר	nahar
sea	ים	yam
stream	נחל	nakhal
valley	עמק	emek
viewpoint	נקודת תצפית	nekudat tatzpit
village	כפר	kfar
vineyard	כרם	kerem
waterfall	מפל מים	mapal mayim
wood	חורשה	khorsha

Leisure

At your hotel or in the tourist information offices you'll often find publications, including free local newspapers listing local attractions and events. You can also consult the English-language newspapers.

TV programs are mostly in Hebrew, but regional stations throughout the Middle East broadcast news in English, which can be received in Israel. Most foreign films are subtitled, with the soundtrack remaining in the original language.

Most major hotels have English-language cable and satellite TV.

Events אירועים

Do you have a program of events?	יש לך תכנית אירועים? *yesh lekha tokhnit eru-im*
Can you recommend a …?	תוכל להמליץ על ...? *tukhal lehamlitz al*
ballet	בלט *balet*
concert	קונצרט *kontzert*
movie [film]	סרט *seret*
opera	אופרה *opera*
play	מחזה *makhaze*

Availability זמינות

When does it start?	מתי זה מתחיל? *matay ze matkhil*
When does it end?	מתי זה נגמר? *matay ze nigmar*
Are there any tickets for tonight?	יש כרטיסים להערב? *yesh kartisim leha-erev*
Where can I get tickets?	איפה אוכל להשיג כרטיסים? *eyfo ukhal lehasig kartisim*
There are … of us.	אנחנו ... אנשים. *anakhnu … anashim*

כרטיסים Tickets

How much are seats?	כמה עולים הכרטיסים? *kama olim hakartisim*
Do you have anything cheaper?	יש לכם משהו זול יותר? *yesh lakhem mashehu zol yoter*
I'd like two tickets for tonight's concert.	אבקש שני כרטיסים לקונצרט הערב. *avakesh shney kartisim lakontzert ha-erev*
I'd like to reserve …	הייתי רוצה להזמין … *hayiti rotze lehazmin*
three tickets for Sunday evening	שלושה כרטיסים ליום ראשון בערב *shlosha kartisim leyom rishon ba-erev*
one ticket for the Friday matinée	כרטיס אחד ליום שישי אחר הצהריים *kartis ekhad leyom shishi akhar hatzohorayim*
Can I pay by credit card?	אפשר לשלם בכרטיס אשראי? *efshar leshalem bekartis ashray*

מה … כרטיס האשראי שלך?	What's your credit card …?
מספר	number
סוג	type
תאריך התפוגה	expiration [expiry] date
תוכל לחתום כאן, בבקשה.	Can you sign here, please.
נא לאסוף את הכרטיסים …	Please pick up the tickets …
לפני … בערב	by … p.m.
בדלפק ההזמנות	at the reservation desk

– *ukhal la-azor lekha?* (Can I help you?)
– *avakesh shney kartisim lakontzert ha-erev.*
(I'd like two tickets for tonight's concert.)
– *beseder.* (Certainly.)
– *efshar leshalem bekartis ashray?*
(Can I pay by credit card?)
ken. (Yes.)
– *im kakh ashalem beviza.* (In that case, I'll pay by Visa.)
– *toda. tukhal lakhtom kan bevakasha?*
(Thank you. Can you sign here, please?)

הכרטיסים אזלו	sold out
כרטיסים להיום	tickets for today
הזמנות מראש	advance reservations

NUMBERS ➤ 216

109

Movies [Cinema] קולנוע

Foreign films are usually shown in their original language with Hebrew subtitles.

Is there a movie theater [cinema] near here?	יש בסביבה קולנוע? yesh basviva kolno-a
What's playing at the movies [on at the cinema] tonight?	מה מציג בקולנוע הערב? ma matzig bakolno-a ha-erev
Is the film dubbed into Hebrew?	יש פסקול עברי? yesh paskol ivri?
Is the film subtitled?	יש תרגום בגוף הסרט? yesh tirgum beguf haseret
Is the film in the original English?	האם הסרט הוא באנגלית המקורית? ha-im haseret hu ba-anglit hamekorit
A ..., please.	..., בבקשה. bevakasha
box [carton] of popcorn	קופסת פופקורן kufsat popkorn
chocolate ice cream [choc-ice]	גלידת שוקולד glidat shokolad
hot dog	נקניקיה naknikiya
soft drink	משקה קל mashke kal
small/regular/large	קטן/רגיל/גדול katan/ragil/gadol

Theater תאטרון

What's playing at the Habimah Theater?	מה מציג בתאטרון הבימה? ma matzig bete-atron habima
Who's the playwright?	מי המחזאי? mi hamakhazay
Do you think I'd enjoy it?	אתה חושב שאהנה מזה? ata khoshev she-ehane mize
I don't know much Hebrew.	אני לא יודע הרבה עברית. ani lo yode-a harbe ivrit

Opera / Ballet / Dance
אופרה / בלט / מחול

Classical and modern dance are popular in Israel. In large cities there are frequent performances by local and visiting troupes. When booking tickets to the opera, you may want to check if it is sung in Hebrew or in the original language.

Where's the theater?	איפה האולם? eyfo ha-ulam
Who's the composer / soloist?	מי המלחין/הסולן? mi hamalkhin/hasolan
Is formal dress required?	דרוש לבוש פורמלי? darush levush formali
Who's dancing?	מי רוקד? mi roked
I'm interested in contemporary dance.	אני מתעניין במחול מודרני. ani mit-anyen bemakhol moderni

Music / Concerts   מוסיקה / קונצרטים

Where's the concert hall?	איפה אולם הקונצרטים? eyfo ulam hakontzertim
Which orchestra / band is playing?	איזו תזמורת/להקה מנגנת? eyzo tizmoret/lahaka menagenet
What are they playing?	מה הם מנגנים? ma hem menagnim
Who's the conductor / soloist?	מי המנצח/הסולן? mi hamenatze-akh/hasolan
Who's the support band?	מי להקה המלווה? mi halahaka hamelava
I really like …	אני מאד אוהב ... ani me-od ohev
folk music / country music	מוסיקת עם/מוסיקת קנטרי musikat am/musikat kantri
jazz	ג'ז jaz
music of the sixties	מוסיקה של שנות הששים musika shel shnot hashishim
pop / rock music	מוסיקת פופ/רוק musikat pop/rok
soul music	מוסיקת נשמה musikat neshama
Have you ever heard of her / him / them?	האם שמעת אי פעם עליה/עליו/עליהם? ha-im shamata ey pa-am aleyha/alav/aleyhem
Are they popular?	הם פופולריים? hem populariyim

111

Nightlife חיי לילה

What is there to do in the evenings?	מה יש לעשות בערבים? *ma yesh la-asot ba-aravim*
Can you recommend a …?	תוכל להמליץ על ...? *tukhal lehamlitz al*
Is there a …?	יש ...? *yesh*
bar / restaurant	בר/מסעדה *bar/mis-ada*
cabaret / casino	קברט/קזינו *kabaret/kazino*
discotheque	דיסקוטק *diskotek*
gay club	מועדון לעליזים *mo-adon le-alizim*
nightclub	מועדון לילה *mo-adon layla*
What type of music do they play?	איזה סוג מוסיקה הם מנגנים? *eyze sug musika hem menagnim*
How do I get there?	איך אגיע לשם? *eykh agi-a lesham*
Is there an admission charge?	צריך לשלם דמי כניסה? *tzarikh leshalem dmey knisa*

Admission כניסה

What time does the show start?	מתי מתחיל המופע? *matay matkhil hamofa*
Is there a cover charge?	יש תשלום שרות מינימלי? *yesh tashlum sherut minimali*
Is a reservation necessary?	נחוץ להזמין מקום? *nakhutz lehazmin makom*
Do we need to be members?	אנחנו צריכים להיות חברים? *anakhnu tzrikhim lihiyot khaverim*
Can you have dinner there?	אפשר לאכול שם ארוחת ערב? *efshar le-ekhol sham arukhat erev*
How long will we have to stand in line [queue]?	כמה זמן נצטרך לעמוד בתור? *kama zman nitztarekh la-amod bator*
I'd like a good table.	אבקש שולחן טוב. *avakesh shulkhan tov*

TIME ➤ 220; TAXI ➤ 84

Children ילדים

Can you recommend something for the children?	תוכל להמליץ על משהו לילדים? *tukhal lehamlitz al mashehu liyladim*
Are there changing facilities here for babies?	יש פה מתקני החלפת חיתולים? *yesh po mitkaney hakhlafat khitulim*
Where are the bathrooms [toilets]?	איפה השרותים? *eyfo hasherutim*
amusement arcade	מועדון מכונות משחק *mo-adon mekhonot miskhak*
fairground	לונה פארק *luna park*
kiddie [paddling] pool	בריכה לפעוטות *brekha lif-otot*
playground	מגרש משחקים *migrash miskhakim*
play group	פעוטון *pa-oton*
zoo	גן חיות *gan khayot*

Baby-sitting שמרטף

Can you recommend a reliable baby-sitter?	תוכל להמליץ על שמרטף אמין? *tukhal lehamlitz al shmartaf amin*
Is there constant supervision?	יש השגחה קבועה? *yesh hashgakha kvu-a*
Is the staff properly trained?	האם הצוות מיומן? *ha-im hatzevet meyuman*
When can I bring them?	מתי אוכל להביא אותם? *matay ukhal lehavi otam*
I'll pick them up at ...	אאסוף אותם ב... *e-esof otam be*
We'll be back by ...	נחזור לפני ... *nakhzor lifney*
She's 3, and he's 18 months.	היא בת שלוש והוא בן שנה וחצי. *hi bat shalosh vehu ben shana vakhetzi*

113

ספורט Sports

Soccer is very popular in Israel, as is basketball, though to a lesser extent. Local soccer teams are supported vocally and enthusiastically: watching such a game can be an experience and is something you can enjoy without needing to know the language. Games are usually held on Saturdays.

Tennis, volleyball, badminton and squash are offered by many major hotels, most of which also have a swimming pool even if they are on the beach. Some hotels can arrange horseback riding, too.

Spectator צופים

Is there a soccer [football] game [match] this Saturday?	יש משחק כדורגל בשבת זו? _yesh miskhak kaduregel beshabat zo_
Which teams are playing?	אילו קבוצות משחקות? _eylu kvutzot mesakhakot_
Can you get me a ticket?	תוכל להשיג לי כרטיס? _tukhal lehasig li kartis_
What's the admission charge?	מה דמי הכניסה? _ma dmey haknisa_

aerobics	אירוביקה	_erobika_
angling	דייג בחכה	_dayig bekhaka_
archery	קשתות	_kashatut_
athletics	אתלטיקה	_atletika_
badminton	בדמינטון	_bedminton_
basketball	כדורסל	_kadursal_
boxing	איגרוף	_igruf_
canoeing	שייט בקנו	_shayit bekanu_
cycling	רכיבה באופניים	_rekhiva be-ofanayim_
gliding	דאייה	_de-iya_

golf	גולף golf
horse racing	מירוצי סוסים merutzey susim
judo	ג'ידו judo
rappeling [abseiling]	סנפלינק sneplink
rock climbing	טיפוס בצוקים tipus betzukim
rowing	חתירה khatira
skiing	סקי ski
soccer	כדורגל kaduregel
squash	סקווש skwosh
swimming	שחיה skhiya
table tennis	טניס שולחן tenis shulkhan
tennis	טניס tenis
volleyball	כדורעף kadur-af

Participating משתתפים

Is there a ... nearby?	יש ... בסביבה? yesh ... basviva
golf course	מגרש גולף migrash golf
sports club	מועדון ספורט mo-adon sport
Are there any tennis courts?	יש מגרשי טניס? yesh migrashey tenis
What's the charge per ...?	מה המחיר ל...? ma hamekhir le
day / round / hour	יום/סיבוב/שעה yom/sivuv/sha-a
Do I need to be a member?	אני צריך להיות חבר? ani tzarikh lihiyot khaver
Where can I rent ...?	איפה אוכל לשכור ...? eyfo ukhal liskor
boots	נעליים na-alayim
clubs	מקלות maklot
equipment	ציוד tziyud
a racket	מחבט makhbet

115

Can I get lessons?	אפשר לקבל שיעורים? _efshar lekabel shi-urim_
Do you have a fitness room?	יש לכם חדר כושר? _yesh lakhem khadar kosher_
May I join in?	אפשר להצטרף? _efshar lehitztaref_

מצטער, אנחנו מלאים.	I'm sorry. We're booked.
יש להשאיר פקדון של ...	There is a deposit of ...
מה המידה שלך?	What size are you?
אתה זקוק לתצלום דרכון.	You need a passport-size photo.

| חדרי הלבשה | changing rooms |

At the beach בחוף

Most resort beaches are supervised, with a system of white, red, and black flags denoting *Safe, Take care,* and *No swimming* respectively. Do not swim in unprotected areas, and always assess conditions beforehand, particularly where children are concerned.

Wear plastic shoes to protect your feet in coral reef areas in the Red Sea, and be careful not to break off any of the coral, which is protected by law.

Water sports of excellent quality are offered at beach resorts along the Mediterranean, Sea of Galilee and Red Sea coasts, including waterskiing, windsurfing, and paragliding.

Is the beach pebbly/sandy?	זה חוף חלוקים/חולי? *ze khof khalukim/kholi*
Is there a … here?	יש פה …? *yesh po*
children's pool	בריכה לילדים *brekha liyladim*
swimming pool	בריכת שחייה *brekhat skhiya*
indoor/open-air	מכוסה/פתוחה *mekhusa/ptukha*
Is it safe to swim/dive here?	בטוח לשחות/לצלול פה? *batu-akh liskhot/litzlol po*
Is it safe for children?	זה בטוח לילדים? *ze batu-akh liyladim*
Is there a lifeguard?	יש מציל? *yesh matzil*
I want to rent a(n)/some …	אני רוצה לשכור … *ani rotze liskor*
deck chair	כסא נוח *kise no-akh*
diving equipment	ציוד צלילה *tziyud tzlila*
jet-ski	סקי ממונע *ski memuna*
motorboat	סירת מנוע *sirat mano-a*
umbrella [sunshade]	שמשיה *shimshiya*
surfboard	גלשן *galshan*
water skis	סקי מים *ski mayim*
for … hours	ל… שעות *le … sha-ot*
I'm an experienced windsurfer.	אני גלשן מנוסה. *ani galshan menuse*
I'm a beginner.	אני מתחיל. *ani matkhil*

Making friends התיידדות

Israelis have first and last names as Westerners do, and they may also have a middle name, which is rarely used. The given name is supposed to come first, followed by the surname – but there is an alternative custom of starting with the surname, so be on your guard! Most married women take on their husband's surname. However, since Israel is one of the most informal of all societies, you will often only know your companion's first name, except in very formal circumstances, and he or she will expect to use yours almost from the very moment you meet.

There is a variety of different greetings and replies for special occasions. However, tourists are better off sticking to one of the general greetings such as **shalom** (hello) and **lehitra-ot** (good-bye). It's also usual to shake hands when you meet people – though you should wait for them to offer their hand first, in case they are prevented from doing so because of a religious custom.

Hello. We haven't met.	שלום. עוד לא הכרנו. shalom. od lo hikarnu
My name is …	שמי … shmi
May I introduce …?	אוכל להכיר לך את …? ukhal lehakir lekha et
Pleased to meet you.	נעים מאד. na-im me-od
What's your name?	מה שמך? ma shimkha
How are you?	מה שלומך? ma shlomkha
Fine, thanks. And you?	טוב, תודה. ואתה? tov toda ve-ata

– shalom. ma shlomkha?
(Hello. How are you?)

– tov toda. ve-ata?
(Fine, thanks. And you?)

– tov toda. (Fine, thanks.)

Where are you from? ‏מאיפה אתה?‏

Where are you from?	‏מאיפה אתה?‏ me-eyfo ata
Where were you born?	‏איפה נולדת?‏ eyfo noladeta
I'm from …	‏אני מ...‏ ani mi
Australia	‏אוסטרליה‏ ostraliya
Britain	‏בריטניה‏ britaniya
Canada	‏קנדה‏ kanada
England	‏אנגליה‏ angliya
Ireland	‏אירלנד‏ irland
Scotland	‏סקוטלנד‏ skotland
South Africa	‏דרום אפריקה‏ drom afrika
the U.S.	‏ארה"ב‏ artzot habrit
Wales	‏ויילס‏ weyls
Where do you live?	‏איפה אתה גר?‏ eyfo ata gar
What part of Israel are you from?	‏מאיזה איזור בישראל אתה?‏ me-eyze ezor be-israel ata
We come here every year.	‏אנחנו באים הנה כל שנה.‏ anakhnu ba-im hena kol shana
It's my/our first visit.	‏זה הביקור הראשון שלי/שלנו.‏ ze habikur harishon sheli/shelanu
Have you ever been to …?	‏היית אי פעם ב...?‏ hayita ey pa-am be
the U.K./U.S.	‏בריטניה/ארה"ב‏ britaniya/artzot habrit
Do you like it here?	‏מוצא חן בעיניך פה?‏ motze khen be-eynekha po
What do you think of the …?	‏מה דעתך על ...?‏ ma da-atkha al
I love the … here.	‏אני אוהב את ה... פה.‏ ani ohev et ha… po
I don't really like the … here.	‏אני לא כל-כך מחבב את ה... פה.‏ ani lo kol kakh mekhabev et ha… po
food/people	‏אוכל/אנשים‏ okhel/anashim

Who are you with? ‏עם מי אתה?‏

Who are you with?	‏עם מי אתה?‏	im mi ata
I'm on my own.	‏אני לבד.‏	ani levad
I'm with a friend.	‏אני עם חבר.‏	ani im khaver
I'm with …	‏אני עם ...‏	ani im
my husband/wife	‏בעלי/אשתי‏	ba-ali/ishti
my family	‏המשפחה‏	hamishpakha
my children/parents	‏הילדים/ההורים‏	hayladim/hahorim
my boyfriend/girlfriend	‏החבר/החברה‏	hakhaver/hakhavera
my father/son	‏אבי/בני‏	avi/bni
my mother/daughter	‏אמי/בתי‏	imi/biti
my brother/uncle	‏אחי/דודי‏	akhi/dodi
my sister/aunt	‏אחותי/דודתי‏	akhoti/dodati
What's your son's/wife's name?	‏מה שם בנך/אשתך?‏	ma shem binkha/ishtekha
Are you married?	‏אתה נשוי?‏	ata nasuy
I'm …	‏אני...‏	ani
married/single	‏נשוי/רווק‏	nasuy/ravak
divorced/separated	‏גרוש/חי בנפרד‏	garush/khay benifrad
engaged	‏מאורס‏	me-oras
We live together.	‏אנחנו חיים יחד.‏	anakhnu khayim yakhad
Do you have any children?	‏יש לך ילדים?‏	yesh lekha yeladim
We have two boys and a girl.	‏יש לנו שני בנים ובת.‏	yesh lanu shney banim uvat
How old are they?	‏בני כמה הם?‏	bney kama hem
They're 10 and 12.	‏הם בני עשר ושתים עשרה.‏	hem bney eser ushteym esre

What do you do? מה אתה עושה?

What do you do?	מה אתה עושה? ma ata ose
What are you studying?	מה אתה לומד? ma ata lomed
I'm studying …	אני לומד … ani lomed
I'm in …	אני ב…‏ ani be
business	עסקים asakim
engineering	הנדסה handasa
sales	מכירות mekhirot
Who do you work for?	אצל מי אתה עובד? etzel mi ata oved
I work for …	אני עובד אצל … ani oved etzel
I'm (a/an) …	אני … ani
accountant	רואה חשבון ro-e kheshbon
housewife	עקרת בית akeret bayit
student	סטודנט student
retired	בגימלאות begimla-ot
self-employed	עצמאי atzma-i
between jobs	לא עובד כרגע lo oved karega
What are your interests/ hobbies?	מה שטחי ההתעניינות/התחביבים שלך? ma shitkhey hahit-anyenut/ hatakhbivim shelkha
I like …	אני אוהב … ani ohev
music	מוסיקה musika
reading	קריאה kri-a
sports	ספורט sport
Would you like to play …?	אתה רוצה לשחק …?‏ ata rotze lesakhek
cards	קלפים klafim
chess	שחמט shakhmat
backgammon	שש-בש sheshbesh

What a lovely day!	איזה יום נפלא!	*eyze yom nifla*
What terrible weather!	איזה מזג אוויר נורא!	*eyze mezeg avir nora*
It's hot/cold today!	חם/קר היום!	*kham/kar hayom*
Is it usually this warm?	בדרך כלל חם כל כך?	*bederekh klal kham kol kakh*
Do you think it's going to … tomorrow?	אתה חושב ש... מחר?	*ata khoshev she… makhar*
be a nice day	יהיה יום יפה	*yihiye yom yafe*
rain	ירד גשם	*yered geshem*
snow	ירד שלג	*yered sheleg*
What's the weather forecast for tomorrow?	מה תחזית מזג האוויר למחר?	*ma takhazit mezeg ha-avir lemakhar*
It's cloudy.	מעונן.	*me-unan*
It's foggy.	מעורפל.	*me-urpal*
It's stormy.	סוער.	*so-er*
It's windy.	נושבת רוח.	*noshevet ru-akh*
It's raining.	יורד גשם.	*yored geshem*
It's snowing.	יורד שלג.	*yored sheleg*
It's sunny.	השמש זורחת.	*hashemesh zorakhat*
Has the weather been like this for long?	מזג האוויר כזה כבר הרבה זמן?	*mezeg ha-avir kaze kvar harbe zman*
What's the pollen count?	מה ריכוז אבקת הפרחים באוויר?	*ma rikuz avkat haprakhim ba-avir*
high/medium/low	גבוה/בינוני/נמוך	*gavo-ha/beynoni/namukh*
Will it be good weather for swimming?	יהיה מזג אוויר טוב לשחייה?	*yihiye mezeg avir tov liskhiya*

אתה בחופשה?	Are you on vacation?
איך הגעת/נסעת הנה?	How did you get/ travel here?
איפה אתה שוהה?	Where are you staying?
כמה זמן אתה כבר פה?	How long have you been here?
לכמה זמן תשאר?	How long are you staying?
מה כבר עשית?	What have you done so far?
לאן תיסע אחרי זה?	Where are you going next?
אתה נהנה מהחופשה?	Are you enjoying your vacation?

I'm here on …	אני פה ל...	_ani_ po le
business	עסקים	asa_kim_
vacation [holiday]	חופשה	khuf_sha_
We came by …	באנו ב...	_banu_ be
train/bus/plane	רכבת/אוטובוס/מטוס	_ra_kevet/_o_tobus/ma_tos_
car	מכונית	mekho_nit_
I have a rental car.	יש לי מכונית שכורה.	yesh li mekho_nit_ skhura
We're staying in/at …	אנחנו שוהים ב...	ana_khnu_ sho_him_ be
a campsite	אתר קמפינג	atar _kemping_
a guest house	בית הארחה	beyt ha-ar_akha_
a hotel	מלון	ma_lon_
a youth hostel	אכסניית נוער	akhsa_nyat no_-ar
with friends	אצל ידידים	_etzel_ yedi_dim_
Can you suggest …?	תוכל להמליץ על ...?	tu_khal_ leham_litz_ al
things to do	דברים לעשות	dva_rim_ la-asot
places to eat	מקומות לארוחה	meko_mot_ le-aru_kha_
places to visit	מקומות לבקר	meko_mot_ leva_ker_
We're having a great time.	אנחנו עושים חיים.	ana_khnu_ osim kha_yim_
We're having a terrible time.	אנחנו נורא לא נהנים.	ana_khnu_ nora lo nehe_nim_

Invitations הזמנות

Would you like to have dinner with us on …?	?תרצה לאכול ארוחת ערב איתנו ב... *tirtze le-ekhol arukhat erev itanu be*
May I invite you to lunch?	?אוכל להזמין אותך לארוחת צהריים *ukhal lehazmin otkha le-arukhat tzohorayim*
Can you come for a drink this evening?	?תוכל לבוא למשקה הערב *tukhal lavo lemashke ha-erev*
We are having a party. Can you come?	?אנחנו עושים מסיבה. תוכל לבוא *anakhnu osim mesiba. tukhal lavo*
May we join you?	?נוכל להצטרף אליך *nukhal lehitztaref elekha*
Would you like to join us?	?תרצה להצטרף אלינו *tirtze lehitztaref eleynu*

Going out בילויים

What are your plans for …?	?מה התכניות שלך ל... *ma hatokhniyot shelkha le*
today / tonight	היום/הערב *hayom/ha-erev*
tomorrow	מחר *makhar*
Are you free this evening?	?אתה פנוי הערב *ata panuy ha-erev*
Would you like to …?	?אתה רוצה ... *ata rotze*
go dancing	ללכת לרקוד *lalekhet lirkod*
go for a drink	ללכת לשתות *lalekhet lishtot*
go out for a meal	ללכת לאכול *lalekhet le-ekhol*
go for a walk	ללכת לטייל *lalekhet letayel*
go shopping	ללכת לקניות *lalekhet likniyot*
I'd like to go to …	...הייתי רוצה ללכת ל *hayiti rotze lalekhet le*
I'd like to see …	... הייתי רוצה לראות *hayiti rotze lir-ot*
Do you enjoy …?	?... אתה אוהב *ata ohev*

124

Accepting/Declining הסכמה/סירוב

Thank you. I'd love to.	תודה. ברצון. toda beratzon
Thank you, but I'm busy.	תודה, אבל אני עסוק. toda aval ani asuk
May I bring a friend?	אוכל להביא ידיד? ukhal lehavi yadid
Where shall we meet?	איפה ניפגש? eyfo nipagesh
I'll meet you …	אפגוש אותך ... efgosh otkha
in front of your hotel	בחזית המלון שלך bekhazit hamalon shelkha
I'll call for you at 8.	אבוא לקחת אותך ב-8. avo lakakhat otkha bishmone
Could we make it a bit later/earlier?	נוכל להיפגש קצת יותר מאוחר/מוקדם? nukhal lehipagesh ktzat yoter me-ukhar/ mukdam
How about another day?	מה עם יום אחר? ma im yom akher
That will be fine.	זה יהיה יופי. ze yihiye yofi

Dining out/in ארוחות במסעדה/בבית

Hospitality is taken very seriously, and if you are invited out to a meal in a restaurant you are not expected to pay – though it never hurts to offer. Being invited for a family meal at home means you have been accepted as a friend, and you should take a gift. A bottle of wine or flowers for the house are always welcome.

Expect to have your plate piled high and to be bombarded with encouragements to have more. At the very least you should try to taste everything placed on the table, which often is a selection of bowls for everyone to help themselves.

May I buy you a drink?	אפשר לקנות לך משקה? efshar liknot lekha mashke
Do you like …?	אתה אוהב ...? ata ohev
What are you going to have?	מה תרצה? ma tirtze
That was a lovely meal.	זו היתה ארוחה נהדרת. zo hayta arukha nehederet

Encounters פגישות

Do you mind if …?	?...אכפת לך אם *ikhpat lekha im*
I sit here/I smoke	אשב פה/אעשן *eshev po/a-ashen*
Can I get you a drink?	?אוכל להביא לך שתיה *ukhal lehavi lekha shtiya*
I'd love to have some company.	.אשמח להיות בחברת מישהו *esmakh lihiyot bekhevrat mishehu*
What's so funny?	?מה כל כך מצחיק *ma kol kakh matzkhik*
Is my Hebrew that bad?	?העברית שלי כל כך גרועה *ha-ivrit sheli kol kakh gru-a*
Shall we go somewhere quieter?	?אולי נלך למקום יותר שקט *ulay nelekh lemakom yoter shaket*
Leave me alone, please!	!עזוב אותי, בבקשה *azov oti bevakasha*
You look great!	!אתה נראה נפלא *ata nir-e nifla*
Would you like to come home with me?	?תרצה לבוא אלי הביתה *tirtze lavo elay habayta*
I'm not ready for that.	.אני עוד לא מוכן לזה *ani od lo mukhan leze*
I'm afraid we have to leave now.	.לצערי נצטרך לעזוב עכשיו *letza-ari nitztarekh la-azov akhshav*
Thanks for the evening.	.תודה על הערב *toda al ha-erev*
It was great.	.היה נהדר *haya nehedar*
Can I see you again tomorrow?	?אוכל לראות אותך שוב מחר *ukhal lir-ot otkha shuv makhar*
See you soon.	.להתראות בקרוב *lehitra-ot bekarov*
Can I have your address?	?אוכל לקבל את הכתובת שלך *ukhal lekabel et haktovet shelkha*

SAFETY ➤ 65

Telephoning טלפונים

Most places in Israel are linked to the international telephone system, with direct dialing offered by several competing companies. Telephone cards for use in public phones are sold at many outlets including post offices and newsstands. You can also use an international calling card.

Can I have your telephone number?	אוכל לקבל את מספר הטלפון שלך? *ukhal* lekab*el* et mis*par* ha*telefon* shel*kha*
Here's my number.	הנה המספר שלי. *hine hamispar sheli*
Please call me.	אנא צלצל אלי. *ana tzaltzel elay*
I'll give you a call.	אתן לך צלצול. *eten lekha tziltzul*
Where's the nearest telephone booth?	איפה תא הטלפון הקרוב? *eyfo* ta ha*telefon hakarov*
May I use your phone?	אוכל להשתמש בטלפון שלך? *ukhal* lehishta*mesh* bate*lefon* shel*kha*
It's an emergency.	זה מקרה חירום. *ze mikre kherum*
I'd like to call someone in England.	אבקש לצלצל למישהו באנגליה. ava*kesh* letzal*tzel* lemishehu be-*angliya*
What's the area [dialling] code for …?	מה הקידומת ל... *ma* hakid*omet* le
I'd like a phone card.	אבקש טלכרט. ava*kesh telekart*
What's the number for Information [Directory Enquiries]?	מה המספר לשרות מודיעין? *ma* hamis*par* lesh*erut* modi-*in*
I'd like the number for …	אבקש את המספר של ... ava*kesh* et hamis*par* shel
I'd like to call collect [reverse the charges].	אני רוצה לחייג בגוביינא. *ani rotze* lekha*yeg* beguv*ayna*

מדברים Speaking

Hello. This is …	הלו. מדבר … *halo. medaber*
I'd like to speak to …	אבקש לדבר עם … *avakesh ledaber im*
Extension …	שלוחה … *shlukha*
Speak louder, please.	דבר בקול רם יותר, בבקשה. *daber bekol ram yoter bevakasha*
Speak more slowly, please.	דבר לאט יותר, בבקשה. *daber le-at yoter bevakasha*
Could you repeat that, please?	תוכל לחזור על זה, בבקשה. *tukhal lakhzor al ze bevakasha*
I'm afraid he's/she's not in.	לצערי הוא/היא לא פה. *letza-ari hu/hi lo po*
You have the wrong number.	חייגת מספר לא נכון. *khiyagta mispar lo nakhon*
Just a moment, please.	רק רגע, בבקשה. *rak rega bevakasha*
Hold on, please.	הישאר על הקו, בבקשה. *hisha-er al hakav bevakasha*
When will he be back/ she be back?	מתי הוא יחזור/היא תחזור? *matay hu yakhzor/hi takhzor*
Will you tell him/her that I called?	תוכל לומר לו/לה שצלצלתי? *tukhal lomar lo/la shetziltzalti*
My name is …	שמי … *shmi*
Would you ask him/her to call me?	תוכל לומר לו/לה להתקשר אלי? *tukhal lomar lo/la lehitkasher elay*
I must go now.	אני צריך ללכת עכשיו. *ani tzarikh lalekhet akhshav*
Thank you for calling.	תודה על הצלצול. *toda al hatziltzul*
I'll be in touch.	אהיה בקשר. *eheye bekesher*
Bye.	להתראות. *lehitra-ot*

Stores & Services

In most cities and large towns you will find shopping malls, department stores, supermarkets, and hypermarkets alongside a large variety of specialty stores. However, you may find it more interesting to buy souvenirs in the markets (**shuk**; **suk** in Arabic). Here you can shop for everything from fruit and spices to carpets and gold. You'll have to use your judgment about how hard to bargain, and don't overdo it in case you end up making an insulting offer.

ESSENTIAL

I'd like …	אבקש … *avakesh*
Do you have …?	יש לכם …? *yesh lakhem*
How much is that?	כמה זה? *kama ze*
Thank you.	תודה. *toda*

פתוח	open
סגור	closed
מכירה	sale

Stores and services
חנויות ושרותים
Where is ...? ...? איפה

Where's the nearest ...?	?איפה ה... הקרוב *eyfo ha... hakarov*
Is there a good ...?	?יש ... טוב *yesh ... tov?*
Where's the main shopping mall [centre]?	איפה מרכז הקניות הראשי? *eyfo merkaz hakniyot harashi*
Is it far from here?	?זה רחוק מפה *ze rakhok mipo*
How do I get there?	?איך מגיעים לשם *eykh magi-im lesham*

Stores חנויות

bakery	מאפיה *ma-afiya*
bank	בנק *bank*
bookstore	חנות ספרים *khanut sfarim*
butcher	אטליז *itliz*
camera store	חנות צילום *khanut tzilum*
clothing store [clothes shop]	חנות בגדים *khanut begadim*
convenience store	צרכניה *tzarkhaniya*
department store	חנות כלבו *khanut kolbo*
fish store [fishmonger]	חנות דגים *khanut dagim*
florist	חנות פרחים *khanut prakhim*
gift store	חנות מתנות *khanut matanot*
greengrocer	ירקן *yarkan*
health food store	חנות למזון טבעוני *khanut lemazon tiv-oni*

jeweler	צורף *tzoref*
music store	חנות תקליטים *khanut taklitim*
newsstand [newsagent]	חנות עיתונים *khanut itonim*
pastry shop	קונדיטוריה *konditoriya*
pharmacy [chemist]	בית מרקחת *beyt merkakhat*
shoe store	חנות נעליים *khanut na-alayim*
souvenir store	חנות מזכרות *khanut mazkarot*
sporting goods store	חנות למוצרי ספורט *khanut lemutzrey sport*
supermarket	סופרמרקט *supermarket*
tobacconist [cigarette kiosk]	חנות למוצרי טבק *khanut lemutzrey tabak*
toy store	חנות צעצועים *khanut tza-atzu-im*

Services שרותים

clinic	מרפאה *mirpa-a*
dentist	רופא שיניים *rofe shina-yim*
doctor	רופא *rofe*
dry cleaner	מכבסה לניקוי יבש *mikhbasa lenikuy yavesh*
hairdresser/barber	מספרה *mispara*
hospital	בית חולים *beyt kholim*
laundromat	מכבסה בשרות עצמי *mikhbasa besherut atzmi*
optician	אופטיקאי *optikay*
police station	תחנת משטרה *takhanat mishtara*
post office	סניף דואר *snif do-ar*
travel agency	סוכנות נסיעות *sokhnut nesi-ot*

Opening hours שעות פתיחה

Hours for stores and banks vary but tend to be from 8 or 9 a.m. until 7 p.m. – though banks and some post offices close much earlier. Some stores close in the middle of the day and re-open in the afternoon. On Fridays and days preceding festivals, stores tend to close early at 2 to 4 p.m. On festival days themselves, they are often closed completely.

Saturday is the official closing day in Jewish areas, Friday in Muslim areas, and Sunday in Christian areas.

When does the … open/close?	מתי ה... נפתח/נסגר? *matay ha... niftakh/nisgar*
Are you open in the evening?	אתם פתוחים בערב? *atem ptukhim ba-erev*
Where is the …	...איפה ה *eyfo ha*
cashier [cash desk]	קופה *kupa*
escalator	מדרגות נעות *madregot na-ot*
elevator [lift]	מעלית *ma-alit*
store directory [guide]	לוח מידע *lu-akh meyda*
first [ground (U.K.)] floor	קומת קרקע *komat karka*
second [first (U.K.)] floor	קומה ראשונה *koma rishona*
Where's the … department?	...איפה מחלקת ה *eyfo makhleket ha*

שעות עסקים	business hours
כניסה	entrance
מדרגות נעות	escalator
יציאה	exit
יציאת חירום	emergency/fire exit
מעלית	elevator [lift]
מדרגות	stairs
שרותים	restroom [toilet]

Service שרות

Can you help me?	?תוכל לעזור לי _tukhal la-azor li_
I'm looking for …	… אני מחפש _ani mekhapes_
I'm just browsing.	.אני רק מסתכל _ani rak mistakel_
It's my turn.	זה התור שלי _ze hator sheli_
Do you sell any …?	?… אתם מוכרים _atem mokhrim_
I'd like to buy …	… הייתי רוצה לקנות _hayiti rotze liknot_
Could you show me …?	?… תוכל להראות לי _tukhal lehar-ot li_
How much is this/that?	?כמה זה/ההוא _kama ze/hahu_
That's all, thanks.	.זה הכל, תודה _ze hakol toda_

בוקר טוב/שלום גבירתי/אדוני.	Good morning/afternoon, madam/sir.
?אוכל לעזור לך	Can I help you?
?זה הכל	Is that everything?
?עוד משהו	Anything else?

– _ukhal la-azor lekha?_ (Can I help you?)
– lo, to_da_. _ani_ rak mista_kel_.
(No, thanks. I'm just browsing.)
– be_seder_. (Fine.)
– slikha. (Excuse me.)
– ken. _ukhal_ la-_azor_ lekha?
(Yes. Can I help you?)
– _kama_ ze? (How much is this?)
– _rega_ rak ev_dok_. … ze shmo_nim shekel_.
(Um, I'll just check. … That's 80 shekels.)

שרות עצמי	self-service
מכירת חיסול	clearance

133

I want something ... | ... אני רוצה משהו | *ani rotze mashehu*
It must be ... | ... זה חייב להיות | *ze khayav lihiyot*
big/small | גדול/קטן | *gadol/katan*
cheap/expensive | זול/יקר | *zol/yakar*
dark/light (color) | כהה/בהיר | *kehe/bahir*
light/heavy | קל/כבד | *kal/kaved*
oval/round/square | אליפטי/עגול/מרובע | *ellipti/agol/meruba*
genuine/imitation | מקורי/חיקוי | *mekori/khikuy*
I don't want anything too expensive. | אני לא רוצה שום דבר יקר מדי. | *ani lo rotze shum davar yakar miday*
in the area of ... shekels | בסביבות ... שקל | *bisvivot ... shekel*

איזה ... אתה רוצה?	What ... would you like?
צבע/צורה	color/shape
איכות/כמות	quality/quantity
כמה אתה רוצה?	How many would you like?
איזה סוג אתה רוצה?	What kind would you like?
על איזה טווח מחירים חשבת?	What price range are you thinking of?

Do you have anything ...? | ...? יש לכם משהו | *yesh lakhem mashehu*
larger/smaller | יותר גדול/יותר קטן | *yoter gadol/yoter katan*
better quality | באיכות יותר טובה | *be-eykhut yoter tova*
cheaper | יותר זול | *yoter zol*
Can you show me ...? | ...? תוכל להראות לי | *tukhal lehar-ot li*
this one/these | את זה/אלה | *et ze/ele*
that one/those | את ההוא/ההם | *et hahu/hahem*
the one in the window/ display case | את זה שבחלון/בארון התצוגה | *et ze shebakhalon/be-aron hatetzuga*
some others | אחרים | *akherim*

COLOR ➤ 143

Conditions of purchase תנאי רכישה

Is there a guarantee?	יש אחריות? yesh akhrayut
Are there any instructions with it?	יש עם זה הוראות שימוש? yesh im ze hora-ot shimush

Out of stock אזל

מצטער, אין לנו.	I'm sorry, we don't have any.
המלאי אזל.	We're out of stock.
אוכל להראות לך משהו אחר/סוג שונה?	Can I show you something else/ a different kind?
נוכל להזמין את זה בשבילך?	Shall we order it for you?

Can you order it for me?	תוכלו להזמין את זה בשבילי? tukhlu lehazmin et ze bishvili
How long will it take?	כמה זמן זה יקח? kama zman ze yikakh
Is there another store that sells …?	יש חנות אחרת המוכרת ...? yesh khanut akheret hamokheret

Decisions החלטה

That's not quite what I want.	זה לא בדיוק מה שאני רוצה. ze lo bediyuk ma she-ani rotze
No, I don't like it.	לא, זה לא מוצא חן בעיני. lo ze lo motze khen be-enay
That's too expensive.	זה יותר מדי יקר. ze yoter miday yakar
I'd like to think about it.	אני רוצה לחשוב על זה. ani rotze lakhshov al ze
I'll take it.	אקח את זה. ekakh et ze

– boker tov. ani mekhapes khultzat meyza.
(Good morning. I'm looking for a sweatshirt.)

– beseder. eyze tzeva tirtze?
(Certainly. What color would you like?)

– katom. ve-ani rotze mashehu gadol.
(Orange. And I want something big.)

– hine. ze arba-im shekel.
(Here you are. That's 40 shekels.)

– ah, ze lo bediyuk ma she-ani rotze. toda.
(Hmm, that's not quite what I want. Thank you.)

Paying תשלום

Where do I pay?	איפה משלמים? _eyfo_ meshal_mim_
How much is that?	כמה זה? _kama_ ze
Could you write it down, please?	תוכל לכתוב את זה בשבילי, בבקשה? _tukhal likhtov_ et ze bishvi_li_ bevaka_sha_
Do you accept traveler's checks [cheques]?	אתם מקבלים המחאות נוסעים? _atem_ mekablim hamkha-_ot_ nos-_im_
I'll pay by …	אשלם ב... asha_lem_ be
cash	מזומן mezu_man_
credit card	כרטיס אשראי _kartis ashray_
I don't have any smaller change.	אין לי כסף יותר קטן. eyn li _kesef yoter katan_
Sorry. I don't have enough money.	סליחה. אין לי מספיק כסף. sli_kha_. eyn li maspik _kesef_

איך אתה משלם?	How are you paying?
פעולה זו לא אושרה/התקבלה.	This transaction has not been approved/accepted.
כרטיס זה אינו בתוקף.	This card is not valid.
אפשר לראות תעודה מזהה נוספת?	May I have further identification?
יש לך כסף יותר קטן?	Do you have any smaller change?

Could I have a receipt, please?	אפשר לתת לי קבלה, בבקשה? ef_shar_ la_tet_ li kabala bevaka_sha_
I think you've given me the wrong change.	נדמה לי שנתת לי עודף לא נכון. nid_me_ li shena_tata_ li _odef_ lo na_khon_

נא לשלם פה	please pay here

136

Complaints תלונות

This doesn't work.	זה לא פועל. ze lo po-el
Can you exchange this, please?	תוכל להחליף את זה בבקשה? tukhal lehakhlif et ze bevakasha
I'd like a refund.	אבקש החזר. avakesh hekhzer
Here's the receipt.	הנה הקבלה. hine hakabala
I don't have the receipt.	אין לי הקבלה. eyn li hakabala
I'd like to see the manager.	אבקש לראות את המנהל. avakesh lir-ot et hamenahel

Repairs/Cleaning תיקונים/ניקוי

This is broken. Can you repair it?	זה שבור. תוכלו לתקן אותו? ze shavur. tukhlu letaken oto
Do you have ... for this?	יש לכם ... בשביל זה? yesh lakhem ... bishvil ze
a battery	סוללה solela
replacement parts	חלפים khalafim
There's something wrong with ...	משהו לא בסדר עם ... mashehu lo beseder im
Can you ... this?	תוכלו ... את זה? tukhlu ... et ze
clean	לנקות lenakot
press	לגהץ legahetz
patch	להטליא lehatli
Could you alter this?	תוכלו לשנות את זה? tukhlu leshanot et ze
When will it be ready?	מתי זה יהיה מוכן? matay ze yihiye mukhan
This isn't mine.	זה לא שלי. ze lo sheli
There's ... missing.	חסר ... khaser

Bank/Currency exchange
בנק/החלפת מטבע

Most banks have ATMs (cash machines) where you can usually withdraw money using an international credit card.

Currency exchange regulations vary from time to time, so take your passport with you when converting foreign currency to shekels and vice versa. Avoid anyone offering to exchange currency on the black market.

Most hotels, and large stores and restaurants, will accept credit cards. Traveler's checks [cheques] from well-known companies are also usually accepted. To play it safe, try to carry a combination of cash and checks/cards.

Where's the nearest …?	איפה ה... הקרוב? _eyfo ha... hakarov_
bank	בנק _bank_
currency exchange office [bureau de change]	משרד להחלפת מטבע _misrad lehakhlafat matbe-a_

החלפת מטבע	currency exchange
פתוח/סגור	open/closed
קופה	cashiers

Changing money החלפת כסף

Can I exchange foreign currency here?	אפשר להחליף פה מטבע זר? _efshar lehakhlif po matbe-a zar_
I'd like to change some dollars/pounds into shekels.	אני רוצה להחליף דולרים/לירות שטרלינג לשקלים. _ani rotze lehakhlif dolarim/lirot sterling lishkalim_
I want to cash some traveler's checks [cheques].	אני רוצה להמיר המחאות נוסעים. _ani rotze lehamir hamkha-ot nos-im_
What's the exchange rate?	מה שער החליפין? _ma sha-ar hakhalifin_
How much commission do you charge?	כמה עמלה אתם דורשים? _kama amala atem dorshim_
Could I have some small change, please?	אפשר לקבל קצת כסף קטן, בבקשה? _efshar lekabel ktzat kesef katan bevakasha_
I've lost my traveler's checks. These are the numbers.	איבדתי את המחאות הנוסעים שלי. אלה המספרים. _ibadeti et hamkha-ot hanos-im sheli. ele hamisparim_

Security ביטחון

?... אפשר לראות	Could I see ...?
את דרכונך	your passport
תעודה מזהה כלשהי	some identification
את כרטיס הבנק שלך	your bank/credit card
?מה כתובתך	What's your address?
?איפה אתה שוהה	Where are you staying?
נא למלא טופס זה, בבקשה.	Fill out this form, please.
לחתום כאן, בבקשה.	Please sign here.

ATMs (Cash machines) כספומט

Can I withdraw money on my credit card here?	אוכל למשוך פה כסף על כרטיס האשראי שלי? *ukhal limshokh po kesef al kartis ha-ashray sheli*
Where are the ATMs (cash machines)?	איפה הכספומטים? *eyfo hakaspomatim*
Can I use my ... card in the cash machine?	אוכל להשתמש בכרטיס ... שלי בכספומט? *ukhal lehishtamesh bekartis ... sheli bakaspomat*
The cash machine has eaten my card.	הכספומט בלע את הכרטיס שלי. *hakaspomat bala et hakartis sheli*

> כספומט   automated teller (ATM)

Currency

The basic unit of currency in Israel is the **shekel** (plural: **shkalim**). The symbol for the **shekel** is ₪. It is divided into 100 **agorot** (singular: **agora**).

Coins: 1, 5, 10, 50 **agorot**; 1, 5, 10 **shkalim**

Notes: 20, 50, 100, 500, 1000 **shkalim**

Pharmacy בית מרקחת

Pharmacies offer a wide range of imported toiletries and medicines, as well as excellent local ones that are considerably cheaper.

Although medications are strictly controlled, you may find that you can obtain drugs over the counter that would be prescription only back home, or vice versa. The pharmacist will usually be both qualified and happy to offer advice.

Where's the nearest (all-night) pharmacy?	?(איפה בית המרקחת הקרוב (התורן *eyfo* beyt hamer*kakh*at haka*rov* (hato*ran*)
What time does the pharmacy open/close?	?מתי בית המרקחת נפתח/נסגר *matay* beyt hamer*kakh*at nif*takh*/nis*gar*
Can you make up this prescription for me?	?תוכלו להכין את המירשם הזה בשבילי *tukh*lu leha*khin* et hamir*sham* haze bishvi*li*
Shall I wait?	?לחכות *lekhakot*
I'll come back for it.	.אחזור לקחת את זה *ekhzor* la*kakh*at et ze

Dosage instructions הוראות מינון

How much should I take?	?כמה עלי לקחת *kama* a*lay* la*kakh*at
How many times a day should I take it?	?כמה פעמים ביום עלי לקחת את זה *kama* pe-a*mim* be*yom* a*lay* la*kakh*at et ze
Is it suitable for children?	?זה מתאים לילדים ze mat-*im* liyla*dim*

קח ...	Take ...
... טבליות/... כפיות	... tablets/... teaspoons
לפני/אחרי הארוחות	before/after meals
עם מים	with water
בלי לפורר	whole
בבוקר/לפני השינה	in the morning/at night
במשך ... ימים	for ... days

for external use only	לשימוש חיצוני בלבד
not to be taken internally	אין לבלוע
do not drive after taking medication	אין לנהוג ברכב אחרי נטילת התרופה

Asking advice בקשת עצה

I'd like some medicine for ...	... אבקש תרופה נגד ava*kesh* trufa *neged*
a cold	הצטננות hitztanenut
a cough	שיעול shi-ul
diarrhea	שלשול shilshul
a hangover	הנג-אובר heng over
hay fever	קדחת השחת kadakhat hashakhat
insect bites	עקיצות חרקים akitzot kharakim
a sore throat	כאב גרון ke-ev garon
sunburn	כוויית שמש kviyat shemesh
motion [travel] sickness	מחלת נסיעה makhalat nesi-a
an upset stomach	קלקול קיבה kilkul keyva
Can I get it without a prescription?	אוכל לקבל את זה בלי מירשם? ukhal lekabel et ze bli mirsham
Can I have some ...?	אוכל לקבל ...? ukhal lekabel
antiseptic cream	משחה אנטיספטית mishkha antiseptit
aspirin	אספירין aspirin
condoms	קונדומים kondomim
cotton [cotton wool]	צמר גפן tzemer gefen
gauze [bandages]	תחבושות takhboshot
insect repellent	דוחה חרקים dokhe kharakim
painkillers	תרופה נגד כאבים trufa neged ke-evim
bandaid® [plasters]	פלסטרים plasterim
vitamins	גלולות ויטמינים glulot vitaminim

141

Toiletries תכשירי טיפוח

I'd like some …	אבקש ...	avakesh
after-shave	מי גילוח	mey gilu-akh
after-sun lotion	משחה לאחרי שיזוף	mishkha le-akharey shizuf
deodorant	דיאודורנט	de-odorant
razor blades	סכיני גילוח	sakiney gilu-akh
sanitary napkins [towels]	תחבושות היגייניות	takhboshot higiyeniyot
soap	סבון	sabon
sun block	חוסם קרינה	khosem krina
suntan lotion	משחת שיזוף	mishkhat shizuf
factor …	מקדם ...	mekadem
tampons	טמפונים	tamponim
tissues	מטפחות נייר	mitpakhot neyar
toilet paper	נייר טואלט	neyar to-alet
toothpaste	משחת שיניים	mishkhat shinayim

Haircare לשיער

comb	מסרק	masrek
conditioner	קונדישנר	kondishener
hair mousse/gel	ג'יל לשיער	jel lese-ar
hair spray	ספריי לשיער	sprey lese-ar
shampoo	שמפו	shampu

For the baby לתינוק

baby food	מזון לתינוקות	mazon letinokot
baby wipes	ניגוביות לתינוק	niguviyot letinok
diapers [nappies]	חיתולים	khitulim
sterilizing solution	תמיסת חיטוי	tmisat khituy

142

Clothing ביגוד

Israel produces many beautiful textiles, and you will find a
wide range of locally made clothes. Many stores also import
Western labels. Markets are a good place to buy traditional
items, such as robes and head scarfs.

General כללי

I'd like …	... אבקש	*avakesh*
Do you have any …?	?... יש לכם	*yesh lakhem*

בגדי נשים	ladieswear
בגדי גברים	menswear
בגדי ילדים	childrenswear

Color צבעים

I'm looking for something in …	אני מחפש משהו ב...	
	ani mekhapes mashehu be	
beige	בז'	*bezh*
black	שחור	*shakhor*
blue	כחול	*kakhol*
brown	חום	*khum*
green	ירוק	*yarok*
gray	אפור	*afor*
orange	כתום	*katom*
pink	ורוד	*varod*
purple	אַרגמן	*argaman*
red	אדום	*adom*
white	לבן	*lavan*
yellow	צהוב	*tzahov*
light …	... בהיר	… *bahir*
dark …	... כהה	… *ke-he*
I want a darker/lighter shade.	אבקש גוון יותר כהה/יותר בהיר.	
	avakesh gavan yoter kehe/yoter bahir	
Do you have the same in …?	?... יש לכם אותו דבר ב	
	yesh lakhem oto davar be	

Clothes and accessories בגדים ואביזרים

belt	חגורה	khagora
bikini	ביקיני	bikini
blouse	חולצה	khultza
bra	חזיה	khaziya
briefs	תחתונים	takhtonim
cap	כומתה	kumta
coat	מעיל	me-il
dress	שמלה	simla
handbag	תיק יד	tik yad
hat	כובע	kova
jacket	ז'קט	zhaket
jeans	ג'ינס	jins
leggings	מכנסי גרבונים	mikhnasey garbonim
pants (U.S.)	מכנסיים	mikhnasayim
panty hose [tights]	גרבונים	garbonim
raincoat	מעיל גשם	me-il geshem
scarf	צעיף	tza-if
shirt (men's)	חולצה (לגברים)	khultza (ligvarim)
shorts	מכנסיים קצרים	mikhnasayim ktzarim
skirt	חצאית	khatza-it
socks	גרביים	garbayim
stockings	גרבי נשים	garbey nashim
suit	חליפה	khalifa
sweater	סודר	sudar
sweatshirt	חולצת מיזע	khultzat meyza
swimming trunks	בגד ים לגברים	beged yam ligvarim
swimsuit	בגד ים לנשים	beged yam lenashim
T-shirt	חולצת טי	khultzat ti
tie	עניבה	aniva
trousers	מכנסיים	mikhnasayim
underpants	תחתונים	takhtonim
with long/short sleeves	עם שרוולים ארוכים/קצרים	im sharvulim arukim/ktzarim
with a V-/round neck	עם צוארון וי/עגול	im tzavaron vi/agol

144

Shoes נעליים

boots	נעליים גבוהות *na-alayim gvohot*
flip-flops	סנדלי אילת *sandaley eylat*
running [training] shoes	נעלי ספורט *na-aley sport*
sandals	סנדלים *sandalim*
shoes	נעליים *na-alayim*
slippers	נעלי בית *na-aley bayit*

Walking/Hiking gear ציוד לטיולים/מחנאות

knapsack	תרמיל גב *tarmil gav*
walking boots	נעלי הליכה *na-aley halikha*
waterproof jacket [anorak]	אנורק *anorak*
windbreaker [cagoule]	מעיל רוח *me-il ru-akh*

Fabric בד

I want something in …	אני רוצה משהו ב... *ani rotze mashehu be*
cotton	כותנה *kutna*
denim	דנים *denim*
lace	תחרה *takhara*
leather	עור *or*
linen	פשתן *pishtan*
wool	צמר *tzemer*
Is this …?	?...זה *ze*
pure cotton	כותנה טהורה *kutna tehora*
synthetic	סינטטי *sinteti*
Is it hand/machine washable?	זה כביס ביד/במכונה *ze kavis bayad/bimkhona*

ניקוי יבש בלבד	dry clean only
כביסת-יד בלבד	handwash only
אין לגהץ	do not iron
לא לניקוי יבש	do not dry clean

Does it fit? ‏זה מתאים?

Can I try this on?	‏אפשר למדוד את זה? *efshar limdod et ze*
Where's the fitting room?	‏איפה חדרי ההלבשה? *eyfo khadrey hahalbasha*
It fits well. I'll take it.	‏זה מתאים מאד. אקח את זה. *ze mat-im me-od. ekakh et ze*
It doesn't fit.	‏זה לא מתאים. *ze lo mat-im*
It's too …	‏זה יותר מדי … *ze yoter miday*
short/long	‏קצר/ארוך *katzar/arokh*
tight/loose	‏הדוק/חופשי *haduk/khofshi*
What size is this?	‏איזו מידה זה? *eyzo mida ze?*
Could you measure me, please?	‏תוכל למדוד אותי, בבקשה? *tukhal limdod oti bevakasha*
I don't know Israeli sizes.	‏אני לא מתמצא במידות ישראליות. *ani lo mitmatze bemidot isra-eliyot*

Size ‏מידה

Israel, like most of the Middle East, uses Continental sizes and metric measures.

Dresses/Suits							Women's shoes			
American	8	10	12	14	16	18	6	7	8	9
British	10	12	14	16	18	20	$4^{1/2}$	$5^{1/2}$	$6^{1/2}$	$7^{1/2}$
Continental	36	38	40	42	44	46	37	38	40	41

Shirts					Men's shoes							
American } **British }**	15	16	17	18	5	6	7	8	$8^{1/2}$	9	$9^{1/2}$	10	11
Continental	38	41	43	45	38	39	41	42	43	43	44	44	45

‏גדול אקסטרה	extra large (XL)
‏גדול	large (L)
‏בינוני	medium (M)
‏קטן	small (S)

1 centimeter (cm.) = 0.39 in.	1 inch = 2.54 cm.
1 meter (m.) = 39.37 in.	1 foot = 30.5 cm.
10 meters = 32.81 ft.	1 yard = 0.91 m.

Health and beauty בריאות ויופי

I'd like a …	abakesh ... אבקש
facial	tipul panim טיפול פנים
manicure	manikur מניקור
massage	isuy עיסוי
waxing	sha-ava שעווה

Hairdresser מספרה

It is common to tip 10% if you are happy with the service.

I'd like to make an appointment for …	...אני רוצה להזמין תור ל ani rotze lehazmin tor le
Can you make it a bit earlier/later?	?אפשר קצת יותר מוקדם/מאוחר efshar ktzat yoter mukdam/me-ukhar
I'd like a …	abakesh ... אבקש
cut and blow-dry	tisporet vefen תספורת ופן
shampoo and set	חפיפה וסידור khafifa vesidur
trim	tikun תיקון
I'd like my hair …	אבקש לעשות לשיער שלי ... avakesh la-asot lase-ar sheli
highlighted	pasim behirim פסים בהירים
permed	silsul tmidi סלסול תמידי
Don't cut it too short.	נא לא לקצר יותר מדי. na lo lekatzer yoter miday
A little more off the …	קצת להוריד ... ktzat lehorid
back/front	מאחור/מלפנים me-akhor/milfanim
neck/sides	בעורף/בצדדים ba-oref/batzdadim
top	lema-la למעלה
That's fine, thanks.	זה יופי, תודה. ze yofi toda

Household articles כלי בית

I'd like a(n)/some … … אבקש *avakesh*

adapter	מתאם	*mat-em*
alumin(i)um foil	נייר אלומיניום	*neyar aluminiyum*
bottle opener	פותחן בקבוקים	*potkhan bakbukim*
can [tin] opener	פותחן קופסאות	*potkhan kufsa-ot*
clothes pins [pegs]	אטבי כביסה	*itvey kvisa*
corkscrew	חולץ פקקים	*kholetz pkakim*
light bulb	נורה	*nura*
matches	גפרורים	*gafrurim*
paper napkins	מפיות נייר	*mapiyot neyar*
plastic wrap [cling film]	עטיפת ניילון	*atifat naylon*
plug	תקע	*teka*
scissors	מספריים	*misparayim*
screwdriver	מברג	*mavreg*

Cleaning items חומרי ניקוי

bleach	מלבין	*malbin*
dishcloth	מטלית ניקוי	*matlit nikuy*
dishwashing [washing-up] liquid	סבון נוזלי	*sabon nozli*
garbage [refuse] bags	שקי אשפה	*sakey ashpa*
detergent [washing powder]	אבקת כביסה	*avkat kvisa*
sponge	ספוג	*sfog*

Dishes [Crockery]/Utensils [Cutlery] חרסינה/סכו"ם

bowls	קערות	*ke-arot*
cups	ספלים	*sfalim*
forks	מזלגות	*mazlegot*
glasses	כוסות	*kosot*
knives	סכינים	*sakinim*
mugs	ספלים גדולים	*sfalim gdolim*
plates	צלחות	*tzalakhot*
spoons	כפות	*kapot*
teaspoons	כפיות	*kapiyot*

<u>Jeweler</u> צורף

Could I see …?	אוכל לראות את ...? ukhal lir-ot et
this/that	זה/ההוא ze/hahu
It's in the window/ display cabinet.	זה בחלון/בארון התצוגה. ze bakhalon/ba-aron hatetzuga
alarm clock	שעון מעורר sha-on me-orer
battery	סוללה solela
bracelet	צמיד tzamid
brooch	סיכה sika
chain	שרשרת sharsheret
clock	שעון sha-on
earrings	עגילים agilim
necklace	מחרוזת makharozet
ring	טבעת taba-at
watch	שעון יד she-on yad

<u>Materials</u> חומרים

Is this real silver/gold?	זה כסף/זהב אמיתי? ze kesef/zahav amiti
Is there a certificate for it?	יש על זה תעודה? yesh al ze te-uda
Do you have anything in …?	יש לכם משהו ב...? yesh lakhem mashehu be
copper	נחושת nekhoshet
crystal (quartz)	קריסטל kristal
cut glass	זכוכית פיתוחים zkhukhit pitukhim
diamond	יהלום yahalom
enamel	אמייל emayl
gold	זהב zahav
gold plate	ציפוי זהב tzipuy zahav
pearl	פנינה pnina
pewter	בדיל-עופרת bdil oferet
platinum	פלטינה platina
silver	כסף kesef
silver plate	ציפוי כסף tzipuy kesef
stainless steel	פלדת אלחלד pildat alkheled

Newsstand [Newsagent]/ Tobacconist
חנות עיתונים/מוצרי טבק

Larger newsstands will carry English-language newspapers and magazines, although they will be expensive and often a few days old. Israel's oldest established English-language daily newspaper is the *Jerusalem Post*.

Do you sell English-language books/newspapers?	אתם מוכרים ספרים/עיתונים באנגלית?	*atem mokhrim sfarim/itonim be-anglit*
I'd like a(n)/some …	אבקש …	*avakesh*
book	ספר	*sefer*
candy [sweets]	ממתקים	*mamtakim*
chewing gum	מסטיק	*mastik*
chocolate bar	טבלת שוקולד	*tavlat shokolad*
cigarettes (pack of)	(חפיסת) סיגריות	*(khafisat) sigariyot*
cigars	סיגרים	*sigarim*
dictionary	מילון	*milon*
English–Hebrew	אנגלי/עברי	*angli/ivri*
envelopes	מעטפות	*ma-atafot*
guidebook of …	מדריך ל…	*madrikh le*
lighter	מצית	*matzit*
magazine	מגזין	*magazin*
map	מפה	*mapa*
map of the town	מפת העיר	*mapat ha-ir*
matches	גפרורים	*gafrurim*
newspaper	עיתון	*iton*
American/English	אמריקאי/אנגלי	*amerika-i/angli*
pen	עט	*et*
road map of …	מפת דרכים של …	*mapat drakhim shel*
stamps	בולים	*bulim*
tobacco	טבק	*tabak*
writing paper	נייר כתיבה	*neyar ktiva*

Photography צילום

I'm looking for a(n) ... camera.	... אני מחפש מצלמה	*ani mekhapes matzlema*
automatic	אוטומטית	*otomatit*
compact	קומפקטית	*kompaktit*
disposable	חד-פעמית	*khad pe-amit*
SLR (i.e. single lens reflex)	רפלקס	*refleks*
I'd like a(n) ...	אבקש	*avakesh*
battery	סוללה	*solela*
camera case	תיק למצלמה	*tik lematzlema*
electronic flash	מבזק אלקטרוני	*mavzek elektroni*
filter	מסנן	*masnen*
lens	עדשה	*adasha*
lens cap	מכסה עדשה	*mikhse adasha*

Film/Processing סרטים/פיתוח

I'd like ... film.	... אבקש סרט	*avakesh seret*
black and white	שחור-לבן	*shakhor lavan*
color	צבע	*tzeva*
24/36 exposures	עשרים וארבע/שלושים ושש תמונות	*esrim ve-arba/shloshim veshesh tmunot*
I'd like this film developed, please.	אבקש לפתח את הסרט הזה, בבקשה.	*avakesh lefate-akh et haseret haze bevakasha*
Would you enlarge this, please?	תוכלו להגדיל את זה, בבקשה?	*tukhlu lehagdil et ze bevakasha*
How much do ... exposures cost?	כמה עולות ... תמונות?	*kama olot ... tmunot*
When will the photos be ready?	מתי יהיו הצילומים מוכנים?	*matay yihiyu hatzilumim mukhanim*
I'd like to collect my photos.	אבקש לקחת את הצילומים שלי.	*avakesh lakakhat et hatzilumim sheli*
Here's the receipt.	הנה הקבלה.	*hine hakabala*

Post office סניף דואר

Mailboxes are red, or sometimes yellow for local items only. Post offices usually have separate counters for packages, registered mail, and special services. Sometimes hotels have their own mailboxes for postcards and letters, and these are usually safe and reliable.

General queries שאלות כלליות

Where is the post office?	איפה סניף הדואר? *eyfo snif hado-ar*
What time does the post office open/close?	מתי סניף הדואר נפתח/נסגר? *matay snif hado-ar niftakh/nisgar*
Does it close for lunch?	הוא נסגר בצהריים? *hu nisgar batzohorayim*
Where's the mailbox?	איפה תיבת הדואר? *eyfo tevat hado-ar*
Is there any mail for me?	יש דואר בשבילי? *yesh do-ar bishvili*

Buying stamps קניית בולים

I'd like to send these postcards to …	אבקש לשלוח גלויות אלה ל... *avakesh lishlo-akh gluyot ele le*
A stamp for this postcard/letter, please.	בול לגלויה/למכתב הזה, בבקשה. *bul lagluya/lamikhtav haze bevakasha*
A … agorot stamp, please.	בול של ... אגורות, בבקשה. *bul shel … agorot bevakasha*
What's the postage for a letter to …?	כמה עולה מכתב ל... *kama ole mikhtav le*

– shalom. ava*kesh* lish*lo*-akh glu*yot* ele le-artzot hab*rit*.
(Hello. I'd like to send these postcards to the U.S.)

– *kama?* (How many?)

– *tesha*, bevakasha. (Nine, please.)

– *ze* tish-*im* ago*rot* kaful *tesha*: shmo*na shekel*
ve-eser ago*rot*, bevaka*sha*.
(That's 90 agorot times nine: 8 shekels and 10 agorot, please.)

Sending packages משלוח חבילות

I want to send this package [parcel] by …	אני רוצה לשלוח חבילה זו ב... *ani rotze lishlo-akh khavila zo be*
airmail	דואר אויר *do-ar avir*
special delivery	מסירה מיוחדת *mesira meyukhedet*
registered mail	דואר רשום *do-ar rashum*
It contains …	היא מכילה *hi mekhila*

נא למלא את הצהרת המכס.	Please fill out the customs declaration form.
מה הערך?	What's the value?
מה יש בפנים?	What's inside?

Telecommunications בזק

Some hotels, office service bureaus, and post offices offer photocopying, wordprocessing, fax, and e-mail facilities.

(See also Telephoning ➤ 127.)

I'd like a phone card, please.	טלכרט, בבקשה. *telekart bevakasha*
10/20/50 units	עשר/עשרים/חמישים יחידות *eser/esrim/khamishim yekhidot*
Do you have a photocopier?	יש לכם מכונת צילום? *yesh lakhem mekhonat tzilum*
I'd like to send a message …	אני רוצה לשלוח הודעה ... *ani rotze lishlo-akh hoda-a*
by e-mail/fax	בדואר אלקטרוני/בפקס *bedoa-ar elketroni/befaks*
What's your e-mail address?	מה כתובת הדואר האלקטרוני שלכם? *ma ktovet hado-ar ha-elektroni shelakhem*
Can I access the Internet here?	יש מפה גישה לאינטרנט? *yesh mipo gisha la-internet*
What are the charges per hour?	מה המחיר לשעה? *ma hamekhir lesha-a*
How do I log on?	איך מתחברים? *eykh mitkhabrim*

153

Souvenirs מזכרות

The following are some suggestions for souvenirs to take
home. Many of these items can be found at the local markets
(**shuk/suk**), which offer a huge range of interesting articles.
You may need to bargain, but try to find out price ranges before
you go so you have some idea of what you should be paying.

dolls	בובות	*bubot*
perfume	בושם	*bosem*
ceramics	קרמיקה	*keramika*
antiques	עתיקות	*atikot*
wine	יין	*yayin*
liqueur	ליקר	*liker*
copperware	חפצי נחושת	*kheftzey nekhoshet*
silverware	חפצי כסף	*kheftzey kesef*
olive-wood artifacts	חפצי עץ זית	*kheftzey etz zayit*
picture books	ספרי תמונות	*sifrey tmunot*
religious articles	תשמישי קדושה	*tashmishey kdusha*
rugs	שטיחים	*shtikhim*
embroidery	ריקמה	*rikma*
diamonds	יהלומים	*yahalomim*

Gifts מתנות

bottle of wine	בקבוק יין	*bakbuk yayin*
box of chocolates	קופסת שוקולד	*kufsat shokolad*
calendar	לוח שנה	*lu-akh shana*
key ring	מחזיק מפתחות	*makhzik maftekhot*
postcards	גלויות	*gluyot*
scarf	צעיף	*tza-if*
souvenir guide	מדריך למזכרת	*madrikh lemazkeret*
tea towel	מגבת מטבח	*magevet mitbakh*
T-shirt	חולצת טי	*khultzat ti*

מוסיקה Music

I'd like a ...   ... אבקש *avakesh*

cassette   קלטת *kaletet*

compact disc   תקליטור *taklitor*

record   תקליט *taklit*

video cassette   קלטת וידאו *kaletet vide-o*

Who are the popular local singers?   מי הזמרים המקומיים הפופולריים? *mi hazamarim hamekomiyim hapopulariyim*

Toys and games צעצועים ומשחקים

I'd like a toy/game ...   ... אבקש צעצוע/משחק *avakesh tza-atzu-a/miskhak*

for a boy   לילד *leyeled*

for a 5-year-old girl   לילדה בת חמש *leyalda bat khamesh*

ball   כדור *kadur*

chess set   משחק שחמט *miskhak shakhmat*

doll   בובה *buba*

electronic game   משחק אלקטרוני *miskhak elektroni*

teddy bear   דובי *dubi*

pail and shovel [bucket and spade]   דלי ואת *dli ve-et*

Antiques עתיקות

How old is this?   מלפני כמה זמן זה? *milifney kama zman ze*

Do you have anything from the ... era?   יש לכם משהו מתקופת ה...? *yesh lakhem mashehu mitkufat ha*

Can you send it to me?   תוכלו לשלוח את זה אלי? *tukhlu lishlo-akh et ze elay*

Will I have problems with customs?   תהיינה לי בעיות במכס? *tihiyena li ba-ayot bamekhes*

Is there a certificate of authenticity?   יש תעודת אותנטיות? *yesh te-udat otentiyut*

WHO?/WHAT?/WHEN? ➤ 104

Supermarket/Minimart
סופרמרקט/מינימרקט

Most supermarkets offer a mix of imported/Western goods and locally-made products.

At the supermarket בסופרמרקט

Excuse me. Where can I find …?	סליחה. איפה אוכל למצוא ...?
	slikha. eyfo ukhal limtzo
Do I pay for this here?	אפשר לשלם על זה פה?
	efshar leshalem al ze po
Where are the carts [trolleys]/baskets?	איפה העגלות/הסלים?
	eyfo ha-agalot/hasalim
Is there a … here?	יש פה ...? yesh po
pharmacy	בית מרקחת beyt merkakhat
delicatessen	מעדניה ma-adaniya

מזון משומר	canned foods
מוצרי חלב	dairy products
דגים טריים	fresh fish
בשר טרי	fresh meat
מוצרים טריים	fresh produce
מזון קפוא	frozen foods
מוצרים לבית	household goods
עוף	poultry
יינות ומשקאות חריפים	wines and spirits
לחם ועוגות	breads and cakes

Weights and measures
- **1 kilogram** or **kilo** (**kg.**) = **1000 grams** (g.); **100 g.** = 3.5 oz.; **1 kg.** = 2.2 lb
  1 oz. = **28.35 g.**; 1 lb. = **453.60 g.**
- **1 liter** (**l.**) = 0.88 imp. quart or 1.06 U.S. quart 1 imp. quart = **1.14 l.**
  1 U.S. quart = **0.951 l.** 1 imp. gallon = **4.55 l.** 1 U.S. gallon = **3.8 l.**

Food hygiene היגיינת מזון

לאכול תוך ... ימים	eat within ... days
מהפתיחה	of opening
לשמור בקירור	keep refrigerated
מתאים למיקרוגל	microwaveable
מתאים לצמחוניים	suitable for vegetarians
להשתמש עד ...	use by ...

At the minimart במינימרקט

I'd like some of that/those.	אבקש קצת מזה/מזאלה.
	avakesh ktzat mize/me-ele
this one/that one	זה/ההוא *ze/hahu*
these/those	אלה/ההם *ele/hahem*
to the left/right	שמאלה/ימינה *smola/yemina*
over there/here	שם/פה *sham/po*
Where is/are the ...?	...?איפה ה *eyfo ha*
I'd like some ...	אבקש ... *avakesh*
a kilo (of)/half a kilo (of)	קילו/חצי קילו *kilo/khatzi kilo*
a liter (of)/half a liter (of)	ליטר/חצי ליטר *liter/khatzi liter*
apples	תפוחים *tapukhim*
beer	בירה *bira*
bread	לחם *lekhem*
coffee	קפה *kafe*
cheese	גבינה *gvina*
cookies [biscuits]	ביסקוויטים *biskvitim*
eggs	ביצים *beytzim*
jam	ריבה *riba*
milk	חלב *khalav*
potato chips [crisps]	טוגנים *tuganim*
soft drinks	משקאות קלים *mashka-ot kalim*
tomatoes	עגבניות *agvaniyot*
That's all, thanks.	זה הכל, תודה. *ze hakol toda*

– <u>le</u>khem, bevaka<u>sh</u>a.
(Some bread, please.)

– ze? *(This one?)*

– ken ha<u>hu</u>. (Yes, that one.)

– <u>be</u>seder. ze ha<u>kol</u>?
(Certainly. Is that all?)

– veka<u>ma</u> bey<u>tzim</u>. (And some eggs.)

– <u>hi</u>ne. *(Here you are.)*

Provisions/Picnic צידה/פיקניק

beer	בירה *bira*
butter	חמאה *khem-a*
cakes	עוגות *ugot*
cheese	גבינה *gvina*
cooked meats	בשר מבושל *basar mevushal*
cookies [biscuits]	ביסקוויטים *biskvitim*
grapes	ענבים *anavim*
instant coffee	קפה נמס *kafe names*
lemonade	לימונדה *limonada*
margarine	מרגרינה *margarina*
olives	זיתים *zeytim*
oranges	תפוזים *tapuzim*
rolls (bread)	לחמניות *lakhmaniyot*
sausages	נקניק *naknik*
tea bags	שקיות תה *sakiyot te*
wine	יין *yayin*
yogurt	יוגורט *yogurt*

There are many varieties of bread (**lekhem**), one of which, **challah**, mainly eaten on the Sabbath and on Jewish festivals, is a braided, soft, white bread, slightly sweet, glazed on top and often covered in poppy seeds. It is normally eaten plain, and also forms a part of religious rituals.

Police משטרה

You will need to report accidents, thefts, and other crimes to the police ☎ 100.

Where's the nearest police station?	איפה תחנת המשטרה הקרובה? _eyfo takhanat hamishtara hakrova_
Does anyone here speak English?	מישהו פה דובר אנגלית? _mishehu po dover anglit_
I want to report a(n) …	... אני רוצה לדווח על _ani rotze ledave-akh al_
accident	תאונה te-_una_
attack	תקיפה _tkifa_
mugging	שוד ברחוב _shod barkhov_
rape	אונס _ones_
My child is missing.	ילדי הלך לאיבוד _yaldi halakh le-ibud_
Here's a photo of him/her.	הנה תצלום שלו/שלה. _hine tatzlum shelo/shela_
Someone's following me.	מישהו עוקב אחרי. _mishehu okev akharay_
I need an English-speaking lawyer.	אני צריך עורך דין דובר אנגלית. _ani tzarikh orekh din dover anglit_
I need to make a phone call.	אני צריך לטלפן. _ani tzarikh letalpen_
I need to contact the … consulate.	...אני צריך להתקשר לקונסוליה ה _ani tzarikh lehitkasher lakonsulya ha_
American/British	אמריקאית/בריטית amerika-_it_/_britit_

תוכל לתאר אותו/אותה?	Can you describe him/her?
זכר/נקבה	male/female
בלונדיני/שיער חום	blond(e)/brunette
שיער אדום/אפור	red-headed/gray-haired
שיער ארוך/קצר/מקריח	long/short hair/balding
... גובה בקירוב	approximate height …
... גיל (בקירוב)	aged (approximately) …
... הוא/היא לבש(ה)	He/She was wearing …

Lost property/Theft רכוש אבוד/גניבה

I want to report a theft.	אני רוצה לדווח על גניבה.
	ani rotze ledave-akh al gneva
My bag was snatched.	התיק שלי נחטף.
	hatik sheli nekhtaf
I've been robbed.	שדדו אותי. *shadedu oti*
I've been mugged.	שדדו אותי ברחוב. *shadedu oti barekhov*
I've lost my …	איבדתי את ה.... שלי. *ibadeti et ha... sheli*
My … has been stolen.	ה... שלי נגנב. *ha... sheli nignav*
bicycle	אופניים *ofanayim*
camera	מצלמה *matzlema*
car	מכונית *mekhonit*
credit cards	כרטיסי אשראי *kartisey ashray*
handbag	תיק יד *tik yad*
money	כסף *kesef*
passport	דרכון *darkon*
purse	ארנק *arnak*
rental car	מכונית שכורה *mekhonit skhura*
ticket	כרטיס *kartis*
wallet	ארנק *arnak*
watch	שעון יד *she-on yad*
What shall I do?	מה אני צריך לעשות?
	ma ani tzarikh la-asot
I need a police report for my insurance claim.	אני צריך דו"ח משטרתי עבור תביעת הביטוח שלי.
	ani tzarikh du-akh mishtarti avur tvi-at habitu-akh sheli

מה חסר?	What's missing?
מה נלקח?	What's been taken?
מתי זה נגנב?	When was it stolen?
מתי זה קרה?	When did it happen?
איפה אתה שוהה?	Where are you staying?
מאיפה זה נלקח?	Where was it taken from?
איפה היית באותו זמן?	Where were you at the time?
אנחנו משיגים בשבילך מתורגמן.	We're getting an interpreter for you.
אנחנו נטפל בעניין.	We'll look into the matter.
נא למלא טופס זה.	Please fill out this form.

Health

Before you leave, make sure your health insurance policy covers illness and accidents while away from home. A system of state health care has recently been introduced in Israel, but, as a tourist, you will need to have your own health insurance to use it.

Almost all doctors will have some command of English, or at least know medical terms. However, there may be occasions when you will need to explain your problem in Hebrew or use the tables (➤ 164–165).

Doctor (general) רופא (כללי)

Where can I find a hospital/ dental office [surgery]?	?איפה יש בית חולים/מרפאת שיניים *eyfo yesh beyt kholim/mirpa-at shinayim*
Where's there a doctor/ dentist who speaks English?	איפה יש רופא/רופא שיניים דובר אנגלית? *eyfo yesh rofe/rofe shinayim dover anglit*
What are the office [surgery] hours?	?מה שעות הקבלה *ma she-ot hakabala*
Could the doctor come to see me here?	?האם הרופא יוכל לבוא לראות אותי פה *ha-im harofe yukhal lavo lir-ot oti po*
Can I make an appointment for …?	?אוכל להזמין תור ל... *ukhal lehazmin tor le*
today/tomorrow	היום/מחר *hayom/makhar*
as soon as possible	בהקדם האפשרי *bahekdem ha-efshari*
It's urgent.	.זה דחוף *ze dakhuf*
I have an appointment with Doctor …	... יש לי תור לדוקטור *yesh li tor ledoktor*

– ukhal lehazmin tor bahekdem ha-efshari?
(Can I make an appointment as soon as possible?)

– anakhnu legamrey mele-im hayom. ze dakhuf?
(We're fully booked today. Is it urgent?)

– ken. (Yes.)

– tov ma im eser vareva im doktor sela?
(Well, how about at 10:15 with Doctor Sela?)

– eser vareva. toda raba. (10:15. Thank you very much.)

Accident and injury   תאונות ופגיעות

My ... is hurt/injured.	ה... שלי נפגע/נפצע.
	ha ... sheli nifga/niftza
husband/wife	בעל/אשה ba-al/isha
son/daughter	בן/בת ben/bat
friend	ידיד yadid
child	ילד yeled
He/She is ...	הוא/היא ... hu/hi
unconscious	ללא הכרה lelo hakara
(seriously) injured	נפצע (קשה) niftza (kashe)
bleeding (heavily)	מדמם (קשה) medamem (kashe)
I have a(n) ...	יש לי ... yesh li
blister	בועה bu-a
boil	פצע מוגלתי petza muglati
bruise	חבורה khabura
burn	כוייה kviya
cut	חתך khatakh
graze	שפשוף shifshuf
insect bite/sting	עקיצת חרק akitzat kharak
lump	גוש gush
rash	פריחה prikha
strained muscle	שריר מתוח shrir matu-akh
swelling	נפיחות nefikhut
My ... hurts.	ה... שלי כואב. ha ... sheli ko-ev

PARTS OF THE BODY ➤ 166

Symptoms סימני מחלה

I've been feeling ill for ... days.	אני מרגיש רע מזה ... ימים. *ani margish ra mize ...* *yamim*
I feel faint.	אני מרגיש חולשה. *ani margish khulsha*
I have a fever.	יש לי חום גבוה. *yesh li khom gavoha*
I've been vomiting.	אני סובל מהקאות. *ani sovel mehaka-ot*
I have diarrhea.	יש לי שלשול. *yesh li shilshul*
It hurts here.	כואב לי פה. *ko-ev li po*
I have (a/an) ...	יש לי ... *yesh li*
backache	כאב גב *ke-ev gav*
cold	הצטננות *hitztanenut*
cramps	עוויתות *avitot*
earache	כאב אזניים *ke-ev oznayim*
headache	כאב ראש *ke-ev rosh*
sore throat	כאב גרון *ke-ev garon*
stomachache	כאב בטן *ke-ev beten*
sunstroke	מכת שמש *makat shemesh*

Conditions מחלות

I have arthritis.	יש לי דלקת פרקים. *yesh li daleket prakim*
I have asthma.	יש לי אסתמה. *yesh li astma*
I am ...	אני ... *ani*
deaf	חירש *kheresh*
diabetic	חולה סכרת *khole sakeret*
epileptic	אפילפטי *epilepti*
handicapped	נכה *nekhe*
(... months) pregnant	בהריון (... חודשים) *beherayon (... khodashim)*
I have a heart condition.	יש לי מחלת לב. *yesh li makhalat lev*
I have high/low blood pressure.	יש לי לחץ דם גבוה/נמוך. *yesh li lakhatz dam gavoha/namukh*
I had a heart attack ... years ago.	היה לי התקף לב לפני ... שנים. *haya li hetkef lev litney ... shanim*

163

Doctor's inquiries שאלות הרופא

כמה זמן אתה כבר מרגיש ככה?	How long have you been feeling like this?
זו הפעם הראשונה שאתה סובל מזה?	Is this the first time you've had this?
אתה לוקח תרופות אחרות כלשהן?	Are you taking any other medication?
אתה אלרגי למשהו?	Are you allergic to anything?
קיבלת חיסון נגד טטנוס?	Have you been vaccinated against tetanus?
התאבון שלך בסדר?	Is your appetite okay?

Examination בדיקה

אבדוק את הטמפרטורה/לחץ הדם שלך.	I'll take your temperature/ blood pressure.
הפשל את השרוול, בבקשה.	Roll up your sleeve, please.
התפשט עד המתניים, בבקשה.	Please undress to the waist.
שכב, בבקשה.	Please lie down.
פתח את הפה.	Open your mouth.
נשום עמוקות.	Breathe deeply.
השתעל, בבקשה.	Cough, please.
איפה כואב?	Where does it hurt?
כואב פה?	Does it hurt here?

Diagnosis אבחנה

אני רוצה שתעבור צילום רנטגן.	I want to have an X-ray done.
אני רוצה לקחת דגימת דם/צואה/שתן.	I'm taking a specimen of your blood/stool/urine.
אני רוצה שתראה מומחה.	I want you to see a specialist.
אני רוצה שתלך לבית חולים.	I want you to go to a hospital.
זה שבור/נקוע.	It's broken/sprained.
זה פרוק/קרוע.	It's dislocated/torn.

... יש לך	You have (a/an) ...
דלקת תוספתן	appendicitis
דלקת שלפוחית השתן	cystitis
שפעת	flu
הרעלת מזון	food poisoning
שבר	fracture
דלקת קיבה	gastritis
טחורים	hemorrhoids
בקע	hernia
... דלקת	inflammation of ...
חצבת	measles
דלקת ריאות	pneumonia
נשית	sciatica
דלקת שקדים	tonsilitis
גידול	tumor
מחלת מין	venereal disease
זה מזוהם.	It's infected.
זה מידבק.	It's contagious.

טיפול Treatment

... אתן לך	I'll give you some ...
חומר אנטיספטי	antiseptic
תרופה נגד כאבים	painkillers
... ארשום לך	I'm going to prescribe ...
טיפול באנטיביוטיקה	a course of antibiotics
נרות	some suppositories
אתה אלרגי לתרופה כלשהי?	Are you allergic to any medication?
... קח גלולה אחת	Take one pill ...
כל ... שעות	every ... hours
... פעמים ביום	... times a day
לפני/אחרי כל ארוחה	before/after each meal
במקרה של כאבים	if you are in pain
למשך ... ימים	for ... days
התייעץ ברופא כאשר תגיע הביתה.	Consult a doctor when you get home.

Parts of the body אברי הגוף

appendix	תוספתן	toseftan
arm	זרוע	zaro-a
back	גב	gav
bladder	שלפוחית שתן	shalpukhit sheten
bone	עצם	etzem
breast	שד	shad
chest	חזה	khaze
ear	אוזן	ozen
eye	עין	ayin
face	פנים	panim
finger	אצבע	etzba
foot	כף רגל	kaf regel
gland	בלוטה	baluta
hand	יד	yad
head	ראש	rosh
heart	לב	lev
jaw	לסת	leset
joint	פרק	perek
kidney	כליה	kilya
knee	ברך	berekh
leg	רגל	regel
lip	שפה	safa
liver	כבד	kaved
mouth	פה	pe
muscle	שריר	shrir
neck	צואר	tzavar
nose	אף	af
rib	צלע	tzela
shoulder	כתף	katef
skin	עור	or
stomach	קיבה	keyva
thigh	ירך	yerekh
throat	גרון	garon
thumb	אגודל	agudal
toe	בוהן	bohen
tongue	לשון	lashon
tonsils	שקדים	shkedim
vein	וריד	varid

Gynecologist גינקולוג

I have …	יש לי ... yesh li
abdominal pains	כאבי בטן ke-evey beten
period pains	כאבי מחזור ke-evey makhzor
a vaginal infection	זיהום בנרתיק zihum banartik
I haven't had my period for … months.	לא קיבלתי מחזור כבר ... חודשים. lo kibalti makhzor kvar ... khodashim
I'm on the Pill.	אני לוקחת את הגלולה. ani lokakhat et haglula

Hospital בית חולים

Please notify my family.	אנא הודיעו למשפחתי. ana hodi-u lemishpakhti
I'm in pain.	אני סובל מכאבים. ani sovel mike-evim
I can't eat/sleep.	אינני מסוגל לאכול/לישון. eyneni mesugal le-ekhol/lishon
When will the doctor come?	מתי יבוא הרופא? matay yavo harofe
Which section [ward] is … in?	באיזו מחלקה ...? be-eyzo makhlaka
I'm visiting …	באתי לבקר את ... bati levaker et

Optician אופטיקאי

I'm near- [short-] sighted/ far- [long-] sighted.	אני קצר-/רחוק-ראייה. ani ketzar/rekhok re-iya
I've lost …	איבדתי ... ibadeti
one of my contact lenses	את אחת מעדשות המגע שלי et akhat me-adshot hamaga sheli
my glasses/a lens	את משקפי/עדשה et mishkafay/adasha
Could you give me a replacement?	תוכל לתת לי תחליף? tukhal latet li takhlif

167

רופא שיניים Dentist

I have a toothache.	יש לי כאב שיניים. yesh li ke-ev shinayim
This tooth hurts.	השן הזו כואבת. hashen hazo ko-evet
I've lost a filling/tooth.	איבדתי סתימה/שן. ibadeti stima/shen
Can you repair this denture?	תוכל לתקן את השיניים התותבות האלה? tukhal letaken et hashinayim hatotavot ha-ele
I don't want it extracted.	אני לא רוצה שתעקור אותה. ani lo rotze sheta-akor ota

אתן לך זריקה/חומר הרדמה.	I'm going to give you an injection/some anesthesia.
אתה זקוק לסתימה/כתר.	You need a filling/cap [crown].
אצטרך להוציא אותה.	I'll have to take it out.
אני יכול לתקן את זה רק זמנית.	I can only fix it temporarily.
אל תאכל שום דבר במשך ... שעות.	Don't eat anything for ... hours.

תשלום וביטוח Payment and insurance

How much do I owe you?	כמה אני חייב לך? kama ani khayav lekha
I have insurance.	יש לי ביטוח. yesh li bitu-akh
Can I have a receipt for my insurance?	תוכל לתת לי קבלה לביטוח? tukhal latet li kabala labitu-akh
Would you fill out this insurance form, please?	תוכל למלא טופס ביטוח זה, בבקשה? tukhal lemale tofes bitu-akh ze bevakasha

Dictionary
English – Hebrew

To enable correct usage, most terms in this dictionary are either followed by an example or cross-referenced to pages where the word appears in a phrase. These notes provide some basic grammar guidelines.

Nouns

Nouns are either masculine or feminine. It is not always easy to tell them apart, but many feminine nouns end with **-a** or refer to female people. **ha-** ("the") is used for both genders, in the singular and the plural. There is no equivalent of the English "a(n)."

masculine	**ha-ish**	the man	*feminine*	**ha-isha**	the woman
masculine	**kise**	(a) chair	*feminine*	**mita**	(a) bed

Plurals are complicated and can sound significantly different from the singular. However, many masculine plurals are made by adding **-im** to the singular, and feminine plurals by adding **-ot**:

masculine	**bakbuk**	(a) bottle	**bakbukim**	bottles
feminine	**kos**	(a) glass	**kosot**	glasses

Adjectives

Adjectives come after the noun, and agree in gender and number. Adjectives are shown in the masculine singular. To make an adjective feminine, you usually add an **-a**, **-im** for masculine plural, and **-ot** for feminine plural. If the noun starts with **ha-**, then so should the adjective:

bakbuk gadol	(a) big bottle		**bakbukim gdolim**	big bottles
hakos hagdola	the big glass		**hakosot hagdolot**	the big glasses

Verbs

Verbs are generally shown in the dictionary in the infinitive with the equivalent of "to" (**le-**, **la-**, or **li-**): **le-daber** ("to speak"). Different prefixes and suffixes are added to a "root" to make the past, present, and future forms. Although there are many variations, the following are typical:

li-sgor (to close)	*past*	*present*	*future*
ani (I, m)	sagarti	soger	esgor
ani (I, f)	sagarti	sogeret	esgor
ata (you, m)	sagarta	soger	tisgor
at (you, f)	sagart	sogeret	tisgeri
hu (he)	sagar	soger	yisgor
hi (she)	sagra	sogeret	tisgor
anakhnu (we, m)	sagarnu	sogrim	nisgor
anakhnu (we, f)	sagarnu	sogrot	nisgor
atem (you, mpl)	sagartem	sogrim	tisgeru
aten (you, fpl)	sagarten	sogrot	tisgorna
hem (they, m)	sagru	sogrim	yisgeru
hen (they, f)	sagru	sogrot	tisgorna

A a.m. בבוקר *baboker*

abroad חוץ לארץ *khutz la-aretz*

accept, to לקבל *lekabel* 136; do you ~ ...? אתם מקבלים ...? *atem mekablim* 136

accident *(road)* f תאונה *te-una* 92, 152

accidentally במקרה *bemikre* 28

accompany, to ללוות *lelavot* 65

accountant m רואה חשבון *ro-e kheshbon* 121

acne mpl פצעי בגרות *pitz-ey bagrut*

across מעבר *me-ever* 12

acrylic *(fabric)* m אקרילן *akrilan*

actor/actress שחקן/שחקנית *sakhkan/sakhkanit*

adapter m מתאם *mat-em* 26, 148

address f כתובת *ktovet* 23, 84, 93, 126

adjoining room m חדר צמוד *kheder tzamud* 22

admission charge mpl דמי כניסה *dmey knisa* 114

adult *(noun)* m מבוגר *mevugar* 81, 100

afraid: I'm ~ *(I'm sorry)* לצערי *letza-ari* 126

after אחרי *akharey* 13, 95, 165

after shave mpl מי גילוח *mey gilu-akh* 142

after-sun lotion f משחה לאחרי שיזוף *mishkha le-akharey shizuf* 142

afternoon: in the ~ אחרי הצהריים *akharey hatzohorayim* 221

aged: to be ~ להיות בגיל *lihiyot begil* 159

ago לפני *lifney* 221; ... years ~ לפני ... שנים *lifney ... shanim* 163

agree: I don't ~ אני לא מסכים *ani lo maskim*

air: ~ conditioning m מיזוג אוויר *mizug avir* 22, 25; ~ mattress m מזרון אוויר *mizron avir* 31; ~ pump f משאבת אוויר *mash-evat avir* 87; ~ sickness bag f שקית למחלת אוויר *sakit lemakhalat avir* 70; ~ mail m דואר אוויר *do-ar avir* 153; ~port m נמל תעופה *nemal te-ufa* 84, 96

aisle seat m מושב במעבר *moshav bama-avar* 69

alarm clock m שעון מעורר *sha-on me-orer* 149

all כל *kol*

allergic: to be ~ להיות אלרגי *lihiyot alergi* 164, 165

allergy f אלרגיה *alergiya*

allowance f מיכסה *mikhsa* 67

almost כמעט *kim-at*

alone לבד *levad*

alone: leave me alone! עזוב אותי! *azov oti* 126

already כבר *kvar* 28

also גם *gam* 19

alter, to לשנות *leshanot* 137

alumin(i)um foil m נייר אלומיניום *neyar aluminiyum* 148

always תמיד *tamid* 13

amazing מפליא *mafli* 101

ambassador m שגריר *shagrir*

ambulance m אמבולנס *ambulans* 92

American *(adj.)* אמריקאי *amerika-i* 150, 159

American Plan [A.P.] פנסיון מלא *pensiyon male* 24

amount *(money)* m סכום *skhum* 42

amusement arcade m מועדון מכונות משחק *mo-adon mekhonot miskhak* 113

and -ו *ve* 19

anesthetic m חומר הרדמה *khomer hardama* 168

animal f חיה *khaya* 106

anorak m אנורק *anorak*

another אחר *akher* 21, 25, 125

antibiotics אנטיביוטיקה *antibiyotika* 165

antiques (noun) fpl עתיקות *atikot* 155

antiseptic (noun) m חומר אנטיספטי *khomer antisepti* 165; **~ cream** f משחה אנטיספטית *mishkha aniseptit* 141

anyone מישהו *mishehu* 67; **does ~ speak English?** מישהו מדבר אנגלית? *mishehu medaber anglit*

anything else? עוד משהו *od mashehu*

apartment f דירה *dira* 28

apologize: I apologize אני מתנצל *ani mitnatzel*

appendicitis f דלקת תוספתן *daleket toseftan* 165

appendix m תוספתן *toseftan* 166

appetite m תאבון *te-avon* 164

apples mpl תפוחים *tapukhim* 157

appointment: to make an ~ להזמין תור *lehazmin tor* 147

approximately בערך *be-erekh* 159

April אפריל *april* 218

Arab ערבי *aravi*

architect m אדריכל *adrikhal* 104

area code f קידומת *kidomet* 127

arm f זרוע *zaro-a* 166

around (approximately) בערך *be-erekh* 13; (time) ב- *be'erekh be*; (place) מסביב *misaviv* 12

arrive, to להגיע *lehagi-a* 13, 68, 70, 71

art gallery f גלריית אמנות *galeriyat omanut* 99

arthritis f דלקת פרקים *daleket prakim* 163

artificial sweetener m ממתיק מלאכותי *mamtik melakhuti* 38

artist m אמן *oman* 104

ashtray f מאפרה *ma-afera* 39

ask: I asked for ... ... ביקשתי *bikashti* 41

aspirin m אספירין *aspirin* 141

asthma f אסתמה *astma* 163

at last! סוף סוף *sof sof* 19

at (place) ב- *be/bi* 12, 84, 221

at least לפחות *lefakhot* 23

athletics f אתלטיקה *atletika* 114

attack f תקיפה *tkifa* 159

attractive מושך *moshekh*

audioguide f הדרכה מוקלטת *hadrakha mukletet* 100

August אוגוסט *ogust* 218

aunt f דודה *doda* 120

Australia f אוסטרליה *ostraliya* 119

authentic: is it ~? זה מקורי? *ze mekori*

authenticity f אותנטיות *otentiyut* 155

automated teller (ATM) m כספומט *kaspomat* 139

automatic (car) f מכונית עם הילוכים אוטומטיים *mekhonit im hilukhim otomatiyim* 86; **~ camera** f מצלמה אוטומטית *matzlema otomatit* 151

autumn m סתיו 219

available (free) פנוי *panuy* 76

B **baby** m תינוק *tinok* 39, 113; **~ food** m מזון לתינוקות *mazon letinokot* 142; **~ wipes** fpl ניגובים לתינוק *niguviyot letinok* 142; **~sitter** m שמרטף *shmartaf* 113

back (body) m גב *gav* 166; **~ache** m כאב גב *ke-ev gav* 166

back: to be ~ לחזור *lakhazor* 98; **at the ~** מאחור *me-akhor* 147

backgammon m שש-בש *sheshbesh* 121

backpacking m מסע תרמילים masa tarmilim

bad רע ra 14

bag m תיק tik 160

baggage fpl מזוודות mizvadot 32, 71, 73; **~ reclaim** f קבלת מזוודות מהיתסה kabalat mizvadot mehatisa 71

bakery f מאפיה ma-afiya 130

balcony f מרפסת mirpeset 29

ball m כדור kadur 155

ballet m בלט balet 108, 111

band (musical) f להקה lahaka 111

bandage f תחבושת takhboshet 141

bank m בנק bank 96, 130, 138

bar (hotel) m בר bar 26, 112

barber (shop) f מספרה mispara 131; (person) m ספר sapar

basement f קומת מרתף komat martef

basket m סל sal 156

basketball m כדורסל kadursal 114

bath f אמבטיה ambatya 21; **~ towel** f מגבת רחצה magevet rakhatza 27; **~room** (with tub) m חדר אמבטיה khadar ambatya 29, 98, 113; (restrooms) mpl שרותים sherutim 26

battery (car) m מצבר matzber 88, 149, 151; (camera, etc.) f סוללה solela 137

battle site m שדה קרב sde krav 99

be, to להיות lihiyot

beach m חוף khof 107, 116

beam (headlights) fpl אורות orot 86

beard m זקן zakan

beautiful יפה yafe 14, 101

because בגלל ש- biglal she 14; **~ of** בגלל biglal 14

bed f מיטה mita 21; **~ and breakfast** לינה וארוחת בוקר lina ve-arukhat boker 24

bedding mpl כלי מיטה kley mita 29

bedroom m חדר שינה khadar sheyna 29

beer f בירה bira 40, 157

before (time) לפני lifney 13, 165, 221

begin, to להתחיל lehatkhil

beginner m מתחיל matkhil 117

behind מאחורי me-akhorey 95

beige בז' bezh 143

belong: this belongs to me זה שייך לי ze shayakh li

belt f חגורה khagora 144

best הטוב ביותר hatov beyoter

better יותר טוב yoter tov 14

between jobs (unemployed) לא עובד כרגע lo oved karega 121

between בין beyn 221

bib m סינור לתינוק sinor letinok

bicycle mpl אופניים ofanayim 74, 83, 160

bidet m בידה bide

big גדול gadol 14, 134; **bigger** יותר גדול yoter gadol 24

bikini m ביקיני bikini 144

bill m חשבון kheshbon 32, 42

bin liner m שק אשפה sak ashpa

binoculars f משקפת mishkefet

bird m ציפור tzipor 106

birthday m יום הולדת yom huledet 219

biscuits mpl ביסקויטים biskvitim 157, 160

bite (insect) f עקיצה akitza

bitten: I've been ~ by a dog נשך אותי כלב nashakh oti kelev

bitter מר mar 41

black שחור shakhor 40; 143; **~ and white film** (camera) m סרט שחור-לבן seret shakhor lavan 151

bladder f שלפוחית שתן shalpukhit sheten 166

blanket f שמיכה smikha 27

bleach m מלבין _malbin_ 148

bleeding: he's ~ הוא מדמם _hu medamem_ 162

blind m צילון _tzelon_ 25

blister f בועה _bu-a_ 162

blocked סתום _satum_ 25

blood m דם _dam_ 164; **~ group** m סוג דם _sug dam_; **~ pressure** m לחץ דם _lakhatz dam_ 163, 164

blouse f חולצה _khultza_ 144

blow-dry m פן _fen_ 147

blue כחול _kakhol_ 143

boarding card m כרטיס עליה למטוס _kartis aliya lamatos_ 70

boat (ship) f ספינה _sfina_ 81; **~ trip** m טיול בספינה _tiyul bisfina_ 81, 97

boil (medical) m פצע מוגלתי _petza muglati_ 162

boiled מבושל _mevushal_

boiler m דוד חימום _dud khimum_ 29

bone m עצם _etzem_ 166

book m ספר _sefer_ 150; **~store** f חנות ספרים _khanut sfarim_ 130

book of tickets f כרטיסיה _kartisiya_ 79

booted: my car has been ~ שמו סנדל על המכונית שלי _samu sandal al hamekhonit sheli_ 87

boots fpl נעליים גבוהות _na-alayim gvohot_ 145; (sports) fpl נעליים _na-alayim_ 115

boring משעמם _mesha-amem_ 101

born: to be ~ להיוולד _lehivaled_ 119; **I was ~ in** נולדתי ב- _noladeti be_

borrow: may I ~ your ...? אוכל לשאול את ה ... שלך? _ukhal lish-ol et ha ... shelkha_

botanical garden m גן בוטני _gan botani_ 99

bottle f בקבוק _bakbuk_ 37; **~ of wine** m בקבוק יין _bakbuk yayin_ 154; **~-opener** m פותחן בקבוקים _potkhan bakbukim_ 148

bowel mpl מעיים _me-ayim_

bowls fpl קערות _ke-arot_ 148

box f קופסה _kufsa_ 110; **~ of chocolates** f קופסת שוקולד _kufsat shokolad_ 154

boy (young child) m ילד _yeled_ 155; (teenager) m נער _na-ar_

boyfriend m חבר _khaver_ 120

bra f חזיה _khaziya_ 144

bracelet f צמיד _tzamid_ 149

brakes mpl בלמים _blamim_ 83

bread m לחם _lekhem_ 38, 157

break down: to ~ (go wrong) להתקלקל _lehitkalkel_ 88; **the stove has broken down** תנור הבישול מקולקל _tanur habishul mekulkal_ 28

break, to לשבור _lishbor_ 28

breakdown truck m רכב גורר _rekhev gorer_ 88

breakfast f ארוחת בוקר _arukhat boker_ 27

breast m שד _shad_ 166

breathe, to לנשום _linshom_ 92, 164

bridge m גשר _gesher_ 95, 107

briefs mpl תחתונים _takhtonim_ 144

bring, to להביא _lehavi_ 113, 125

Britain f בריטניה _britaniya_ 119

British (adj.) בריטי _briti_ 159

broken שבור _shavur_ 25, 137; **to be ~** להיות שבור _lihiyot shavur_ 164

brooch f סיכה _sika_ 149

brother m אח _akh_ 120

brown חום _khum_ 143

browse, to (in shop) להסתכל _lehistakel_ 133

bruise f חבורה _khabura_ 162

bucket m דלי _dli_ 155

building m בנין _binyan_

A-Z

built: to be ~ להיבנות *lehibanot* 104

bulletin board m לוח הדעות *lu-akh hoda-ot* 26

bureau de change m משרד להחלפת מטבע *misrad lehakhlafat matbe-a* 138

burger m המבורגר *hamburger* 40; **~ stand** m מזנון המבורגר *miznon hamburger* 35

burn f כוייה *kviya* 162

bus m אוטובוס *otobus* 70, 71, 79, 123; **~ route** m קו אוטובוס *kav otobus* 96; **~ station** f תחנה מרכזית *takhana merkazit* 77; **~ stop** f תחנת אוטובוס *takhanat otobus* 65, 96

business mpl עסקים *asakim* 121, 123; **~ class** f מחלקת עסקים *makhleket asakim* 68; **on ~** לעסקים *le-asakim* 66

busy עמוס *amus* 36; (occupied) עסוק *asuk* 125

but אבל *aval* 19

butane gas m גז לבישול *gaz lebishul* 30

butcher m אטליז *itliz* 130

butter f חמאה *khem-a* 38, 160

button m כפתור *kaftor*

buy, to לקנות *liknot* 79, 80, 81, 98, 125, 133

by (method) ב *be* 94; (near) ליד *leyad* 36; (time) עד *ad* 13; לא יאוחר מ *lo ye-ukhar mi* 221; **~ bus** באוטובוס *be-otobus* 17; **~ car** במכונית *bimkhonit* 17, 94; **~ cash** במזומן *bimzuman* 17; **~ credit card** בכרטיס אשראי *bekartis ashray* 17; **~ train** ברכבת *berakevet* 17

bye! להתראות! *lehitra-ot* 17

C **cabaret** m קברט *kabaret* 112

cabin m תא *ta* 81

café m בית קפה *beyt kafe* 35

cagoule m מעיל רוח *me-il ru-akh*

cake f עוגה *uga* 40; **cakes** fpl עוגות *ugot* 160

calendar m לוח שנה *lu-akh shana* 154

call collect, to לחייג בגובייינא *lekhayeg beguvayna* 127

call: to ~ לקרוא *likro* 92; (telephone) להתקשר *lehitkasher* 87, 127; **to ~ for someone** לבוא לקחת *lavo lakakhat* 125; **to be called** להיקרא *lehikare* 94; **~ the police!** קרא למשטרה! *kra lamishtara* 92

camera f מצלמה *matzlema* 151, 160; **~ case** m תיק למצלמה *tik lematzlema* 151; **~ store** f חנות צילום *khanut tzilum* 130

camp: ~site m אתר קמפינג *atar kemping* 30, 123; **~bed** f מיטת שדה *mitat sade* 31

can: I can אני יכול *ani yakhol* 18; **I can't** אני לא יכול *ani lo yakhol* 18

can opener m פותחן קופסאות *potkhan kufsa-ot* 148

Canada קנדה *kanada* 119

canal f תעלה *te-ala* 107

cancel, to לבטל *levatel* 68

cancer (disease) m סרטן *sartan*

candy mpl ממתקים *mamtakim* 150

cap (hat) f כומתה *kumta* 144; (dental) m כתר *keter* 168

car f מכונית *mekhonit* 30, 73, 81, 86, 88, 93, 123, 160; **~ park** f חנייה *khanaya* 26, 96; **~ rental** f שכירת מכוניות *skhirat mekhoniyot* 70; (train compartment) m קרון *karon* 74

carafe m קנקן *kankan* 37

caravan m קרוון *karavan* 30, 81

cards (game) mpl קלפים *klafim* 121

careful: be ~! היזהר! *hizaher*

carpenter m נגר *nagar*

carpet (rug) m שטיח *shati-akh*

carrier bag f שקית קניות *sakit kniyot*

carry-cot m עריסת-סל *arisat sal*

cart f עגלה *agala* 156

carton f קופסה *kufsa* 110

case (suitcase) f מזוודה *mizvada* 69

cash (money) m כסף מזומן *kesef mezuman* 42, 136; **~ desk** f קופה *kupa* 132; **~ machine** m כספומט *kaspomat* 139; **to ~** (convert) להמיר *lehamir* 138

cashier f קופה *kupa* 132

casino m קזינו *kazino* 112

cassette f קלטת *kaletet* 155

castle f מצודה *metzuda* 99

catch, to לתפוס *litpos*

cathedral f קתדרלה *katedrala* 99

Catholic קתולי *katoli* 105

cave f מערה *me-ara* 107

CD m תקליטור *taklitor*; **CD-player** m מנגן תקליטורים *menagen taklitorim*

cemetery m בית קברות *beyt kvarot* 99

center of town m מרכז העיר *merkaz ha-ir* 21

central heating f הסקה מרכזית *hasaka merkazit*

ceramics f קרמיקה *keramika*

certificate f תעודה *te-uda* 149, 155

chain f שרשרת *sharsheret* 149

change (coins) m כסף קטן *kesef katan* 87, 136; (remainder of money) m עודף *odef* 84

change, to להחליף *lehakhlif* 39, 74, 79, 138; (reservation) לשנות *leshanot* 68

changing facilities mpl מתקני החלפת חיתולים *mitkaney hakhlafat khitulim* 113

charcoal mpl פחמים *pekhamim* 31

charge m מחיר *mekhir* 30, 115, 153

charter flight f טיסת שכר *tisat sekher*

cheap זול *zol* 14, 134; **cheaper** יותר זול *yoter zol* 21, 24, 109, 134

check: please ~ the ... ... בבקשה בדוק את *bevakasha bdok et*; **to ~ in** להירשם לטיסה *leherashem latisa* 68; **to ~ out** (hotel) לצאת *latzet* 32

checkbook m פנקס ציקים *pinkas chekim*

check-in הרשמה לטיסה *harshama latisa* 69

cheers! לחיים! *lekhayim*

cheese f גבינה *gvina* 157, 160

chemist f בית מרקחת *beyt merkakhat* 131

cheque book m פנקס ציקים *pinkas chekim*

chess m שחמט *shakhmat* 121; **~ set** m משחק שחמט *miskhak shakhmat* 155

chest m חזה *khaze* 166

chewing gum m מסטיק *mastik* 150

child f ילדה *yalda* 159, 162; m ילד *yeled* 159; **children** mpl ילדים *yeladim* 22, 24, 39, 66, 74, 81, 100, 113, 116, 120, 140

child's cot f עריסה *arisa* 22

child's seat m כסא לילד *kise leyeled* 39

childminder f מטפלת *metapelet*

Chinese סיני *sini* 35

chocolate שוקולד *shokolad* 40; **~ bar** f טבלת שוקולד *tavlat shokolad* 150; **~ ice cream [choc-ice]** f גלידת שוקולד *glidat shokolad* 110

church f כנסיה *knesiya* 96, 99, 105

cigarette kiosk f
חנות למוצרי טבק
khanut lemutzrey
tabak 130

cigarettes fpl סיגריות
sigariyot 150

cigars mpl סיגרים sigarim 150

cinema m קולנוע kolno-a 110

claim check תווית קבלה tavit kabala 71

clamped: my car has been ~
שמו סנדל על המכונית שלי
samu sandal al hamekhonit
sheli 87

clean (adj.) נקי naki 14, 39

clean, to לנקות lenakot 137

cliff m צוק tzuk 107

cling film ניילון עטיפת atifat
naylon 148

clinic f מרפאה mirpa-a 131

clock m שעון sha-on 149

close (near) קרוב karov 93, 95

close, to (shut something) לסגור
lisgor 100; (be shut) להיסגר
lehisager 140, 152;

clothes pins [pegs] mpl אטבי כביסה
itvey kvisa 148

clothing store [clothes shop] f
חנות בגדים khanut begadim 130

cloudy: to be ~ מעונן להיות lihiyot
me-unan 122

clubs (golf) mpl מקלות maklot 115

coach (train compartment) קרון
karon 74; (long-distance bus) m
אוטובוס בינעירוני otobus beyn-ironi
77; **~ station** f תחנה מרכזית takhana
merkazit 77

coast m חוף khof

coat m מעיל me-il 144; **~hanger** m
קולב kolav

cockroach m מקק makak

coffee m קפה kafe 40, 157

coin f מטבע matbe-a

cold קר kar 14, 41, 122; (illness) f
הצטננות hitztanenut 141, 163

collapse: he's collapsed התמוטט הוא
hu hitmotet

collect, to לאסוף le-esof 113, 151

color m צבע tzeva 143; **~ film** m
צבע סרט seret tzeva 151

comb m מסרק masrek 142

come, to לבוא lavo 36, 124, 126;
to ~ back (return) לחזור lakhazor
36, 140

commission f עמלה amala 138

compact camera f מצלמה קומפקטית
matzlema kompaktit 151

compact disc m תקליטור taklitor 155

company (business) f חברה khevra 93;
(companionship) f חברה khevra 126

compartment (train) m תא ta

composer m מלחין malkhin 111

computer m מחשב makhshev;
~ consultant m למחשבים יועץ yo-etz
lemakhshevim

concert m קונצרט kontzert 108, 111;
~ hall m קונצרטים אולם ulam
kontzertim 111

concussion: he has a ~ מוח זעזוע לו יש
yesh lo za-azu-a mo-akh

conditioner m קונדישנר kondishener 142

condom m קונדום kondom 141

conductor m מנצח menatze-akh 111

confirm, to לאשר le-asher 22, 68

congratulations! טוב מזל mazal tov 219

connection (train) f ממשיכה רכבת
rakevet mamshikha 76

conscious: he's ~ בהכרה הוא hu
behakara

constant קבוע kavu-a 113

constipation f עצירות atzirut

Consulate f קונסוליה konsulya 159

consult, to להיוועץ lehitya-etz 165

contact lens f עדשת מגע adshat maga 167

contact, to להתקשר lehitkasher 28

contagious: to be ~ להיות מידבק lihiyot midabek 165

contain, to להכיל lehakhil 39, 69, 153

contemporary dance m מחול מודרני makhol moderni 111

contraceptive m אמצעי מניעה emtza-i meni-a

cook (chef) m טבח tabakh

cook, to לבשל levashel

cooked meats בשר מבושל basar mevushal 160

cooker m תנור בישול tanur bishul 28

cookies mpl ביסקוויטים biskvitim 157, 160

cooking (noun) m בישול bishul; (cuisine) m מטבח mitbakh; ~ **facilities** mpl מתקני בישול mitkaney bishul 30

coolbox f צידנית tzedanit

cooler m יותר קריר yoter karir

copper f נחושת nekhoshet 149

copy m העתק he-etek

corkscrew f חולץ פקקים kholetz pkakim 148

correct נכון nakhon

cosmetics f קוסמטיקה kosmetika

cost, to לעלות la-alot 84, 89

cottage m קוטג' kotej 28

cotton כותנה kutna 145; (cotton wool) m צמר גפן tzemer gefen 141

cough, to להשתעל lehishta-el 164; (noun) m שיעול shi-ul 141

could I have ...? אפשר לקבל ...? efshar lekabel 18

country (nation) f ארץ eretz

country music f מוסיקת קנטרי musikat kantri 111

courier (guide) m מדריך madrikh

course (meal) f מנה mana; (track, path) m מסלול maslul 106

cousin m (f) דוד (בת) בן ben (bat) dod

cover: ~ charge תשלום שרות מינימלי tashlum sherut minimali 112

craft shop f חנות לדברי אומנות khanut ledivrey umanut

cramps fpl עוויתות avitot 163

crèche m פעוטון pa-oton

credit card m כרטיס אשראי kartis ashray 42, 109, 136, 139, 160; ~ **number** מספר כרטיס אשראי mispar kartis ashray 109

crib f עריסה arisa 22

crisps mpl טוגנים tuganim 157

crockery mpl כלי חרס kley kheres 29

cross, to לחצות lakhatzot 95

crown (dental) m כתר keter 168

cruise (noun) m שייט shayit

crutches mpl קביים kabayim

crystal (quartz) m קריסטל kristal 149

cup m ספל sefel 39

cupboard m ארון aron

cups mpl ספלים sfalim 148

currency exchange (transaction) f החלפת מטבע hakhlafat matbe-a 70, 73; (office) m משרד להחלפת מטבע misrad lehakhlafat matbe-a 138

currency m מטבע matbe-a 67, 138

curtains mpl וילונות vilonot

customs m מכס mekhes 67, 155

cut (hair) f תספורת tisporet 147

cut glass f זכוכית פיתוחים zkhukhit pitukhim 149

cut m חתך khatakh 162

cutlery m סכו"ם sakum 29

cycle route m מסלול אופניים maslul ofanayim 106

cycling f רכיבה באופניים
rekhiva be-ofanayim 114

cystitis f
דלקת שלפוחית השתן
daleket shalpukhit
hasheten 165

D **daily** יומי yomi
damaged ניזוק nizok 28;
to be ~ להינזק lehinazek 71

damp (noun/adj.) לחות/לח lakhut/lakh

dance (as an art form) m מחול makhol
111; (disco) m ריקוד rikud

dance, to לרקוד lirkod 111

dancing: to go ~ ללכת לרקוד lalekhet
lirkod 124

dangerous מסוכן mesukan

dark (place) חשוך khashukh 24; (color)
כהה kehe 14, 134, 143; **darker**
(color) יותר כהה yoter kehe 143

daughter בת bat 120, 162

dawn m שחר shakhar 221

day m יום yom 23, 97, 122, 221

dead (battery) שבת shovet 88

deaf: to be ~ להיות חירש lihiyot
kheresh 163

December דצמבר detzember 218

deck chair m כסא נוח kise no-akh 116

declare, to להצהיר lehatzhir 67

deduct, to (money) לנכות lenakot

deep freeze (noun) m מקפיא עמוק
makpi amok

deep עמוק amok

defrost, to להפשיר lehafshir

degrees (temperature) fpl מעלות
ma-alot

delay m עיכוב ikuv 70

delicatessen f מעדנייה ma-adaniya 156

delicious נפלא nifla 14

deliver, to למסור limsor

denim m דנים denim 145

dental floss m חוט דנטלי khut dentali

dentist m רופא שיניים rofe shina-yim
131, 168

denture mpl שיניים תותבת shinayim
totavot 168

deodorant דיאודורנט
de-odorant 142

department store f חנות כלבו khanut
kolbo 96, 130

departure lounge m אולם יוצאים ulam
yotz-im

deposit m פקדון pikadon 24, 83

describe, to לתאר leta-er 159

destination m יעד ya-ad

details mpl פרטים pratim

detergent (washing powder)
אבקת כביסה avkat kvisa 148;
(washing-up liquid) m סבון נוזלי
sabon nozli 148

develop, to לפתח lefate-akh 151

diabetes f סכרת sakeret

diabetic (noun) m חולה סכרת khole
sakeret 39; **to be ~** סכרת חולה להיות
lihiyot khole sakeret 163

dialling code f קידומת kidomet 127

diamond m יהלום yahalom 149

diapers mpl חיתולים khitulim 142

diarrhea m שלשול shilshul 141, 163

dice fpl קוביות kubiyot

dictionary m מילון milon 150

diesel דיזל dizel 87

diet: I'm on a ~ אני בדיאטה
ani bedi-eta

difficult קשה kashe 14

dining car m מזנון miznon 74, 77

dining room m חדר אוכל khadar
okhel 26, 23

dinner: to have ~ לאכול ארוחת ערב
le-ekhol arukhat erev 124

direct (train, journey, etc.) ישר
yashir 74

direct, to (to a place) להדריך lehadrikh 18

direction: in the ~ of ... בכיוון ... bekivun ... 95

director (company) m מנהל menahel

directory (telephone) m מדריך טלפון madrikh telefon

dirty מלוכלך melukhlakh 14, 28

disabled (noun) mpl נכים nekhim 22, 100

discotheque דיסקוטק diskotek 112

dish (meal) m מאכל ma-akhal 37

dishcloth f מטלית ניקוי matlit nikuy 148

dishes mpl כלי חרס kley kheres 29

dishwashing liquid m סבון נוזלי sabon nozli 148

dislocated: to be ~ להיות נקוע lihiyot naku-a 164

display case m ארון תצוגה aron tetzuga 134, 149

disposable camera f מצלמה חד-פעמית matzlema khad pe-amit 151

distilled water mpl מים מזוקקים mayim mezukakim

disturb: don't ~ לא להפריע lo lehafri-a

dive, to לצלול litzlol 116

diving equipment m ציוד צלילה tziyud tzlila 116

divorced: to be ~ להיות גרוש lihiyot garush 120

dizzy: I feel ~ יש לי סחרחורת yesh li skharkhoret

do, to לעשות la-asot 123; **what do you do?** מה אתה עושה? ma ata ose 121

doctor m רופא rofe 92, 131, 167

doll f בובה buba 155

dollar m דולר dolar 67, 138

door f דלת delet 25, 29

double: ~ bed f מיטה זוגית mita zugit 21; **~ room** m חדר לזוג kheder lezug 21

downtown (town center) m מרכז העיר merkaz ha-ir 83; **~ area** m מרכז העיר merkaz ha-ir 99

dozen, a תריסר treysar 217

draft [draught] מחהבית mehakhavit 40

dress f שמלה simla 144

drink (noun) m משקה mashke 125, 126; f שתיה shtiya 70; **drinks** mpl משקאות mashka-ot 37

drinking water mpl מי שתיה mey shtiya 30

drip: the faucet [tap] drips הברז מטפטף haberez metaftef

drive, to לנהוג linhog

driver m נהג nahag

driver's license m רשיון נהיגה rishyon nehiga 93

drop: to ~ someone off להוריד lehorid 83

drowning: someone is ~ מישהו טובע mishehu tove-a

drunk שיכור shikor

dry-clean, to לעשות ניקוי יבש la-asot nikuy yavesh

dry cleaner f מכבסה לניקוי יבש mikhbasa lenikuy yavesh 131

dubbed: to be ~ (into Hebrew) עם פסקול (עברי) im paskol (ivri) 110

dummy (pacifier) m מוצץ motzetz

during במשך bemeshekh 221

dustbins mpl פחי אשפה pakhey ashpa 30

duvet f שמיכת פוך smikhat pukh

E **e-mail** m דואר אלקטרוני do-ar elektroni 153; **~ address** m כתובת דואר אלקטרוני ktovet do-ar elektroni 153

ear drops fpl טיפות אזניים tipot oznayim

ear f אוזן _ozen_ 166;
~ache m כאב אוזניים _ke-ev oznayim_ 163; **~rings**
mpl עגילים _agilim_ 149

early מוקדם _mukdam_ 14,
221; **earlier** יותר מוקדם _yoter mukdam_ 125, 147

east מזרח _mizrakh_ 95

easy קל _kal_ 14

eat, to לאכול _le-ekhol_ 123, 167

economy class f מחלקת תיירים _makhleket tayarim_ 68

eggs fpl ביצים _beytzim_ 157

Egypt מצרים _mitzrayim;_ **Egyptian** מצרי _mitzri_

elastic (adj.) אלסטי _elasti;_ (noun) גומייה _gumiya_

electric shaver f מכונת גילוח _mekhonat gilu-akh_

electrical outlets mpl שקעי חשמל _shik-ey khashmal_ 30

electricity meter m שעון חשמל _sha-on khashmal_ 28

electronic אלקטרוני _elektroni_ 69;
~ flash m מבזק אלקטרוני _mavzek elektroni_ 151; **~ game** m משחק אלקטרוני _miskhak elektroni_ 155

elevator f מעלית _ma-alit_ 26, 132

else: something ~ משהו אחר _mashehu akher_

embassy f שגרירות _shagrirut_

emerald m איזמרגד _izmaragd_

emergency f מקרה חירום _mikre kherum_ 127; **~ exit** f יציאת חרום _yetzi-at kherum_ 132

empty ריק _rek_ 14

enamel m אמייל _emayl_ 149

end, to להיגמר _lehigamer_ 108; **at the ~** בסוף _basof_ 95

engaged: to be ~ להיות מאורס _lihiyot me-oras_ 120

engine m מנוע _mano-a_ 82, 91

engineering f הנדסה _handasa_ 121

England f אנגליה _angliya_ 119

English (language) f אנגלית _anglit_ 11,
67, 100, 110, 150, 159; **~-speaking**
דובר אנגלית _dover anglit_ 98, 159

enjoy, to ליהנות _lehanot_ 110, 124

enjoyable נעים _na-im_ 32

enlarge, to להגדיל _lehagdil_ 151

enough מספיק _maspik_ 15, 42, 136

ensuite bathroom m חדר אמבטיה צמוד _khadar ambatya tzmud_

entertainment guide m מדריך בידור _madrikh bidur_

entrance fee mpl דמי כניסה _dmey knisa_ 100

entry visa f אשרת כניסה _ashrat knisa_

envelope f מעטפה _ma-atafa_ 150

epileptic: to be ~ להיות אפילפטי _lihiyot epilepti_ 163

equipment m ציוד _tziyud_ 115

era f תקופה _tkufa_ 155

error f טעות _ta-ut_

escalator fpl מדרגות נעות _madregot na-ot_ 132

essential הכרחי _hekhrekhi_ 89

EU m האיחוד האירופי _ha-ikhud ha-eropi_

Eurocheque m יורוצ'יק _yurocheck_

evening m ערב _erev_ 109, 124, 132; **in the ~** בערב _ba-erev_ 221

every כל _kol_ 119; **~ day** כל יום _kol yom;_ **~ hour** כל שעה _kol sha-a_ 76;
~ week כל שבוע _kol shavu-a_ 13

examination (medical) f בדיקה _bdika_

example: for ~ לדוגמה _ledugma_

except מלבד _milvad_

excess baggage m מטען עודף _mit-an odef_ 69

exchange, to להחליף _lehakhlif_ 137, 138

exchange rate m שער חליפין _sha-ar khalifin_ 138

excursion m טיול _tiyul_ 97

excuse me! סליחה! _slikha_ 10, 11, 94

exhausted: I'm ~ אני תשוש _ani tashush_ 106

exit f יציאה _yetzi-a_ 70, 83, 132

expensive יקר _yakar_ 14, 134

experienced מנוסה _menuse_ 117

expiration [expiry] date m תאריך תפוגה _ta-arikh tfuga_ 109

exposure (photos) תמונה _tmuna_ 151

extension f שלוחה _shlukha_ 128

extra עוד _od_ 23, 27

extract, to (tooth) לעקור _la-akor_ 168

eye f עין _ayin_ 166

F fabric m בד _bad_ 145

face mpl/fpl פנים _panim_ 166

facial m טיפול פנים _tipul panim_ 147

facilities mpl אמצעים _emtza-im_ 22; mpl מתקנים _mitkanim_ 30

factor ... m מקדם _mekadem_ 142

faint: to feel ~ להרגיש חולשה _lehargish khulsha_ 163

fairground m לונה פארק _luna park_ 113

fall (autumn) m סתיו _stav_ 219

family f משפחה _mishpakha_ 66, 74, 120, 167

famous מפורסם _mefursam_

fan (air: manual) f מניפה _menifa_; (electric) m מאוורר _me-avrer_ 25

far רחוק _rakhok_ 12, 95, 130; **how ~ is it?** מה המרחק _ma hamerkhak_ 94, 106; **how ~ is it to there?** מה המרחק לשם _ma hamerkhak lesham_ 72

farm f חווה _khava_ 107

fast מהר _maher_ 17, 93; (clock) ממהר _memaher_ 221; **~-food restaurant** m מזנון מהיר _miznon mahir_ 35

father m אב _av_ 120

faucet m ברז _berez_ 25

faulty: this is ~ זה פגום _ze pagum_

favorite (adj.) האהוב _ha-ahuv_

fax m פקס _faks_ 22, 153

February פברואר _febru-ar_ 218

feed, to (baby) להניק _lehanik_ 39

feeding bottle m בקבוק הנקה _bakbuk hanaka_

feel: to ~ ill להרגיש רע _lehargish ra_ 163

female נקבה _nekeva_ 159

ferry f מעבורת _ma-aboret_ 81, 123

fever m חום גבוה _khom gavoha_ 163

few מעט _me-at_ 15; **a ~ of ...** מעטים... _me-atim me/mi_ 15

fiancé(e) m (f) ארוס(ה) _arus/arusa_

field m שדה _sade_ 107

fifth חמישי _khamishi_ 217

fill: to ~ out (a form) למלא _lemale_ 168; **to ~ up** למלא _lemale_ 87

filling (dental) f סתימה _stima_ 168

film m סרט _seret_ 108, 110, 151

filter m מסנן _masnen_ 151

find, to למצוא _limtzo_ 18

fine (penalty) m קנס _knas_ 93

fine (well) טוב _tov_ 19, 118

finger f אצבע _etzba_ 166

fire: ~ alarm f אזעקת שריפה _az-akat srefa_; **~ department [brigade]** mpl כבאים _kaba-im_ 92; **~ escape** m יציאת חרום _yetzi-at kherum_; **~ extinguisher** m מטף _mataf_; **~wood** mpl עצי הסקה _atzey hasaka_; **there's a ~!** שריפה! _srefa_

first ראשון _rishon_ 68, 75, 132, 217; **~ class** f מחלקה ראשונה _makhlaka rishona_ 68

fish: ~ restaurant f מסעדת דגים _mis-adat dagim_ 35; **~ store [~monger]** f חנות דגים _khanut dagim_ 130

fit, to (clothes) להתאים lehat-im 146

fitting room m חדר הלבשה khadar halbasha 146

fix, to (repair) לתקן letaken 168

flashlight m פנס panas 31

flat (puncture) m תקר teker 83, 86, 88

flavor: what flavors do you have? אילו טעמים יש לכם? elu te-amim yesh lakhem

flea m פרעוש par-osh

flight f טיסה tisa 68, 70; **~ number** m מספר טיסה mispar tisa 68

flip-flops mpl סנדלי אילת sandaley eylat 145

floor (level) f קומה koma 132

florist f חנות פרחים khanut prakhim 130

flower m פרח perakh 106

flu f שפעת shapa-at 165

flush: the toilet won't ~ השרותים אינם שוטפים hasherutim eynam shotfim

fly (insect) m זבוב zvuv

foggy: to be ~ להיות מעורפל lihiyot me-urpal 122

folk: ~ art אמנות עם omanut am; **~ music** f מוסיקת עם musikat am 111

follow, to (a road by car) לנסוע לפי linso-a lefi 95; (pursue) לעקוב אחרי la-akov akharey 159

food m מזון mazon 39, m אוכל okhel 119; **~ poisoning** f הרעלת מזון har-alat mazon

foot m כף רגל kaf regel 166; **~ball** (soccer) m כדורגל kaduregel 115; **~ path** m שביל shvil 107

for (of time) למשך lemeshekh 13; ל... le 86, 94, 116

foreign currency m מטבע זר matbe-a zar 138

forest m יער ya-ar 107

forget, to לשכוח lishko-akh 42

fork m מזלג mazleg 39, 40; **forks** mpl מזלגות mazlegot 148

form m טופס tofes 23, 168

formal dress m לבוש פורמלי levush formali 111

fortnight mpl שבועיים shvu-ayim

fortunately למרבה המזל lemarbe hamazal 19

fountain f מזרקה mizraka 99

four-door car f מכונית עם ארבע דלתות mekhonit im arba dlatot 86

four-wheel drive (car) m רכב שטח ארבע על ארבע rekhev shetakh arba al arba 86

fourth רביעי revi-i 217

foyer (hotel, theater) m אולם כניסה ulam knisa

fracture m שבר shever 165

frame f מסגרת misgeret

free (available) פנוי panuy 36, 124; (of charge) ללא תשלום lelo tashlum 69

freezer m תא הקפאה ta hakpa-a 29

French dressing m רוטב חומץ rotev khometz 38

frequent: how ~ ...? מה תדירות ...? ma tadirut 75

frequently לעתים קרובות le-itim krovot

fresh טרי tari 41

Friday m יום שישי yom shishi 218

fried מטוגן metugan

friend m ידיד yadid 123, 125, 162

friendly ידידותי yediduti

fries mpl צ'יפס chips 40; **French ~** mpl צ'יפס chips 38

frightened מבוהל mevohal

from מ... me/mi 12, 70; **where are you ~?** מאיפה אתה? me-_eyfo_ ata 119; **from ... to** (time) מ-... עד mi... ad 13, 221

front (adj.) קדמי kid_mi_ 83

front (fringe) מלפנים milfa_nim_ 147

frying pan f מחבת makha_vat_ 29

fuel (gasoline) דלק _delek_ 86

full (bottle, etc.) מלא ma_le_ 14, 36; **to be ~** (hotel) מלאים mele-_im_ 21; **~ board** פנסיון מלא pensiyon ma_le_ 24

fun: **to have ~** לעשות חיים la-a_sot_ khayim

funny מצחיק matzk_hik_ 126

furniture mpl רהיטים rahi_tim_

fuse m נתיך na_tikh_ 28; **~ box** תיבת נתיכים tey_vat_ netikhim 28

G

gallon m גלון ga_lon_

game (toy) m משחק mis_khak_ 114, 155

garage m מוסך mu_sakh_ 26

garbage bags שקי אשפה sa_key_ ashpa 148

garden (small) f גינה gina 35; (large) m גן gan

gas: **~ bottle** m מיכל גז mey_khal_ gaz 28; **~ station** f תחנת דלק ta_khanat_ _delek_ 87; **I smell ~!** אני מריח גז! _ani_ mari-_akh_ gaz

gastritis f דלקת קיבה da_leket_ _keyva_ 165

gate m שער sha-_ar_ 70

gauze f תחבושת takh_boshet_ 141

gay club m מועדון לעליזים mo-a_don_ le-alizim 112

genuine (original) מקורי meko_ri_ 134

---

get, to (buy, find) להשיג lehasig 30, 84; **to ~ back** (return) לחזור lakha_zor_ 98; **to ~ off** (bus, etc.) לרדת la_redet_ 79; **to ~ to** להגיע lehagi-a 70, 77; **how do I ~ to ...?** איך מגיעים ...? eykh magi-_im_ ... 73, 94

gift f מתנה matana 67, 154; **~ shop** f חנות מתנות kha_nut_ matanot 130

girl (young child) f ילדה yalda 155; (teenager) f נערה na-_ara_

girlfriend f חברה khave_ra_ 120

give, to לתת la_tet_ 136

gland f בלוטה baluta 166

glass f כוס kos 37, 39

glasses (for drinking) fpl כוסות ko_sot_ 148; (optical) mpl משקפיים misha_fayim_ 167

glossy finish (photos) m גימור מבריק gimur mavrik

glove f כפפה kfafa

go, to (on foot) ללכת la_lekhet_ 18; (take away) לקחת la_kakhat_ 40; (travel) לנסוע linso-a 93; **~ away!** לך מפה! lekh mipo; **to ~ for a walk** ללכת לטייל la_lekhet_ letayel 124; **to ~ out for a meal** ללכת לאכול la_lekhet_ le-e_khol_ 124; **to ~ out** (in evening) לצאת la_tzet_; **to ~ shopping** ללכת לקניות la_lekhet_ liknoyot 124; **to ~ to** (travel) לנסוע ל... linso-a le 66; **let's ~!** בוא נלך! bo ne_lekh_; **where does this bus ~?** לאן האוטובוס הזה נוסע? le-_an_ ha-_otobus_ haze nose-a; **go on** תמשיך tamshikh 19

goggles mpl משקפי מגן mishkafey magen

gold m זהב zahav 149; **~ plate** m ציפוי זהב tzipuy zahav 149

---

golf m גולף golf 115;
~ **course** מגרש גולף migrash golf

good m טוב tov 14, 35, 42;
~ **evening** ערב טוב erev tov 10; ~ **morning** בוקר טוב boker tov 10; ~ **night** לילה טוב layla tov 10

good-bye להתראות lehitra-ot 10

grandparents mpl סבים savim

grapes mpl ענבים anavim 160

grass (lawn) f דשא deshe

gray אפור afor 143

graze שפשוף shifshuf 162

great (excellent) מצויין metzuyan 19

Greece יוון yavan; **Greek** יווני yevani

green ירוק yarok 143

grocer חנווני khenvani; **green~** m ירקן yarkan 130

grilled בגריל bigril

ground (earth) f קרקע karka 31

ground floor (U.S. first floor) f קומת קרקע komat karka

groundcloth [groundsheet] f יריעת קרקע yeri-at karka 31

group f קבוצה kvutza 66; **groups** fpl קבוצות kvutzot 100

guarantee f אחריות akhrayut 135

guesthouse m בית הארחה beyt ha-arakha 123

guide (tour) m מדריך madrikh 98, 150; ~**book** חוברת הדרכה khoveret hadrakha 100

guided: ~ **tour** m סיור מודרך siyur mudrakh 100; ~ **walk** m טיול מודרך tiyul mudrakh 106

guitar f גיטרה gitara

gums (part of body) mpl חניכיים khanikhayim

guy rope m חבל חיזוק khevel khizuk 31

gynecologist m גינקולוג ginecolog 167

H **hair** m שיער se-ar 147;
~ **mousse** m ג'ל לשיער jel lese-ar 142; ~ **spray** m ספריי לשיער sprey lese-ar 142; ~**cut** f תספורת tisporet; ~**dresser** f מספרה mispara 131, 147

half (noun) m חצי khetzi 217; ~ **board** חצי פנסיון khatzi pensiyon 24; ~ **past ...** ... וחצי ... vakhetzi 220

hammer m פטיש patish 31

hand f יד yad 166; ~ **luggage** מטען יד mit-an yad 69; ~ **washable** כביס ביד kavis bayad 145

handbag m תיק יד tik yad 144, 160

handicapped: to be ~ להיות נכה lihiyot nekhe 163

handicrafts f מלאכת יד mlekhet yad

handkerchief f מטפחת mitpakhat

hanger m קולב kolav 27

hangover m הנג-אובר heng over 141

happen, to לקרות likrot 93

happy: I'm not ~ with the service אני לא מרוצה מהשרות ani lo merutze mehasherut

harbor m נמל namal

hard קשה kashe 31, 106

hat m כובע kova 144

have, to (receive) לקבל lekabel 70;
could I ~ ...? ...? אפשר לקבל efshar lekabel 38; **does the hotel ~ ...?** ...? יש במלון yesh bamalon 22; **I'll ~ ...** ... אקח ekakh 37

hay fever f קדחת השחת kadakhat hashakhat 141

head m ראש rosh 166; ~**ache** כאב ראש ke-ev rosh 163

head waiter m מלצר ראשי meltzar rashi 41

heading: to be ~ (in a direction) לנסוע לכיוון linso-a lekivun 83

health food store f חנות למזון טבעוני
khanut lemazon tiv-oni 130

hear, to לשמוע _lishmo-a_

hearing aid m מכשיר שמיעה _makhshir shmi-a_

heart m לב _lev_ 166; **~ attack** m התקף לב _hetkef lev_ 163

heat f הסקה _hasaka_ 25

heater m מכשיר חימום _makhshir khimum_

heating f הסקה _hasaka_ 25

heavy כבד _kaved_ 14, 69, 134

Hebrew (language) עברית _ivrit_ 11, 110, 126

height גובה _gova_ 159

hello שלום _shalom_ 10, 118

help: can you ~ me? תוכל לעזור לי? _tukhal la-azor li_ 92, 133; **may I ~ you?** אוכל לעזור לך? _ukhal la-azor lekha_ 18

hemorrhoids mpl טחורים _tkhorim_ 165

her/hers שלה _shela_ 16; **it's hers** זה שלה _ze shela_

here (position) פה _po_ 17, 31, 77, 106, 119; (to here) לפה _lepo_ 12

hernia m בקע _beka_ 165

high גבוה _gavo-ha_ 122

highlights (hair) mpl פסים בהירים _pasim behirim_ 147

highway m כביש מהיר _kvish mahir_ 88, 92, 94

hiking m טיול רגלי _tiyul ragli_

hill f גבעה _giv-a_ 107

his שלו _shelo_ 16; **it's his** זה שלו _ze shelo_

historic site m אתר היסטורי _atar histori_ 99

hobby (pastime) m תחביב _takhbiv_ 121

hold: to ~ on (wait on phone) להישאר על הקו _lehisha-er al hakav_ 128

hole m חור _khor_

holiday f חופשה _khufsha_ 123; **on ~** לחופשה _lekhufsha_ 66; **~ resort** m אתר נופש _atar nofesh_

home: to come ~ לבוא הביתה _lavo habayta_ 126; **we're going ~** אנחנו נוסעים הביתה _anakhnu nos-im habayta_

homosexual (adj.) הומוסקסואלי _homosexu-ali_

honeymoon: we're on our ~ אנחנו בירח דבש _anakhnu beyerakh dvash_

hopefully יש לקוות _yesh lekavot_ 19

horse m סוס _sus_; **~-racing** mpl מירוצי סוסים _merutzey susim_ 115

hospital m בית חולים _beyt kholim_ 96, 131, 164, 167

hot לוהט _lohet_ 14; (weather) חם _kham_ 122; **~ spring** m מעיין חם _ma-ayan kham_; **~ water** mpl מים חמים _mayim khamim_ 25

hot dog f נקניקיה _naknikiya_ 110

hotel m מלון _malon_ 21, 123

hour f שעה _sha-a_ 97, 117; **in an ~** בעוד שעה _be-od sha-a_ 84

house m בית _bayit_; **~wife** f עקרת בית _akeret bayit_ 121

how? איך? _eykh_ 17; **~ are things?** איך העניינים? _eykh ha-inyanim_ 19; **~ are you?** מה שלומך? _ma shlomkha_ 118; **~ long …?** (duration) מה משך _ma meshekh_ 68, 76, 77, 88, 94, 135; **~ many?** כמה? _kama_ 15, 79, 80; **~ many times …?** כמה פעמים …? _kama pe-amim_ 140; **~ much?** כמה _kama_ 15, 21, 65, 68, 79, 89, 100, 109, 136, 140; **~ old?** (people) בן כמה? _ben kama_ 120; (antiques) לפני כמה זמן …? _milifney kama zman_

hundred מאה me-a 217

hungry: I'm ~ אני רעב ani ra-ev

hurry: I'm in a ~ אני ממהר ani memaher

hurt, to לכאוב likh-ov 164; **to be ~** להיפצע lehipatza 92; להיפגע lehipaga 162; **my ... hurts** ה... שלי כואב ha ... sheli ko-ev 162

husband m בעל ba-al 120, 162

I אבקש ... **I'd like ...** avakesh 18

I've lost איבדתי ibadeti

ice m קרח kerakh 38

ice cream גלידה glida 40; **~ parlor** f גלידריה glideriya 35

identification m זיהוי zihuy

ill: I'm ~ אני חולה ani khole

illegal: is it ~? זה לא חוקי? ze lo khuki

imitation חיקוי khikuy 134

in בתוך betokh 88; (place) ב- be/bi 12; (within period of time) בעוד be-od 13; **~ front of** בחזית bekhazit 125

included: to be ~ להיכלל lehikalel 42; **is ... ~?** זה כולל ...? ze kolel 42, 86, 98

including כולל kolel 24

incredible לא יאומן lo ye-uman 101

indicate, to להצביע lehatzbi-a

indigestion קלקול קיבה kilkul keyva

indoor pool f בריכה מכוסה brekha mekhusa 116

inexpensive זול zol 35

infected: to be ~ להיות מזוהם lihiyot mezoham 167

infection m זיהום zihum 167

inflammation f דלקת daleket 165

informal לא פורמלי lo formali

information (knowledge) m מידע meyda 97; **~ desk** m מודיעין modi-in 73; **~ office** m מודיעין modi-in 96

injection f זריקה zrika 168

injured: to be ~ להיפצע lehipatza 92, 162

innocent (not guilty) חף khaf

insect m חרק kharak 25; **~ bite** f עקיצת חרקים akitzat kharakim 141, 162; **~ repellent** דוחה חרקים dokhe kharakim 141

inside בפנים bifnim 12

insist: I insist אני עומד על כך ani omed al kakh

insomnia mpl נדודי שינה nedudey shena

instant coffee m קפה נמס kafe names 160

instead of במקום bimkom

instructions (for use) fpl הוראות שימוש hora-ot shimush 135

instructor m מדריך madrikh

insulin m אינסולין insulin

insurance m ביטוח bituakh 86, 89, 93, 160, 168; **~ card [certificate]** f תעודת ביטוח te-udat bitu-akh 93; **~ claim** f תביעת ביטוח tvi-at bitu-akh 160

interest (hobby) m שטח התעניינות shetakh hit-anyenut 121

interested: to be ~ in להתעניין ב... lehit-anyen be 111

interesting מעניין me-anyen 101

International Student Card m כרטיס סטודנט בינלאומי kartis student beynle-umi 29

Internet m אינטרנט internet 153

interpreter m מתורגמן meturgeman 160

intersection f הצטלבות hitztalvut 95

introduce, to להציג lehatzig 118

invite, to להזמין lehazmin 124

Ireland אירלנד irland 119

is: ~ it ...? ‏?...‏ זה ‏ ze 17; it isn't ... ‏... לא‏ זה ‏ ze lo 17; ~ there ...? ‏?...‏ יש ‏ yesh 17

Israel ישראל ‏ yisra-el; **Israeli** ישראלי ‏ yisra-eli

Italian איטלקי ‏ italki 35

itch: it itches ‏ זה מגרד ‏ ze megared

itemized bill m ‏ חשבון מפורט ‏ kheshbon meforat 32

J **jacket** m ‏ זיקט ‏ zhaket 144

jam f ‏ ריבה ‏ riba 157

jammed: to be ~ ‏ תקוע ‏ taku-a 25

January ‏ ינואר ‏ yanu-ar 218

jaw f ‏ לסת ‏ leset 166

jazz m ‏ ג'ז ‏ jaz 111

jeans mpl ‏ ג'ינס ‏ jins 144

jellyfish f ‏ מדוזה ‏ meduza

jet-ski m ‏ סקי ממונע ‏ ski memuna 116

jeweler m ‏ צורף ‏ tzoref 130, 149

Jewish יהודי ‏ yehudi

job: what's your ~? ‏?מה המקצוע שלך‏ ma hamiktzo-a shelkha

join: to ~ in ‏ להצטרף ‏ lehitztaref 116; can we ~ you ‏ נוכל להצטרף אליך ‏ nukhal lehitztaref elekha 124

joint m ‏ פרק ‏ perek 166; ~ **passport** m ‏ דרכון משותף ‏ darkon meshutaf 66

joke f ‏ בדיחה ‏ bdikha

Jordan ‏ ירדן ‏ yarden; **Jordanian** ‏ ירדני‏ yardeni

journalist m ‏ עיתונאי ‏ itonay

journey f ‏ נסיעה ‏ nesi-a 76, 77

jug (of water) m ‏ כד ‏ kad

July ‏ יולי ‏ yuli 218

jump leads mpl ‏ כבל התנעה ‏ kevel hatna-a

jumper m ‏ סודר ‏ sudar

junction (intersection) m ‏ צומת ‏ tzomet 95

June ‏ יוני ‏ yuni 218

K **keep:** ~ **the change!** ‏!העודף בשבילך‏ ha-odef bishvilkha

kerosene m ‏ נפט ‏ neft; ~ **stove** m ‏ תנור נפט ‏ tanur neft 31

ketchup m ‏ קטשופ ‏ ketchup

kettle m ‏ קומקום ‏ kumkum 29

key m ‏ מפתח ‏ mafte-akh 27, 28, 88; ~ **ring** m ‏ מחזיק מפתחות ‏ makhzik maftekhot 154

kiddie pool f ‏ בריכה לפעוטות ‏ brekha lif-otot 113

kidney f ‏ כליה ‏ kilya 166

kilometer m ‏ קילומטר ‏ kilometer 88

kind (pleasant) ‏ חביב ‏ khaviv

kind: what ~ of ... ‏... איזה סוג של‏ eyze sug shel

kiss, to ‏ לנשק ‏ lenashek

kitchen m ‏ מטבח ‏ mitbakh 29

knapsack m ‏ תרמיל גב ‏ tarmil gav 31, 145

knee f ‏ ברך ‏ berekh 166

knickers mpl ‏ תחתונים ‏ takhtonim

knife m/f ‏ סכין ‏ sakin 39, 40; **knives** fpl/mpl ‏ סכינים ‏ sakinim 148

know, to (be informed) ‏ לדעת ‏ lada-at; (your way around) ‏ להתמצא ‏ lehitmatze 146

kosher ‏ כשר ‏ kasher

L **label** f ‏ תווית ‏ tavit

lace f ‏ תחרה ‏ takhara 145

ladder m ‏ סולם ‏ sulam

lake m ‏ אגם ‏ agam 107

lamp f ‏ מנורה ‏ menora 25, 29

land, to ‏ לנחות ‏ linkhot 70

language course m ‏ קורס שפות ‏ kurs safot

large גדול _gadol_ 40, 69, 110; **larger** יותר גדול _yoter gadol_ 134

last, to להמשיך _lehimashekh_

last: the ~ ... האחרון ... _ha-akharon_ 14, 68, 75, 80, 218

late מאוחר _me-ukhar_ 14, 221; **later** יותר מאוחר _yoter me-ukhar_ 125, 147

laundromat f מכבסה בשרות עצמי _mikhbasa besherut atzmi_ 131

laundry: ~ facilities mpl מתקני כביסה _mitkaney kvisa_ 30; **~ service** m שרות כביסה _sherut kvisa_ 22

lavatory mpl שרותים _sherutim_

lawyer m עורך דין _orekh din_ 159

laxative m חומר משלשל _khomer meshalshel_

lead, to (in a direction) להוביל _lehovil_ 94

lead-free (gas) נטול עופרת _netul oferet_ 87

leader (guide) m מדריך _madrikh_; (group) m מנהיג _manhig_

leak, to לדלוף _lidlof_

learn, to ללמוד _lilmod_

leather m עור or 145

leave, to (depart) לעזוב _la-azov_ 32, 41, 70, 76, 126; (start) לצאת _latzet_ 68, 98; (deposit) להשאיר _lehash-ir_ 72; (sail) להפליג _lehaflig_ 81; **I've left my bag** השארתי את התיק שלי _hish-arti et hatik sheli_

left: on the ~ משמאל _mismol_ 76; בצד שמאל _betzad smol_ 95

left-luggage office שמירת חפצים _shmirat khafatzim_ 71, 73

leg f רגל _regel_ 166

legal: is it ~? זה חוקי? _ze khuki_

leggings mpl מכנסי גרבונים _mikhnasey garbonim_ 144

lemon m לימון _limon_ 38

lemonade f לימונדה _limonada_ 160

lend: could you ~ me ...? (money) ...? תוכל להלוות לי _tukhal lehalvot li_; (object) ...? תוכל להשאיל לי _tukhal lehash-il li_

length (of) אורך (של) _orekh_ (shel)

lens f עדשה _adasha_ 151, 167; **~ cap** m מכסה עדשה _mikhse adasha_ 151

lesbian club m מועדון לסביות _mo-adon lesbiyot_

less פחות _pakhot_ 15

lesson m שיעור _shi-ur_ 116

let: ~ me know! תודיע לי! _todi-a li_

letter m מכתב _mikhtav_ 152; **~box** m תיבת דואר _tevat do-ar_

level (adj.) ישר _yashar_ 31

library f ספריה _sifriya_

lie: to ~ down לשכב _lishkav_ 164

life: ~belt f חגורת הצלה _khagorat hatzala_; **~boat** f סירת הצלה _sirat hatzala_; **~guard** m מציל _matzil_ 116; **~jacket** f חגורת הצלה _khagorat hatzala_

lift f מעלית _ma-alit_ 26, 132; (hitchhiking) m טרמפ _tremp_ 83

light (lamp) m אור or 25; (bicycle) פנס _panas_ 83; (weight) קל _kal_ 14, 134; (color) בהיר _bahir_ 14, 134, 143; **lighter** יותר בהיר _yoter bahir_ 143

light bulb f נורה _nura_ 148

lighter (cigarette) m מצית _matzit_ 150

like: to ~ לחבב _lekhabev_ 119, 121, 125; **I ~ it** זה מוצא חן בעיני _ze motze khen be-eynay_ 101; **I don't ~ it** זה לא מוצא חן בעיני _ze lo motze khen be-eynay_; **I'd like ...** ... אבקש _avakesh_ 18, 37, 40, 141, 157; **we'd like ...** ... נבקש _navakesh_ 18

like this (similar to) כמו זה _kmo ze_

line (bus, etc.) m קו _kav_ 80

linen m פשתן *pishtan* 145

lip f שפה *safa* 166

lipstick m שפתון *sfaton*

liqueur m ליקר *liker*

liter m ליטר *liter* 87

little קטן *katan*; **a little** קצת *ktzat* 15

live together, to לחיות יחד *likhyot yakhad* 120

liver m כבד *kaved* 166

living room m חדר אורחים *khadar orkhim* 29

lobby (theater, hotel) m אולם כניסה *ulam knisa*

local מקומי *mekomi* 37

lock (noun) m מנעול *man-ul* 25

lock, to לנעול *lin-ol* 88; **I've locked myself out of my room** סגרתי את עצמי מחוץ לחדר *sagarti et atzmi mikhutz lakheder* 27

log on, to להתחבר *lehitkhaber* 153

long ארוך *arokh* 144, 146

long-distance bus m אוטובוס בינעירוני *otobus beyn-ironi* 77

look: to ~ for לחפש *lekhapes* 18, 133; **I'm looking for ...** ... אני מחפש *ani mekhapes* 143; **to ~ like** להיראות *lehera-ot* 71; **I'm just looking** אני רק מסתכל *ani rak mistakel*

loose חופשי *khofshi* 146

lorry f משאית *masa-it*

lose, to לאבד *le-abed* 28, 138, 160; **I've lost ...** ... אבדתי *ibadeti* 71, 100, 160; **I'm lost** תעיתי בדרך *ta-iti baderekh* 106

lost-and-found [lost property office] משרד אבדות ומציאות *misrad avedot umtzi-ot* 73

louder בקול רם יותר *bekol ram yoter* 128

love, to לאהוב *le-ehov* 119; **I love you** אני אוהב אותך *ani ohev otkha*

lovely נפלא *nifla* 122, 125

low נמוך *namukh* 122; **~-fat** דל-שומן *dal shuman*

luck: good ~ בהצלחה *behatzlakha* 219

luggage fpl מזוודות *mizvadot*; **~ carts [trolleys]** fpl עגלות מטען *agalot mit-an* 71

lump m גוש *gush* 162

lunch f ארוחת צהריים *arukhat tzohorayim* 98; **~-time** צהריים *tzohorayim* 152

lung f ריאה *re-a*

M **machine washable** כביס במכונה *kavis bimkhona* 145

magazine m מגזין *magazin* 150

magnificent מפואר *mefo-ar* 101

maid f חדרנית *khadranit* 27, 28

mail, to לשלוח בדואר *lishlo-akh bado-ar* 27

mail (noun) m דואר *do-ar* 27, 152; **by ~** בדואר *bado-ar* 22; **~box** f תיבת דואר *tevat do-ar* 152

main ראשי *rashi* 130; **~ street** m רחוב ראשי *rekhov rashi* 95

make: to ~ up (prepare) להכין *lehakhin* 140

make-up m איפור *ipur*

male זכר *zakhar* 159

mallet m פטיש עץ *patish etz* 31

man m איש *ish*

manager m מנהל *menahel* 25, 41, 137

manicure m מניקור *manikur* 147

manual (car) ידני *yadani*

map f מפה *mapa* 94, 106, 150

March מרץ *mertz* 218

margarine f מרגרינה *margarina* 160

market m שוק *shuk* 99

A-Z

married: to be ~ להיות נשוי lihiyot nasuy 120

mascara f מסקרה maskara

mask f מסיכה masekha

mass f מיסה misa 105

massage m עיסוי isuy 147

mat finish (photos) f גימור מט gimur mat

match (sport) משחק miskhak 114

matches mpl גפרורים gafrurim 31, 148, 150

matinée (afternoon show) f הצגת אחר צהריים hatzagat akhar tzohorayim 109

matter: it doesn't ~ זה לא משנה ze lo meshane; **what's the ~?** מה קרה? ma kara

mattress m מזרון mizron

May מאי may 218

may I ...? אוכל ...? ukhal 18

maybe אולי ulay

meal f ארוחה arukha 38, 42, 70, 125, 165

mean: what does this ~? מה זאת אומרת? ma zot omeret 11

measles f חצבת khatzevet 165

measure, to למדוד limdod 146

measurement f מידה mida

meat m בשר basar 41

mechanic m מכונאי mekhonay 88

medication f תרופה trufa 164, 165

medicine f תרופה trufa 141

medium בינוני beynoni 40, 122

meet, to לפגוש lifgosh 125; **pleased to ~ you** נעים מאד na-im me-od 118

meeting place [point] נקודת מפגש nekudat mifgash 12

member (of club, etc.) m חבר khaver 88, 112, 115

men (toilets) גברים gvarim

mention: don't ~ it אין בעד מה eyn be-ad ma 10

menu m תפריט tafrit

message f הודעה hoda-a 27

metal f מתכת matekhet

metro f רכבת תחתית rakevet takhtit 80

microwave (oven) m מיקרוגל mikrogal

midday mpl צהריים tzohorayim

midnight חצות khatzot 13, 220

migraine f מיגרנה migrena

milk m חלב khalav 157; **with ~** בחלב bekhalav 40

million מיליון milyon 217

mind: do you mind? אכפת לך? ikhpat lekha 76, 126

mine שלי sheli 16; **it's ~!** זה שלי! ze sheli

mineral water mpl מים מינרליים mayim mineraliyim

mini-bar m מיני-בר mini bar 32

minimart m מינימרקט minimarket 156

minute f דקה daka

mirror m ראי re-i

missing: to be ~ (to be lacking) להיות חסר lihiyot khaser 137; (to be lost) ללכת לאיבוד lalekhet le-ibud 159

mistake f טעות ta-ut 32, 41

misunderstanding: there's been a ~ היתה אי-הבנה hayta i havana

mobile home m קרוון karavan

Modified American Plan [M.A.P.] חצי פנסיון khatzi pensiyon 24

moisturizer (cream) m קרם לחות krem lakhut

monastery m מנזר minzar 99

Monday יום שני yom sheni 218

money m כסף kesef 139, 160; **~ order** f המחאת כסף hamkha-at kesef

month m חודש khodesh 218

moped mpl אופניים עם מנוע 83

more (comparative) יותר _yoter_ 15, 94;
(additional amount) עוד od 67;
  I'd like some ~ … אבקש עוד …
  avakesh od 39

morning: in the ~ בבוקר _baboker_ 221

mosque m מסגד _misgad_

mosquito bite f עקיצת יתוש _akitzat yatush_

mother f אם _em_ 120

motion sickness f מחלת נסיעה _makhalat nesi-a_ 141

motor: ~bike m אופנוע _ofno-a_ 83;
  ~boat סירת מנוע _sirat mano-a_ 116

motorway m כביש מהיר _kvish mahir_ 88, 92, 94

mountain m הר _har_ 107; **~ bike** אופנוע הרים _ofno-a harim_; **~ pass** m מעבר הרים _ma-avar harim_ 107;
~ range f שרשרת הרים _sharsheret harim_ 107

moustache m שפם _safam_

mouth m פה _pe_ 164, 166; **~ ulcer** m כיב פה _kiv pe_

move, to (hotel room) לעבור _la-avor_ 25;
(someone else) להזיז _lehaziz_ 92; **don't ~ him** אל תזיז אותו _al taziz oto_ 92

movie m סרט _seret_ 108; **~ theater** m קולנוע _kolno-a_ 110

Mr. מר _mar_

Mrs. גברת _gveret_

mugged: to be ~ להישדד ברחוב _lehishaded barkhov_ 160

mugging m שוד ברחוב _shod barkhov_ 159

mugs mpl ספלים גדולים _sfalim gdolim_ 148

mumps f חזרת _khazeret_

muscle m שריר _shrir_ 166

museum m מוזאון _muze-on_ 99

music f מוסיקה _musika_ 112, 121; **~ store** f חנות תקליטים _khanut taklitim_ 131

musician m מוסיקאי _musikay_

must: I must אני מוכרח _ani mukhrakh_

mustard m חרדל _khardal_ 38

my שלי _sheli_ 16

myself: I'll do it ~ אעשה זאת בעצמי _e-ese zot be-atzmi_

N **name** m שם _shem_ 22, 36, 93, 118, 120; **my ~ is** שמי _shmi_ 118;
what's your ~? מה שמך? _ma shimkha_ 118

napkin f מפית _mapit_ 39

nappies חיתולים _khitulim_ 142

national לאומי _le-umi_

nationality f אזרחות _ezrakhut_ 23

nature preserve f שמורת טבע _shmurat teva_ 107

nausea f בחילה _bkhila_

near קרוב _karov_ 12, 35

nearby בסביבה _basviva_ 21, 87, 115

nearest הקרוב _hakarov_ 80, 88, 92, 127, 130, 140

necessary נחוץ _nakhutz_ 112

neck m צואר _tzavar_ 166; (back of head) עורף _oref_ 147; **~lace** f מחרוזת _makharozet_ 149

need: I ~ to … אני צריך … _ani tzarikh_ 18

nephew m בן אח _ben akh_

nerve m עצב _atzav_

nervous system מערכת העצבים _ma-arekhet ha-atzabim_

never לא אף פעם _af pa-am lo_ 13;
~ mind אין דבר _eyn davar_ 10

new חדש _khadash_ 14

news: ~**agent** f חנות עיתונים *khanut itonim* 131; ~**paper** m עיתון *iton* 150; ~**stand** f חנות עיתונים *khanut itonim* 131, 150

next הבא *haba* 14, 75, 77, 80, 94, 100, 218; **next to** ליד *leyad* 12, 95; **the next** הבא *haba* 68; **next stop!** התחנה הבאה! *hatakhana haba-a* 79

niece f בת אח *bat akh*

night m לילה *layla*; **at ~** בלילה *balayla* 221; **for two nights** לשני לילות *lishney leylot* 22; ~**club** m מועדון לילה *mo-adon layla* 112

no לא *lo* 10; **no way!** בשום אופן לא! *beshum ofen lo* 19

no one אף אחד לא *af ekhad lo* 16

noisy רועש *ro-esh* 14, 24

non-alcoholic לא אלכוהולי *lo alkoholi*

non-smoking (adj.) לא מעשן *lo me-ashen* 36

none: there's ~ אין כלום *eyn klum* 15

nonsense! שטויות! *shtuyot* 19

noon שתים עשרה בצהריים *shteym esre batzohorayim* 220

normal רגיל *ragil* 67

north צפון *tzafon* 95

nose אף *af* 166

not: ~ bad לא רע *lo ra* 19; **~ yet** עדיין לא *adayin lo* 13

nothing שום דבר לא *shum davar lo* 16; **~ else** שום דבר אחר לא *shum davar akher lo* 15

notify, to להודיע ל... *lehodi-a le* 167

November נובמבר *november* 218

now עכשיו *akhshav* 13, 32, 84

number: sorry, wrong ~ מצטער, מספר לא נכון *mitzta-er mispar lo nakhon*

nurse f אחות *akhot*

nylon m ניילון *naylon*

---

o'clock: it's ... o'clock עכשיו השעה ... *akhshav hasha-a* 220

occasionally לפעמים *lif-amim*

occupied תפוס *tafus* 14

October אוקטובר *oktober* 218

of course כמובן *kamuvan* 19

off-peak לא בתקופת העומס *lo bitkufat ha-omes*

office m משרד *misrad*

often לעתים קרובות *le-itim krovot*

oil שמן *shemen* 38

okay אוקיי *okey* 19, בסדר *beseder* 10

old (objects) ישן *yashan* 14; (people) זקן *zaken* 14; **~ town** f עיר עתיקה *ir atika* 99

olive oil m שמן זית *shemen zayit*

olives mpl זיתים *zeytim* 160

omelet f חביתה *khavita* 40

on (day, date) ב- *ba/be/bi* 13; **~ foot** ברגל *baregel* 17, 95; **~ the left** בצד שמאל *betzad smol* 12; **~ the right** בצד ימין *betzad yamin* 12; **on/off switch** מפסק ראשי *mafsek rashi*

once פעם אחת *pa-am akhat* 217; **~ a day** פעם ביום *pa-am beyom* 76

one-way בכיוון אחד *bekivun ekhad* 65, 74, 79

open (adj.) פתוח *patu-akh* 14; **~-air pool** f בריכה פתוחה *brekha ptukha* 116

open, to לפתוח *lifto-akh* 76, 100, 132, 140, 164; (be opened) להיפתח *lehipatakh* 152

opening hours fpl שעות פתיחה *she-ot ptikha* 100

opera f אופרה *opera* 108, 111; **~ house** m בית אופרה *beyt opera* 99

operation (medical) ניתוח *nitu-akh*

opposite מול *mul* 12, 95

optician m אופטיקאי *optikay* 131, 167

or או *o* 19

orange (color) כתום *katom* 143

oranges (fruit) mpl תפוזים *tapuzim* 160

orchestra f תזמורת *tizmoret* 111

order, to להזמין *lehazmin* 32, 37, 41, 135

organized hike/walk m טיול מאורגן ברגל *tiyul me-urgan baregel*

our/ours שלנו *shelanu* 16

outdoor בחוץ *bakhutz*

outrageous (price, etc.) לא יתכן *lo yitakhen* 89

outside (of something) - מחוץ ל- *mikhutz le* 12; (outdoors) בחוץ *bakhutz* 36

oval אליפטי *elipti* 134

oven תנור בישול *tanur bishul*

over: ~ here פה *po* 157; **~ there** שם *sham* 36, 157

overcharge: I've been overcharged לקחו ממני מחיר מופרז *lakkhu mimeni mekhir mufraz*

overdone מבושל יותר מדי *mevushal yoter miday* 41

overheat, to להתחמם יותר מדי *lehitkhamem yoter miday*

overnight ללילה אחד *lelayla ekhad* 23

owe, to להיות חייב *lihiyot khayav* 168; **how much do I ~?** כמה אני חייב *kama ani khayav*

own: on my ~ לבדי *levadi* 65; **I'm on my ~** אני לבדי *ani levadi* 66

P

p.m. אחרי צהריים *akharey tzohorayim*

pacifier m מוצץ *motzetz*

pack, to לארוז *le-eroz* 69

package f חבילה *khavila* 153

packed lunch f ארוחה ארוזה *arukha aruza*

paddling pool f בריכה לפעוטות *brekha lif-otot* 113

padlock m מנעול תלוי *man-ul taluy*

pail m דלי *dli* 155

pain: ~killer f תרופה נגד כאבים *trufa neged ke-evim* 141, 165; **to be in ~** לסבול מכאבים *lisbol mike-evim* 167

paint, to (artist) לצייר *letzayer*

painter (artist) m צייר *tzayar*

painting f ציור *tziyur*

pair: a ~ of זוג *zug* 217

palace m ארמון *armon* 99

Palestinian פלשתינאי *palestina-i*

palpitations fpl דפיקות לב *dfikot lev*

panorama f פנורמה *panorama* 107

pants (U.S.) mpl מכנסיים *mikhnasayim* 144

panty hose mpl גרבונים *garbonim* 144

paper napkins mpl מפיות נייר *mapiyot neyar* 148

paraffin m נפט *neft* 31

paralysis m שיתוק *shituk*

parcel f חבילה *khavila* 153

parents mpl הורים *horim* 120

park m פארק *park* 99, 107; גן *gan* 96

parking: ~ lot m מגרש חנייה *migrash khanaya* 26, 87, 96; **~ meter** m מדחן *madkhan* 87

parliament building f כנסת *kneset* 99

partner (in relationship – male/female) m/f בן זוג/בת זוג *ben zug/bat zug*

party (social) f מסיבה *mesiba* 124

pass, to (a place) לעבור *la-avor*

passport m דרכון *darkon* 23, 66, 69, 160; **~ number** m מספר דרכון *mispar darkon* 23

pasta fpl אטריות *itriyot* 38

pastry shop f קונדיטוריה _konditoriya_ 131

patch, to להטליא _lehatli_ 137

patient (noun) m חולה _khole_

pavement: on the ~ על המדרכה _al hamidrakha_

pay: to ~ לשלם _leshalem_ 42, 136; **can I ~ in ...** אפשר לשלם ב... _efshar leshalem be ..._ 67; **~ phone** טלפון ציבורי _telefon tziburi_

payment m תשלום _tashlum_

peak f פיסגה _pisga_ 107

pearl f פנינה _pnina_ 149

pebbles mpl חלוקים _khalukim_ 116

pedestrian: ~ crossing מעבר להולכי רגל _ma-avar leholkhey regel_ 96; **~ zone [precinct]** מדרחוב _midrakhov_ 96

pegs (clothes) mpl אטבי כביסה _itvey kvisa_ 148

pen m עט _et_ 150

people mpl אנשים _anashim_ 119

pepper m פלפל _pilpel_ 38

per: ~ day ליום _leyom_ 30, 83, 86, 87, 115; **~ hour** לשעה _lesha-a_ 87, 115, 155; **~ night** ללילה _lelayla_ 21, 24; **~ round** (golf) לסיבוב _lesivuv_ 115; **~ week** לשבוע _leshavu-a_ 24, 30, 83, 86

perhaps אולי _ulay_ 19

period (menstrual) m מחזור _makhzor_ 167; **~ pains** mpl כאבי מחזור _ke-evey makhzor_ 167

perm m סלסול תמידי _silsul tmidi_ 147

person m אדם _adam_ 93

petrol station f תחנת דלק _takhanat delek_ 87

pewter m בדיל-עופרת _bdil oferet_ 149

pharmacy m בית מרקחת _beyt merkakhat_ 131, 140, 156

phone, to לטלפן _letalpen_; **~ card** m טלכרט _telekart_ 127, 153

photo: to take a ~ לצלם _letzalem_

photocopier f מכונת צילום _mekhonat tzilum_ 153

photographer m צלם _tzalam_

phrase m ביטוי _bituy_ 11

pick up: to ~ לאסוף _le-esof_ 28

picnic m פיקניק _piknik_; **~ area** m אתר פיקניק _atar piknik_ 107

piece (item) m פריט _parit_ 69; **a ~ of ...** ... חתיכת _khatikhat_ 40

pill f גלולה _glula_ 165, 167

pillow m כר _kar_ 27; **~ case** f ציפית _tzipit_

pilot light f להבה תמידית _lehava tmidit_

pink ורוד _varod_ 143

pipe (smoking) f מקטרת _mikteret_

pitch (for camping) m שדה לקמפינג _sade lekemping_

pizza f פיצה _pitza_ 40

pizzeria f פיצריה _pitzeriya_ 35

place m מקום _makom_ 123

plane m מטוס _matos_ 68

plans fpl תכניות _tokhniyot_ 124

plant (noun) m צמח _tzemakh_

plaster m פלסטר _plaster_ 141

plastic: ~ bags mpl שקי ניילון _sakey naylon_; **~ wrap** m עטיפת ניילון _atifat naylon_ 148

plate f צלחת _tzalakhat_ 39; **plates** fpl צלחות _tzalakhot_ 148

platform m רציף _ratzif_ 73, 76

platinum f פלטינה _platina_ 149

play (theater) m מחזה _makhaze_ 108; **~wright** m מחזאי _makhazay_ 110; **~ground** m מגרש משחקים _migrash miskhakim_ 113; **~ group** m פעוטון _pa-oton_ 113

play, to (game) לשחק _lesakhek_ 114, 110, 121; (music) לנגן _lenagen_ 111

playing: to be ~ (movie, etc.) להציג lehatzig 110; **~ field** m מגרש ספורט migrash sport 96

pleasant נעים na-im 14

please בבקשה bevakasha 10

plug (electric) m תקע teka 148

pneumonia f דלקת ריאות daleket re-ot 165

poison m רעל ra-al

police f משטרה mishtara 92, 159; **~ report** m דו"ח משטרתי du-akh mishtarti 160; **~ station** f תחנת משטרה takhanat mishtara 96, 131, 159

pollen: ~ count m ריכוז אבקת הפרחים rikuz avkat haprakhim 122

polyester m פוליאסטר poli-ester

pond f בריכה brekha 107

pop (music) m פופ pop 111

popcorn m פופקורן popkorn 110

popular פופולרי populari 111, 155

port (harbor) m נמל namal

porter m סבל sabal 71

portion f מנה mana 40

possible: as soon as ~ בהקדם האפשרי bahekdem ha-efshari

post, to לשלוח בדואר lishlo-akh bado-ar; (noun) m דואר do-ar; **~ office** m סניף דואר snif do-ar 96, 131, 152; **~card** f גלויה gluya 152, 154

potato chips mpl טוגנים tuganim 157

potatoes mpl תפודים tapudim 38

pottery f קדרות kadarut

pound (sterling) f לירה שטרלינג lira sterling 67, 138

power: ~ cut f הפסקת חשמל hafsakat khashmal; **~ points** mpl שקעי חשמל shik-ey khashmal 30

pregnant: to be ~ להיות בהריון lihiyot beherayon 163, 167

premium (gasoline) m אוקטן גבוה oktan gavoha 87

prescribe, to לרשום lirshom 165

prescription m מירשם mirsham 140, 141

present (gift) f מתנה matana

press, to לגהץ legahetz 137

pretty יפה yafe

price m מחיר mekhir 24

priest (Christian) m כומר komer

prison m כלא kele

profession m מקצוע miktzo-a 23

program f תכנית tokhnit 108, 109

pronounce, to לבטא levate

Protestant פרוטסטנטי protestanti 105

public (noun) m ציבור tzibur 100

pump (gas station) f משאבה mash-eva 87

puncture m תקר teker 83, 86, 88

puppet show f הצגת בובות hatzagat bubot

pure טהור tahor 145

purple ארגמן argaman 143

purse m ארנק arnak 160

push-chair f עגלת ילדים eglat yeladim

put, to (to place) לשים lasim 22; **can you put me up for the night?** תוכלו לארח אותי הלילה? tukhlu le-are-akh oti halayla; **where can I ~ ...?** איפה אוכל לשים ...? eyfo ukhal lasim

Q quality f איכות eykhut 134

quarter: a ~ רבע reva 217; **a ~ past** (after) ... ורבע va... vareva 220; **a ~ to** (before) ... רבע ל... reva le 220

queue, to לעמוד בתור la-amod bator 112

quick מהיר mahir 14; **quickly** מהר maher 17

quickest: what's the ~ way? מה הדרך המהירה ביותר? _ma haderekh hamehira beyoter_

quiet שקט _shaket_ 14; **quieter** יותר שקט _yoter shaket_ 24, 126

R **rabbi** m רב _rav_

racket (tennis, squash) m מחבט _makhbet_ 115

railway f רכבת _rakevet_

rain m גשם _geshem_ 122; **~coat** m מעיל גשם _me-il geshem_ 144

rape m אונס _ones_ 159

rapids mpl אשדות _ashadot_ 107

rare (unusual) נדיר _nadir_; (steak) צלוי למחצה _tzaluy lemekhetza_

rash f פריחה _prikha_ 162

razor blades mpl/fpl סכיני גילוח _sakiney gilu-akh_ 142

reading f קריאה _kri-a_ 121

ready: to be ~ להיות מוכן _lihiyot mukhan_ 89, 126, 137, 151

real (genuine) אמיתי _amiti_ 149

rear אחורי _akhori_ 83

receipt f קבלה _kabala_ 32, 42, 89, 136, 137, 151, 168

reception (desk) f קבלה _kabala_

receptionist m פקיד קבלה _pkid kabala_

reclaim tag f תווית קבלה _tavit kabala_ 71

recommend, to להמליץ _lehamlitz_ 21, 37; **can you ~ ...?** תוכל להמליץ על ...? _tukhlu lehamlitz al ...?_ 35, 97, 108, 112

record (L.P.) m תקליט _taklit_ 155

red אדום _adom_ 143; **~ wine** m יין אדום _yayin adom_ 40

reduction f הנחה _hanakha_ 24, 68, 74, 100

refreshments mpl אוכל ושתיה _okhel ushtiya_ 77

refrigerator m מקרר _mekarer_ 29

refund m החזר _hekhzer_ 137

refuse bags mpl שקי אשפה _sakey ashpa_ 148

region m איזור _ezor_ 106; **in the ~ of ...** m בסביבות _bisvivot_ 134

registered mail m דואר רשום _do-ar rashum_ 153

registration form m טופס הרשמה _tofes harshama_ 23

regular (gasoline) רגיל _ragil_ 87, 110; (medium) בינוני _beynoni_ 40

reliable אמין _amin_ 113

religion f דת _dat_

remember: I don't ~ אני לא זוכר _ani lo zokher_

rent, to לשכור _liskor_ 83, 86, 115, 116, 117; **to ~ out** להשכיר _lehaskir_ 29

repair, to לתקן _letaken_ 89, 137, 168

repairs mpl תיקונים _tikunim_ 89

repeat, to לחזור _lakhazor_ 94, 128

replacement (noun) m תחליף _takhlif_ 167; **~ parts** mpl חלפים _khalafim_ 137

report, to לדווח על _ledave-akh al_ 159, 160

require, to לדרוש _lidrosh_ 83

required דרוש _darush_ 111

reservation f הזמנה _hazmana_ 22, 36, 68, 76, 112; **~ desk** m דלפק הזמנות _dalpak hazmanot_ 109

reserve, to להזמין _lehazmin_ 21, 74, 81, 109; **I'd like to ~ ...** אבקש להזמין ... _avakesh lehazmin_ 36

rest, to לנוח _lanu-akh_ 106

restaurant f מסעדה _mia-ada_ 35, 112

retired: to be ~ להיות בגימלאות _lihiyot begimla-ot_ 121

return, to (come back) לחזור lakhazor 74, 81, 106; (surrender) להחזיר lehakhzir 86

return ticket הלוך ושוב halokh vashov 65, 74

reverse the charges, to לחייג בגוביינא lekhayeg beguvayna 127

revolting מגעיל mag-il 14

rheumatism m ראומטיזם re-umatizm

rib f צלע tzela 166

rice m אורז orez 38

right (correct) נכון nakhon 76, 79, 94; that's ~ זה נכון ze nakhon

right: on the ~ מימין miyamin 76

right of way (in traffic) זכות קדימה zkhut kdima 93; (access) אפשרות מעבר efsharut ma-avar 106

ring f טבעת taba-at 149

river m נהר nahar 107; ~ **cruise** m שייט בנהר shayit banahar 81

road f דרך derekh 94, 95; ~ **map** f מפת דרכים mapat drakhim 150

robbed: to be ~ להישדד lehishaded 160

robbery שוד shod

rock music f מוסיקת רוק musikat rok 111

rolls (bread) fpl לחמניות lakhmaniyot 160

romantic רומנטי romanti 101

roof m גג gag

roof-rack m גגון מזוודות gagon mizvadot

room m חדר kheder 21, 25

rope m חבל khevel

round עגול agol 134; ~ **neck** צוארון עגול tzavaron agol 144

round-trip הלוך ושוב halokh vashov 65, 74, 79

route m מסלול maslul 106

rubbish (trash) f אשפה ashpa 28

rucksack m תרמיל גב tarmil gav

rude גס gas

ruins fpl חורבות khoravot 99

run: to ~ into (crash) לפגוע lifgo-a 93; **to ~ out of** (fuel) להיגמר lehigamer 88

rush hour f שעת העומס she-at ha-omes

S **safe** (lock-up) f כספת kasefet 27; (not dangerous) בטוח batu-akh 116; **to feel ~** להרגיש בטוח lehargish batu-akh 65

safety f בטיחות betikhut; ~ **pins** fpl סיכות ביטחון sikot bitakhon

sailing f הפלגה haflaga 81

salad m סלט salat 38

sales fpl מכירות mekhirot 121; ~ **tax** m מע"מ ma-am 24

salt f מלח melakh 38; **salty** מלוח malu-akh

same אותו oto 74

sand m חול khol

sandals mpl סנדלים sandalim 145

sandwich m כריך karikh 40

sandy חולי kholi 117; ~ **beach** חוף חולי khof kholi

sanitary napkin [towel] f תחבושת היגיינית takhboshet higiyenit 142

satellite TV f טלוויזיית לוויין televizyat lavyan 22

satin m סטין satin

satisfied: I'm not ~ with this אני לא מרוצה מזה ani lo merutze mize

Saturday שבת shabat 218

sauce m רוטב rotev 38

sauna f סאונה sauna 22

sausage m נקניק naknik 160

say: how do you ~ ...? ...? איך אומרים eykh omrim

scarf m צעיף tza-_if_ 144, 154

scheduled flight f טיסה מתוכננת _tisa metukhnenet_

sciatica f נשית _nashit_ 165

scissors mpl מספריים _misparayim_ 148

scooter m קטנוע _katno-a_

Scotland סקוטלנד _skotland_ 119

screwdriver m מברג _mavreg_ 148

sea m ים _yam_ 107; **~front** חוף טיילת _tayelet khof_; **~sick: I feel seasick** יש לי מחלת-ים _yesh li makhalat yam_

season ticket m כרטיס מנוי _kartis manuy_

seat (on train, etc.) m מושב _moshav_ 74, 76

second שני _sheni_ 132, 217; **~ floor** (U.K.: first floor) f קומה ראשונה _koma rishona_; **~hand** יד שניה _yad shniya_

secretary f מזכירה _mazkira_

sedative f תרופת הרגעה _trufat harga-a_

see, to לראות _lir-ot_ 18, 24, 37, 93, 124; **~ you soon!** להתראות בקרוב! _lehitra-ot bekarov_ 126

self-employed: to be ~ להיות עצמאי _lihiyot atzma-i_ 121

self-service (gas station) שרות עצמי _sherut atzmi_ 87

sell, to למכור _limkor_ 133

send, to לשלוח _lishlo-akh_ 153

senior citizen m קשיש _kashish_ 74, 100

separated: to be ~ לחיות בנפרד _likhyot benifrad_ 120

separately בנפרד _benifrad_ 42

September ספטמבר _september_ 218

serious רציני _retzini_

service (in restaurant) m שרות _sherut_ 42; (prayer) f תפילה _tfila_ 105

serviette f מפית _mapit_ 39

set menu m תפריט קבוע _tafrit kavu-a_ 37

shade (color) m גוון _gavan_ 143; (out of the sun) m צל _tzel_

shallow רדוד _radud_

shampoo m שמפו _shampu_ 142; **~ and set** mpl חפיפה וסידור _khafifa vesidur_ 147

share, to (room) להתחלק _lehitkhalek_

sharp חד _khad_ 69

shaving: ~ brush f מברשת גילוח _mivreshet gilu-akh_; **~ cream** f משחת גילוח _mishkhat gilu-akh_

she היא _hi_

sheath (contraceptive) m קונדום _kondom_

sheet (bed) m סדין _sadin_ 28

shekel m שקל _shekel_ 67

shipping m שייט _shayit_ 81

shirt (men's) f חולצה (לגברים) _khultza (ligvarim)_ 144

shock (electric) m מכת חשמל _makat khashmal_

shoe: shoes fpl נעליים _na-alayim_ 145; **~ repair** m תיקון נעליים _tikun na-alayim_; **~ store [shop]** f חנות נעליים _khanut na-alayim_ 131

shop f חנות _khanut_; **~ assistant** m מוכר _mokher_

shopping: to go ~ ללכת לקניות _lalekhet likniyot_; **~ area** m איזור קניות _ezor kniyot_ 99; **~ basket** m סל קניות _sal kniyot_; **~ mall [centre]** m מרכז קניות _merkaz kniyot_ 130; **~ trolley** f עגלת קניות _eglat kniyot_

short (person) נמוך _namukh_ 14; (object) קצר _katzar_ 144, 146, 147

shorts mpl מכנסיים קצרים _mikhnasayim ktzarim_ 144

shoulder f כתף _katef_ 166

shovel f את et 155

show, to להראות lehar-ot 18, 94, 134;
can you ~ me? תוכל להראות לי?
tukhal lehar-ot li 106

shower f מקלחת miklakhat 21;
showers fpl מקלחות miklakhot 30;
~ room חדר מקלחת khadar
miklakhat 26

shut (adj.) סגור sagur 14

shut, to לסגור lisgor 132; **when do
you ~?** מתי אתם סוגרים? matay atem
sogrim

shutter m תריס tris 25

sick: I'm going to be ~ אני עומד להקיא
ani omed lehaki

side: ~ street רחוב צדדי rekhov
tzdadi 95; **at the sides** בצדדים
batzdadim 147

sights mpl אתרי תיירות atarey tayarut

sightseeing: to go ~
לסייר באתרי תיירות lesayer be-atarey
tayarut; **~ tour** m סיור מאורגן siyur
me-urgan 97

sign (road sign) m שלט shelet 93, 95;
~post m שלט דרכים shelet drakhim

silk m משי meshi

silver m כסף kesef 149

silver plate m ציפוי כסף tzipuy
kesef 149

singer m זמר zamar 155

single (ticket) בכיוון אחד bekivun
ekhad 65, 74; **~ room** m חדר ליחיד
kheder leyakhid 21; **to be ~**
להיות רווק lihiyot ravak 120

sink m כיור kiyor 25

sister f אחות akhot 120

sit, to לשבת lashevet 36, 76, 126;
~ down, please שב, בבקשה shev
bevakasha

size (clothes) מידה mida 146

skin m עור or 166

skirt f חצאית
khatza-it 144

sleep, to לישון
lishon 167

sleeping: ~ bag m
שק שינה sak sheyna 31; **~ pill**
f גלולת שינה glulat sheyna

sleeve m שרוול sharvul 144

slice: a ~ of ... ... פרוסת prusat 40

slippers mpl נעלי בית na-aley
bayit 145

slow איטי iti 14; (of clock) מפגר
mefager 221; **~ down!** יותר לאט!
yoter le-at; **slowly** לאט le-at 11, 17,
94, 128

SLR camera f מצלמת רפלקס matzlemat
refleks 151

small קטן katan 14, 24, 40, 110, 134;
~ change m כסף קטן kesef katan
138; **smaller** יותר קטן yoter katan 134

smell: there's a bad ~ יש ריח רע yesh
re-akh ra

smoke, to לעשן le-ashen 126

smoking (adj.) מעשן me-ashen 36

snack bar m מזנון miznon 73

snacks mpl חטיפים khatifim

sneakers fpl נעלי התעמלות na-aley
hit-amlut

snorkel m שנורקל shnorkel

snow m שלג sheleg 122

soap m סבון sabon 27, 142;
~ powder f אבקת סבון avkat sabon

soccer m כדורגל kaduregel 115

socket m שקע sheka

socks mpl גרביים garbayim 144

soft drink m משקה קל mashke kal
110, 157

sole (shoes) f סוליה sulya

soloist m סולן solan 111

soluble aspirin m אספירין נמס aspirin
names

some כמה *kama*

something משהו *mashehu* 16; **~ to eat** m משהו לאכול *mashehu le-ekhol* 70

sometimes לפעמים *lif-amim* 13

son m בן *ben* 120, 162

soon בקרוב *bekarov* 13

sore: ~ throat כאב גרון *ke-ev garon* 141, 163; **it's ~** זה כואב *ze ko-ev*

sorry! *(apology)* סליחה! *slikha* 10

soul music f מוסיקת נשמה *musikat neshama* 111

sour חמוץ *khamutz* 41

South Africa דרום אפריקה *drom afrika* 119

south דרום *darom* 95

souvenir f מזכרת *mazkeret* 98, 154

souvenir: ~ guide m מדריך למזכרת *madrikh lemazkeret* 154; **~ store** f חנות מזכרות *khanut mazkarot* 131

space m מקום *makom* 30

spade f את *et* 155

spare רזרבי *rezervi* 28

speak, to לדבר *ledaber* 11, 18, 41, 67, 128; **to ~ to someone** לדבר עם מישהו *ledaber im mishehu* 128; **do you ~ English?** אתה מדבר [את מדברת] אנגלית? *ata medaber [at medaberet] anglit* 11

special מיוחד *meyukhad* 86; **~ delivery** f מסירה מיוחדת *mesira meyukhedet* 153

specialist m מומחה *mumkhe* 164

specimen f דגימה *dgima* 164

spectacles mpl משקפיים *mishkafayim*

spend, to *(money)* להוציא *lehotzi*

spicy מתובל *metubal*

sponge m ספוג *sfog* 148

spoon f כף *kaf* 39, 41; **spoons** fpl כפות *kapot* 148

sport m ספורט *sport* 121

sporting goods store f חנות למוצרי ספורט *khanut lemutzrey sport* 131

sports: ~ club m מועדון ספורט *mo-adon sport* 115; **~ ground** m מגרש ספורט *migrash sport* 96

spot *(place)* שטח *shetakh* 31

sprained: to be ~ להיות נקוע *lihiyot naku-a* 164

spring m אביב *aviv* 219

square מרובע *meruba* 134

stadium m אצטדיון *itztadyon* 96

staff m צוות *tzevet* 113

stain m כתם *ketem*

stainless steel f פלדת אלחלד *pildat alkheled* 149

stairs fpl מדרגות *madregot* 132

stamp m בול *bul* 152; **stamps** mpl בולים *bulim* 150

stand: to ~ in line לעמוד בתור *la-amod bator* 112

standby ticket כרטיס כוננות *kartis konenut*

start, to *(car)* להתניע *lehatni-a* 88, 108, 112

statement *(to police)* f הודעה *hoda-a* 93

stationer's f חנות למכשירי כתיבה *khanut lemakhshirey ktiva*

statue m פסל *pesel* 99

stay, to *(remain)* להישאר *lehisha-er* 23, 65; *(in hotel, campsite, etc.)* לשהות *lishhot* 123

steak house f מסעדת סטייקים *mis-adat stekim* 35

sterilizing solution f תמיסת חיטוי *tmisat khituy* 142

stiff neck m צוואר נוקשה *tzavar nukshe*

still: I'm ~ waiting אני עדיין מחכה *ani adayin mekhake*

stockings mpl גרבי נשים *garbey nashim* 144

stolen, to be להיגנב *lehiganev* 71, 160

stomach m קיבה *keyva* 166; **~ache** m כאב בטן *ke-ev beten* 163

stool (faeces) f צואה *tzo-a* 164

stop, to לעצור *la-atzor* 77, 98; (bus, etc.) f תחנה *takhana* 80

stopcock m ברז ראשי *berez rashi* 28

store guide m לוח מידע *lu-akh meyda* 132

stormy: to be ~ להיות סוער *lihiyot so-er* 122

stove m תנור בישול *tanur bishul* 28

straight ahead ישר קדימה *yashar kadima* 95

strained muscle m שריר מתוח *shrir matu-akh* 162

strange מוזר *muzar* 101

straw (drinking) f קשית *kashit*

strawberry f תות שדה *tut sade* 40

stream m נחל *nakhal* 107

strong (potent) חזק *khazak*

student m סטודנט *student* 74, 100, 121

study, to ללמוד *lilmod* 121

style m סגנון *signon* 104

subtitled: to be ~ עם תרגום בגוף הסרט *im tirgum beguf haseret* 110

subway (metro) f רכבת תחתית *rakevet takhtit* 80; **~ map** f מפת קווים *mapat kavim* 80

sugar m סוכר *sukar* 38

suit f חליפה *khalifa* 144

suitable מתאים *mat-im* 140; **~ for** מתאים ל... *mat-im le*

summer m קיץ *kayitz* 219

sun f שמש *shemesh*; **~ block** m חוסם קרינה *khosem krina* 142; **to ~bathe** להשתזף *lehishtazef*; **~burn** f כוויית שמש *kviyat shemesh* 141; **~glasses** mpl משקפי שמש *mishkafey shemesh*; **~shade** f שמשיה *shimshiya* 116; **~stroke** f מכת שמש *makat shemesh* 163; **~tan lotion** משחת שיזוף *mishkhat shizuf* 142

sunny: to be ~ השמש זורחת *hashemesh zorakhat* 122

Sunday m יום ראשון *yom rishon* 218

super (gasoline) אוקטן גבוה *oktan gavoha* 87

superb נהדר *nehedar* 101

supermarket m סופרמרקט *supermarket* 131, 156

supervision f השגחה *hashgakha* 113

supplement m היטל *hetel* 68, 69

suppositories mpl נרות *nerot* 165

sure: are you ~? אתה בטוח? *ata batu-akh*

surfboard m גלשן *galshan* 116

surname m שם משפחה *shem mishpakha*

sweater m סודר *sudar* 144

sweatshirt f חולצת מיזע *khultzat meyza* 144

sweet (taste) מתוק *matok*

sweets (candy) ממתקים *mamtakim* 150

swelling f נפיחות *nefikhut* 162

swim, to לשחות *liskhot* 116; **~suit** m בגד ים לנשים *beged yam lenashim* 144

swimming f שחייה *skhiya* 115; **~ pool** f בריכת שחייה *brekhat skhiya* 22, 26, 116; **~ trunks** בגד ים לגברים *beged yam ligvarim* 144

swollen נפוח *nafu-akh*

symptom (illness) mpl סימני מחלה simaney makhala 163

synagogue m בית כנסת beyt kneset 99, 105

synthetic סינטטי sinteti 145

T **T-shirt** חולצת טי khultzat ti 144, 154

table m שולחן shulkhan 36, 112

take, to לקחת lakakhat 24, 71, 140, 165; (require) להצטרך lehitztarekh 86; (time) להימשך lehimashekh 77; **to ~ away** לקחת lakakhat 40; **to ~ out** להוציא lehotzi 168; **to ~ photographs** לצלם letzalem 98, 100; **I'll ~ it** אקח אותו ekakh oto 24; **is this seat taken?** המקום הזה תפוס hamakom haze tafus 76; **~ me to ...** קח אותי ל... kakh oti le 84

talk, to לדבר ledaber

tall גבוה gavoha 14

tampons mpl טמפונים tamponim 142

tan שיזוף shizuf

tap ברז berez 25

taxi f מונית monit 32, 70, 71, 84; **~ stand [rank]** תחנת מוניות takhanat moniyot 96

tea m תה te 40; **~ bags** fpl שקיות תה sakiyot te 160; **~ towel** f מגבת מטבח magevet mitbakh 154

teacher m מורה more

team f קבוצה kvutza 114

teaspoons fpl כפיות kapiyot 148

teddy bear m דובי dubi 155

telephone m טלפון telefon 22, 92; **~ bill** חשבון טלפון kheshbon telefon 32; **~ booth** f תא טלפון ta telefon 127; **~ call** f שיחת טלפון sikhat telefon 32; **~ number** m מספר טלפון mispar telefon 127

tell: to ~ לומר lomar 18; **can you ~ me ...?** ?...תוכל לומר לי tukhal lomar li 79

temperature f טמפרטורה temperatura 164

temple m מקדש mikdash 105

temporarily זמנית zmanit 168

tennis m טניס tenis 115; **~ court** m מגרש טניס migrash tenis 115

tent m אוהל ohel 30, 31; **~ pegs** fpl יתדות yetedot 31; **~ pole** m עמוד לאוהל amud le-ohel 31

terrace f מרפסת mirpeset 35

terrible נורא nora 19, 101, 122

terrific נהדר nehedar 19

tetanus m טטנוס tetanus 164

thank you תודה toda 10

that: ~ one ההוא hahu 16, 134, 157; **~'s true** זה נכון ze nakhon 19; **~'s all** זה הכל ze hakol 133

theater m תיאטרון te-atron 96, 99, 110, 111

theft f גניבה gneva 160

their/theirs שלהם shelahem 16

theme park m פארק שעשועים נושאי park sha-ashu-im temati

then (time) אז az 13

there שם sham 12; **~ isn't/aren't ...** אין ... eyn 17; **over ~** שם sham 76

thermometer m מדחום madkhom

thermos flask m בקבוק תרמוס bakbuk termos

these אלה ele 134; 157

they הם hem

thief m גנב ganav

thigh m ירך yerekh 166

thin (person) רזה raze; (soup) דליל dalil; (string) דק dak

think: I think ... ... אני חושב ani khoshev 42; **to ~ about something** לחשוב על משהו lakhshov al mashehu 135

third שלישי *shlishi* 217

third party insurance m
ביטוח צד שלישי *bitu-akh tzad shlishi*

thirsty: I am ~ אני צמא *ani tzame*

this זה *ze* 84, 218; **~ one** זה *ze* 16, 134, 157; **~ evening** הערב *ha-erev* 36

those ההם *hahem* 134, 157

thousand אלף *elef* 217

throat m גרון *garon* 166

thrombosis f פקקת *pakeket*

through דרך *derekh*

thumb m אגודל *agudal* 166

Thursday יום חמישי *yom khamishi* 218

ticket m כרטיס *kartis* 65, 68, 69, 73, 74, 79, 80, 81, 100, 109, 114, 160; **tickets** mpl כרטיסים *kartisim* 108; **~ office** f קופה *kupa* 73

tie f עניבה *aniva* 144

tight הדוק *haduk* 146

tights mpl גרבונים *garbonim* 144

till: ~ receipt קבלת קופה *kabalat kupa*

time m זמן *zman* 32; **is it on ~?** הוא עומד בלוח הזמנים? *hu omed belu-akh hazmanim* 75; **free ~** m זמן חופשי *zman khofshi* 98; **what's the ~?** מה השעה? *ma hasha-a* 220; **~table** m לוח זמנים *lu-akh zmanim* 75

tin opener m פותחן קופסאות *potkhan kufsa-ot* 148

tire (on wheel) m צמיג *tzamig* 83

tired: I'm ~ אני עייף *ani ayef*

tissue f מטפחת נייר *mitpakhat neyar* 142

to (place) ל- *le/la/li* 12

tobacco m טבק *tabak* 150

tobacconist m חנות למוצרי טבק *khanut lemutzrey tabak* 130

today היום *hayom* 89, 124, 218

toe m/f בוהן *bohen* 166

toilet m בית שימוש *beyt shimush* 25, 98, 113; **toilets** mpl שרותים *sherutim* 26, 29, 77; **~ paper** m נייר טואלט *neyar to-alet* 25, 142

tomatoes fpl עגבניות *agvaniyot* 157

tomb m קבר *kever* 99

tomorrow מחר *makhar* 36, 84, 122, 124, 218

tongue m לשון *lashon* 166

tonight הערב *ha-erev* 108, 124

tonsils mpl שקדים *shkedim* 166

tonsilitis f דלקת שקדים *daleket shkedim* 165

too (extreme) מדי *miday* 17, 41, 93, 135; **~ much** יותר מדי *yoter miday* 15, 146

tooth f שן *shen* 168; **~brush** f מברשת שיניים *mivreshet shinayim*; **~ache** m כאב שיניים *ke-ev shinayim*; **~paste** f משחת שיניים *mishkhat shinayim* 142

top (of head) למעלה *lema-la* 147

torch m פנס *panas* 31

torn: to be ~ להיות קרוע *lihiyot karu-a* 164; **this is ~** זה קרוע *ze karu-a*

tough (food) קשה *kashe* 41

tour m טיול *tiyul* 98; **~ guide** m מדריך טיולים *madrikh tiyulim* 27; **~ operator** f חברת נסיעות *khevrat nesi-ot* 26

tourist m תייר *tayar*; **~ office** m מודיעין לתיירים *modi-in letayarim* 97

tow truck m רכב גורר *rekhev gorer* 88

towards לכיוון *lekivun* 12

towel f מגבת *magevet*

tower m מגדל *migdal* 99

town f עיר *ir* 94; **~ center** m מרכז העיר *merkaz ha-ir* 83; **~ hall** f עירייה *iriya* 99

toy m צעצוע *tza-atzu-a* 155; **~ store** f חנות צעצועים *khanut tza-atzu-im* 131

traffic f תנועה *tnu-a*; **~ jam** m פקק תנועה *pkak tnu-a*; **~ light** m רמזור *ramzor* 95; **~ violation [offence]** f עבירת תנועה *averat tnu-a*

trailer m קרוון *karavan* 30, 81

train m רכבת *rakevet* 13, 73, 74, 76, 123; **~ station** f תחנת רכבת *takhanat rakevet* 72, 84, 96

trained מיומן *meyuman* 113

transfer f העברה *ha-avara*

transit: in ~ במעבר *bema-avar*

translate, to לתרגם *letargem* 11

translation m תרגום *targum*

translator m מתרגם *metargem*

trashcans mpl פחי אשפה *pakhey ashpa* 30

travel: ~ agency f סוכנות נסיעות *sokhnut nesi-ot* 131; **~ sickness** f מחלת נסיעה *makhalat nesi-a* 141

traveler's check [cheque] f המחאת נוסעים *hamkha-at nos-im* 136, 138

tray m מגש *magash*

tree m עץ *etz* 106

trim m תיקון *tikun* 147

trip m נסיעה *nesi-a* 76, 77

trolley f עגלה *agala* 156

trousers mpl מכנסיים *mikhnasayim* 144

truck f משאית *masa-it*

true: that's not ~ זה לא נכון *ze lo nakhon*

try: to ~ on (clothes) למדוד *limdod* 146

Tuesday יום שלישי *yom shlishi* 218

tumor m גידול *gidul* 165

tunnel f מנהרה *minhara*

turn: to ~ down (volume, heat) להוריד *lehorid*; **to ~ off** לכבות *lekhabot* 25; **to ~ on** להדליק *lehadlik* 25; **to ~ up** (volume, heat) להגביר *lehagbir*

TV f טלוויזיה *televizya* 22

tweezers m מלקט *malket*

twice פעמיים *pa-amayim* 217; **~ a day** פעמיים ביום *pa-amayim beyom* 76

twin beds fpl מיטות נפרדות *mitot nifradot* 21

twist: I've twisted my ankle סובבתי את הקרסול *sovavti et hakrsol*

two-door car f מכונית עם שתי דלתות *mekhonit im shtey dlatot* 86

type m סוג *sug* 109; **what ~ of ...?** איזה סוג ...? *eyze sug* 112

typical אופייני *ofyani* 37

tyre m צמיג *tzamig* 83

U U.S. ארה"ב הברית *artztot habrit*

ugly מכוער *mekho-ar* 14, 101

ulcer m כיב *kiv*

umbrella (sunshade) f שמשיה *shimshiya* 116

uncle m דוד *dod* 120

unconscious: to be ~ להיות ללא הכרה *lihiyot lelo hakara* 92; **he's ~** הוא ללא הכרה *hu lelo hakara* 162

under מתחת *mitakhat*

underdone מבושל פחות מדי *mevushal pakhot miday* 41

underpants mpl תחתונים *takhtonim* 144

understand: to ~ להבין *lehavin* 11; **do you ~?** אתה מבין? *ata mevin* 11; **I don't ~** אני לא מבין *ani lo mevin* 11, 67

undress, to להתפשט *lehitpashet* 164

uneven לא ישר *lo yashar* 31

unfortunately למרבה הצער *lemarbe hatza-ar* 19

uniform mpl מדים *madim*

unit f יחידה yekhida 153

United States ארצות הברית artzot habrit 119

unleaded נטול עופרת netul oferet; **~ gas [petrol]** m דלק נטול עופרת delek netul oferet

unlimited mileage m קילומטראז' לא מוגבל kilometrazh lo mugbal

unlock, to לפתוח מנעול lifto-akh man-ul

unpleasant לא נעים lo na-im 14

unscrew, to לפתוח הברגה lifto-akh havraga

until עד ad 221

up to עד ל- ad le/la/li 12

upset: ~ stomach m קלקול קיבה kilkul keyva 141

urine f שתן sheten 164

use, to להשתמש ב... lehishtamesh be 139; **for my personal ~** לשימושי האישי leshimushi ha-ishi 67

utensils m סכו"ם sakum 29

V

V-neck וי צווארון tzavaron vi 144

vacant פנוי panuy 14

vacation f חופשה khufsha 123; **on ~** לחופשה lekhufsha 66

vaccinated: to be ~ against להיות מחוסן נגד lihiyot mekhusan neged 164

vaginal infection m זיהום בנרתיק zihum banartik 167

valid בתוקף betokef 74

validate, to לאמת le-amet

valley m עמק emek 107

valuable יקר-ערך yekar erekh

valve (stopcock) m ברז ראשי berez rashi 28

vanilla (flavor) וניל vanil 40

VAT מע"מ ma-am 24; **~ receipt** f קבלת מע"מ kabalat ma-am

vegan (adj.) טבעוני tiv-oni

vegetables mpl ירקות yerakot 38

vegetarian צמחוני tzimkhoni 35, 39

vein m וריד varid 166

venereal disease f מחלת מין makhalat min 165

ventilator m מאוורר me-avrer

very מאד me-od 17; **~ good** טוב מאד tov me-od 19

video: ~ cassette f קלטת וידאו kaletet vide-o 155; **~ game** m משחק וידאו miskhak vide-o; **~ recorder** m מכשיר וידאו makhshir vide-o

view: with a ~ of the sea עם תצפית על הים im tatzpit al hayam; **~point** f נקודת תצפית nekudat tatzpit 99, 107

village m כפר kfar 107

vinaigrette m רוטב חומץ rotev khometz 38

vinegar m חומץ khometz 38

vineyard m כרם kerem 107

visa f אשרה ashra

visit (noun) m ביקור bikur 119

visit, to לבקר levaker 123, 167

visiting hours fpl שעות ביקור she-ot bikur

vitamin tablet f גלולת ויטמין glulat vitamin 141

volleyball m כדורעף kadur-af 115

voltage m מתח metakh

vomit, to להקיא lehaki 163; **I've been vomiting** אני סובל מהקאות ani sovel mehaka-ot 163

W

wait, to לחכות lekhakot 36, 41, 140; **to ~ for** לחכות ל... lekhakot le 76, 89; **wait!** חכה! khake 98

waiter m מלצר meltzar 37

waiting room m חדר המתנה khadar hamtana 73

A-Z

waitress f מלצרית *meltzarit* 37

wake: to ~ someone להעיר *leha-ir* 27, 70

wake-up call f קריאת השכמה *kri-at hashkama*

Wales וויילס *weyls* 119

walk: to ~ home ללכת הביתה *lalekhet habayta* 65

walking: ~ boots mpl נעלי הליכה *na-aley halikha* 145; **~ route** m מסלול הליכה *maslul halikha* 106

wallet m ארנק *arnak* 42, 160

ward (hospital) f מחלקה *makhlaka* 167

warm חם *kham* 14, 122; **warmer** יותר חם *yoter kham* 24

washbasin m כיור *kiyor*

washing: ~ machine f מכונת כביסה *mekhonat kvisa* 29; **~ powder** f אבקת כביסה *avkat kvisa* 148; **~-up liquid** m סבון נוזלי *sabon nozli* 148

wasp f צירעה *tzir-a*

watch m שעון יד *she-on yad* 149, 160

water mpl מים *mayim* 87; **~ bottle** m בקבוק מים *bakbuk mayim*; **~ heater** m דוד הסקה *dud hasaka* 28; **~ skis** m סקי מים *ski mayim* 116; **~fall** m מפל מים *mapal mayim* 107

waterproof חסין-מים *khasin mayim*; **~ jacket** m אנורק *anorak* 145

wave m גל *gal*

waxing f שעווה *sha-ava* 147

way: I've lost my ~ תעיתי בדרך *ta-iti baderekh* 94; **it's on the ~ to ...** זה בדרך ל... *ze baderekh le* 83

we אנחנו *anakhnu*

wear, to ללבוש *lilbosh* 159

weather m מזג אוויר *mezeg avir* 122; **~ forecast** f תחזית מזג האוויר *takhazit mezeg ha-avir* 122

wedding f חתונה *khatuna*; **~ ring** f טבעת נישואים *taba-at nisu-im*

Wednesday יום רביעי *yom revi-i* 218

week m שבוע *shavu-a* 23, 97, 218

weekend m סוף שבוע *sof shavu-a* 218; **~ rate** m תעריף לסוף שבוע *ta-arif lesof shavu-a* 86

weight: my ~ is... ... משקלי *mishkali*

welcome to ... ברוכים הבאים ל... *brukhim haba-im le*

well f באר *be-er* 99

well-done (steak) צלוי היטב *tzaluy heytev*

west מערב *ma-arav* 95

wetsuit f חליפת צלילה *khalifat tzlila*

what? מה? *ma* 94, 104; **~ kind of ...?** איזה סוג של...? *eyze sug shel* 37, 106; **~ time ...?** באיזו שעה ...? *be-eyzo sha-a* 68, 76, 78, 81

wheelchair m כסא גלגלים *kise galgalim*

when? מתי? *matay* 13, 68, 77, 104

where? איפה? *eyfo* 12, 73, 76, 77, 84, 88, 98; **~ is the ...?** איפה ה...? *eyfo ha* 80, 94, 99; **~ were you born?** איפה נולדת? *eyfo noladeta* 119

which? איזה? *eyze* 16

white לבן *lavan* 143; **~ wine** m יין לבן *yayin lavan* 40

who? מי? *mi* 16, 104

whose? של מי? *shel mi* 16

why? מדוע? *madu-a* 14; **why not?** מדוע לא? *madu-a lo* 14

wife f אשה *isha* 120, 162

wildlife fpl חיות בר *khayot bar*

windbreaker m מעיל רוח *me-il ru-akh* 145

window m חלון *khalon* 25, 76, 134, 149; **~ seat** m מושב ליד החלון *moshav leyad hakhalon* 69

windshield [windscreen] f שימשה קדמית *shimsha kidmit* 90

windy: to be ~ נושבת רוח *noshevet ru-akh* 122

wine m יין *yayin* 40, 160; **~ list** m תפריט יינות *tafrit yeynot* 37

winery m יקב *yekev* 107

winter m חורף *khoref* 219

wishes: best ~ מיטב האיחולים *meytav ha-ikhulim* 219

with עם *im* 17

withdraw, to למשוך *limshokh* 139

within (time) תוך *tokh* 13

without בלי *bli* 17, 38, 141

witness m עד *ed* 93

woman f אישה *isha*

wood f חורשה *khorsha* 107

wool m צמר *tzemer* 145

work, to (operate) לפעול *lif-ol* 28, 83; **it doesn't ~** זה לא פועל *ze lo po-el* 25, 137

worse יותר גרוע *yoter garu-a* 14; **worst** הגרוע ביותר *hagaru-a beyoter*

write: to ~ down לכתוב *likhtov* 136

writing paper m נייר כתיבה *neyar ktiva* 150

wrong (faulty) לא בסדר *lo beseder* 88; (incorrect) לא נכון *lo nakhon* 95, 136; **~ number** m מספר לא נכון *mispar lo nakhon* 128; **there's something ~ with ...** משהו לא בסדר עם ... *mashehu lo beseder im*

X Y Z x-ray m צילום רנטגן *tzilum rentgen* 164

yacht f יאכטה *yakhta*

year f שנה *shana* 119, 218

yellow צהוב *tzahov* 143

yes כן *ken* 10

yesterday אתמול *etmol* 218

yogurt m יוגורט *yogurt* 160

you m/f אתה/את *ata/at*

young צעיר *tza-ir* 14

your(s) (sing./pl.) שלך/שלכם *shelkha/shelakhem* 16

youth hostel f אכסניית נוער *akhsaniyat no-ar* 29, 123

zebra crossing m מעבר להולכי רגל *ma-avar leholkhey regel*

zero m אפס *efes*

zip(per) m רוכסן *rokhsan*

zoo m גן חיות *gan khayot* 113

Glossary
Hebrew–English

This Hebrew-English glossary covers all the areas where you may need to decode written Hebrew: hotels, public buildings, restaurants, stores, ticket offices, airports, and bus and train stations. The Hebrew is written in large type to help you identify the word(s) from the signs you see around you.

General כללי

שמאל	smol	LEFT
ימין	ya<u>min</u>	RIGHT
כניסה	kni<u>sa</u>	ENTRANCE
יציאה	yetzi-<u>a</u>	EXIT
שרותים	sheru<u>tim</u>	TOILETS
גברים	gva<u>rim</u>	MEN (TOILETS)
נשים	na<u>shim</u>	WOMEN (TOILETS)
אסור לעשן	a<u>sur</u> le-a<u>shen</u>	NO SMOKING
סכנה	sa<u>kana</u>	DANGER
אין כניסה	eyn kni<u>sa</u>	NO ENTRY
משוך/דחוף	me<u>shokh</u>/de<u>khof</u>	PULL/PUSH

General כללי

חפצים אבודים	khafa*tzim* avu*dim*	LOST PROPERTY
אסור לשחות	*asur* lis*khot*	NO SWIMMING
מי שתיה	mey shti*ya*	DRINKING WATER
שטח פרטי	*shetakh* pra*ti*	PRIVATE
שריפה	*srefa*	FIRE
אין להשליך אשפה	eyn lehash-*likh* ash*pa*	NO LITTERING
אין לדרוך על הדשא	eyn lid*rokh* al ha*de*she	KEEP OFF THE GRASS
זהירות מדרגה	zehi*rut* madre*ga*	WATCH YOUR STEP
צבע טרי	*tzeva tari*	WET PAINT
מחלקה ראשונה	makhla*ka* risho*na*	FIRST CLASS
מחלקה שניה	makhla*ka* shni*ya*	SECOND CLASS

שילוט בדרכים Road signs

עצור	_atzor_	STOP
סע בצד ימין	sa be<u>tzad</u> ya<u>min</u>	KEEP RIGHT
סע בצד שמאל	sa be<u>tzad</u> smol	KEEP LEFT
דרך חד סטרית	<u>de</u>rekh khad sit<u>rit</u>	ONE WAY
אין עקיפה	eyn aki<u>fa</u>	NO PASSING
אין חניה	eyn khana<u>ya</u>	NO PARKING
דרך מהירה	<u>de</u>rekh mehi<u>ra</u>	HIGHWAY [MOTORWAY]
רמזור	ram<u>zor</u>	TRAFFIC LIGHT
צומת	<u>tzo</u>met	INTERSECTION
האט	ha-<u>et</u>	SLOW

מודיעין	modi-*in*	INFORMATION
רציף 1	rat*zif* e*khad*	PLATFORM 1
שער 1	sha-ar e*khad*	GATE 1
מכס	me*khes*	CUSTOMS
עליה	ali*ya*	IMMIGRATION
באים	ba-*im*	ARRIVALS
יוצאים	yotz-*im*	DEPARTURES
שמירת חפצים	shmi*rat* khafat*zim*	LUGGAGE LOCKERS
קבלת מזודות	kaba*lat* mizva*dot*	BAGGAGE CLAIM
אוטובוס/רכבת	*oto*bus/ra*ke*vet	BUS/TRAIN
שכירת מכוניות	skhi*rat* mekhoni*yot*	CAR RENTAL

מודיעין	modi-_in_	INFORMATION
קבלה	kaba_la_	RECEPTION
שמור	sha_mur_	RESERVED
יציאת חרום	yetzi-_at_ khe_rum_	EMERGENCY EXIT
חם	kham	HOT
קר	kar	COLD
לעובדים בלבד	le-ov_dim_ bil_vad_	STAFF ONLY
מלתחה	melta_kha_	COATCHECK [CLOAKROOM]
מרפסת/גן	mir_peset_/gan	TERRACE/GARDEN
בר	bar	BAR

Stores חנויות

פתוח	patu-akh	OPEN
סגור	sagur	CLOSED
ארוחת צהריים	arukhat tzohorayim	LUNCH
מחלקת ...	makhleket	... DEPARTMENT
קומה	koma	FLOOR
קומת מרתף	komat martef	BASEMENT
מעלית	ma-alit	ELEVATOR [LIFT]
מדרגות נעות	madregot na-ot	ESCALATOR
קופה	kupa	CASHIER
מכירה	mekhira	SALE

הכניסה חינם	haknisa khinam	FREE ADMISSION
מבוגרים	mevugarim	ADULTS
ילדים	yeladim	CHILDREN
הנחות	hanakhot	CONCESSIONS
סטודנטים/ גימלאים	studentim/ gimla-im	STUDENTS/ SENIOR CITIZENS
מזכרות	mazkarot	SOUVENIRS
מזנון	miznon	REFRESHMENTS
לא לגעת	lo laga-at	DO NOT TOUCH
אסור לצלם	asur letzalem	NO PHOTOGRAPHY
שקט	sheket	SILENCE
אין מעבר	eyn ma-avar	DO NOT ENTER

Public Buildings בניני ציבור

בית חולים	*beyt kholim*	HOSPITAL
רופא	*rofe*	DOCTOR
רופא שיניים	*rofe shinayim*	DENTIST
משטרה	*mishtara*	POLICE
בנק	*bank*	BANK
דואר	*do-ar*	POST OFFICE
בריכת שחיה	*brekhat skhiya*	SWIMMING POOL
עיריה	*iriya*	TOWN HALL
תחנת מוניות	*takhanat moniyot*	TAXI STAND [RANK]
מוזאון	*muze-on*	MUSEUM

Numbers

GRAMMAR

1. Unlike the rest of the script, numbers are written from left to right, as in English. The same numerals and conventions are used: two point five = 2.5; one million = 1,000,000.

2. Some nouns have a special "dual" ending in Hebrew, **-ayim**, which replaces the number 2. Thus, "a week" is **shavua**; "two weeks" is **shvu-ayim**; three weeks and above is **shavu-ot**. In the case of many parts of the body, the dual is used as the general plural; thus, "a tooth" is **shen**, (any number of) "teeth" is **shinayim**.

3. Other than that, plurals are formed by using a large number of different patterns and they can sound very different from the singular, e.g. **ir** (town)/**arim** (towns).

4. Large numbers are built up in similar fashion to English, e.g., 1998 is **elef t'sha me-ot tish-im ushmone** = (one) thousand, nine hundred, ninety, and eight.

0	אפס	_efes_	10	עשרה	_asara_
1	אחד	_ekhad_	11	אחד עשר	_akhad asar_
2	שניים	_shnayim_	12	שנים עשר	_shneym asar_
3	שלושה	_shlosha_	13	שלושה עשר	_shlosha asar_
4	ארבעה	_arba-a_	14	ארבעה עשר	_arba-a asar_
5	חמישה	_khamisha_	15	חמישה עשר	_khamisha asar_
6	ששה	_shisha_	16	ששה עשר	_shisha asar_
7	שבעה	_shiv-a_	17	שבעה עשר	_shiv-a asar_
8	שמונה	_shmona_	18	שמונה עשר	_shmona asar_
9	תשעה	_tish-a_	19	תשעה עשר	_tish-a asar_

20	עשרים *esrim*	1,000	אלף *elef*
21	עשרים ואחד *esrim ve-ekhad*	1,000,000	מיליון *milyon*
22	עשרים ושניים *esrim ushnayim*	first	ראשון *rishon*
23	עשרים ושלושה *esrim ushlosha*	second	שני *sheni*
24	עשרים וארבעה *esrim ve-arba-a*	third	שלישי *shlishi*
25	עשרים וחמישה *esrim vekhamisha*	fourth	רביעי *revi-i*
26	עשרים וששה *esrim veshisha*	fifth	חמישי *khamishi*
27	עשרים ושבעה *esrim veshiv-a*	once	פעם אחת *pa-am akhat*
28	עשרים ושמונה *esrim ushmona*	twice	פעמיים *pa-amayim*
29	עשרים ותשעה *esrim vetish-a*	three times	שלוש פעמים *shalosh pe-amim*
30	שלושים *shloshim*	a half	חצי *khetzi*
31	שלושים ואחד *shloshim ve-ekhad*	half an hour	חצי שעה *khatzi sha-a*
32	שלושים ושניים *shloshim ushnayim*	a quarter	רבע *reva*
40	ארבעים *arba-im*	a third	שליש *shlish*
50	חמישים *khamishim*	a pair of ...	זוג ... *zug*
60	ששים *shishim*	a dozen ...	תריסר ... *treysar*
70	שבעים *shiv-im*	1999	אלף תשע מאות תשעים ותשע *elef tsha me-ot tish-im vetesha*
80	שמונים *shmonim*		
90	תשעים *tish-im*	the 1990s	שנת התשעים *shnot hatish-im*
100	מאה *me-a*	the year 2000	שנת אלפיים *shnat alpayim*
101	מאה ואחד *me-a ve-ekhad*		
102	מאה ושניים *me-a ushnayim*	2001	אלפיים ואחת *alpayim ve-akhat*
200	מאתיים *matayim*	the millennium	האלף החדש *ha-elef hakhadash*
500	חמש מאות *khamesh me-ot*		

217

ימים Days

Sunday	יום ראשון	yom rishon
Monday	יום שני	yom sheni
Tuesday	יום שלישי	yom shlishi
Wednesday	יום רביעי	yom revi-i
Thursday	יום חמישי	yom khamishi
Friday	יום ששי	yom shishi
Saturday	שבת	shabat

חודשים Months

January	ינואר	yanu-ar
February	פברואר	febru-ar
March	מרץ, מרס	mertz, mars
April	אפריל	april
May	מאי	may
June	יוני	yuni
July	יולי	yuli
August	אוגוסט	ogust
September	ספטמבר	september
October	אוקטובר	oktober
November	נובמבר	november
December	דצמבר	detzember

תאריכים Dates

It's …	היום ...	hayom
July 10	עשירי ביולי	asiri beyuli
Tuesday, March 1	יום שלישי, אחד במרץ	yom shlishi ekhad bemertz
yesterday	אתמול	etmol
today	היום	hayom
tomorrow	מחר	makhar
this …/last …	הזה/... ... האחרון	haze/... ha-akharon
next week	השבוע הבא	hashavu-a haba
every month/year	כל חודש/שנה	kol khodesh/shana
on [at] the weekend	בסוף השבוע	besof hashavu-a

218

Seasons עונות השנה

spring	אביב	a_viv_
summer	קיץ	_kayitz_
fall [autumn]	סתיו	stav
winter	חורף	_khoref_
in spring	באביב	ba-a_viv_
during the summer	במשך הקיץ	be_me_shekh ha_kayitz_

Greetings ברכות

Happy birthday!	יום הולדת שמח!	yom hu_le_det same-akh
Happy New Year!	שנה טובה!	sha_na to_va_
Best wishes!	מיטב האיחולים!	mey_tav_ ha-ikhu_lim_
Congratulations!	מזל טוב!	_mazal_ tov
Good luck!/All the best!	בהצלחה!	behatz_lakha_
Have a good trip!	נסיעה טובה!	nesi-_a to_va_
Give my regards to …	דרישת שלום ל...	_drishat_ sha_lom_ le

Public holidays חגים

Official public holidays are those of the Jewish calendar, which starts in September/October, plus a few days of recent historical and national significance. However, this will vary in areas that are predominantly Muslim or Christian. The Gregorian calendar is used extensively alongside its Jewish equivalent, in normal business and everyday life. The Jewish months and major festivals are as follows:

Jewish month	Major Jewish/national festivals
tishre (Sep./Oct.)	1st–2nd: **Rosh Ha'Shana** (Jewish New Year)
	10th: **Yom Kippur** (Day of Atonement)
	15th–21st: **Succoth** (Tabernacles)
kheshvan (Oct./Nov.)	
kislev (Nov./Dec.)	25th kislev–2nd tevet: **Khanukah** (Hanuka)
tevet (Dec./Jan.)	
shvat (Jan./Feb.)	
adar (Feb./Mar.)	14th: **Purim** (Purim, the Feast of Lots)
nisan (Mar./Apr.)	15th–21st: **Pessakh** (Passover)
	27th: **Yom Ha'Sho'a Ve'Hagvura** (Holocaust Remembrance Day)
iyar (Apr./May)	5th: **Yom Ha'Atzma'ut** (Independence Day)
sivan (May/Jun.)	6th–7th: **Shavu'ot** (Pentecost)
tamuz (Jun./Jul.)	
av (Jul./Aug.)	9th: **Tish'a Be'Av** (Destruction of the Temple)
elul (Aug./Sep.)	

Time זמן

khamisha li... hasha-a ... ve-khamisha
asara li... ve-asara
reva li... ... vareva
esrim li... ve-esrim
esrim ve-khamisha li... ... vakhetzi ... esrim ve-khamisha

Both the 24-hour clock and the 12-hour clock are used in official contexts and in ordinary conversation, the latter often with the addition of **baboker** (in the morning), **batzohorayim** (at noon), **akharey hatzohorayim** (in the afternoon), **ba-erev** (in the evening), and **balayla** (at night) or **akharey khatzot** (after midnight).

Excuse me. Can you tell me the time?	סליחה. מה השעה?	
	slikha. ma hasha-a	
It's …	עכשיו ... *akhshav*	
five past one	אחת וחמישה *akhat vekhamisha*	
ten past two	שתיים ועשרה *shtayim ve-asara*	
a quarter past three	שלוש ורבע *shalosh vareva*	
twenty past four	ארבע ועשרים *arba ve-esrim*	
twenty-five past five	חמש עשרים וחמישה *khamesh esrim vekhamisha*	
half past six	שש וחצי *shesh vakhetzi*	
twenty-five to seven	עשרים וחמישה לשבע *esrim vekhamisha lesheva*	
twenty to eight	עשרים לשמונה *esrim lishmone*	
a quarter to nine	רבע לתשע *reva letesha*	
ten to ten	עשרה לעשר *asara le-eser*	
five to eleven	חמישה לאחת עשרה *khamisha le-akhat esre*	
twelve o'clock (noon)	שתים עשרה בצהריים *shteym esre batzohorayim*	
midnight	חצות *khatzot*	

220

at dawn	עם שחר *im shakhar*
in the morning	בבוקר *baboker*
during the day	במשך היום *bemeshekh hayom*
before lunch	לפני הצהריים *lifney hatzohorayim*
after lunch	אחרי ארוחת הצהריים *akharey arukhat hatzohorayim*
in the afternoon	אחרי הצהריים *akharey hatzohorayim*
in the evening	בערב *ba-erev*
at night	בלילה *balayla*
I'll be ready in five minutes.	אהיה מוכן תוך חמש דקות. *eheye mukhan tokh khamesh dakot*
He'll be back in a quarter of an hour.	הוא יחזור בעוד רבע שעה. *hu yakhazor be-od reva sha-a*
She arrived half an hour ago.	היא הגיעה לפני חצי שעה. *hi higi-a lifney khatzi sha-a*
The train leaves at …	הרכבת יוצאת ב... *harakevet yotzet be*
13:04	שלוש עשרה וארבע דקות *shlosh esre ve-arba dakot*
00:40	ארבעים דקות אחרי חצות *arba-im dakot akharey khatzot*
The train is 10 minutes late/early.	הרכבת מאחרת/מקדימה בעשר דקות. *harakevet me-akheret/makdima be-eser dakot*
It's 5 minutes fast/slow.	הוא ממהר/מפגר בחמש דקות. *hu memaher/mefager bekhamesh dakot*
from 9:00 to 5:00	מתשע עד חמש *mitesha ad khamesh*
between 8:00 and 2:00	בין שמונה ושתיים *beyn shmone ushtayim*
I'll be leaving by …	אעזוב לא יאוחר מ... *e-ezov lo ye-ukhar mi*
Will you be back before …?	תחזור לפני ...? *takhazor lifney*
We'll be here until …	נהיה פה עד ... *nihiye po ad*

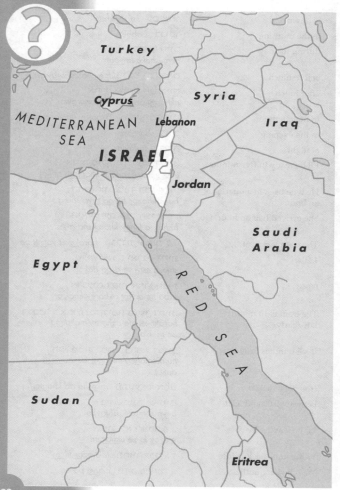

Good morning.	בוקר טוב.	_boker_ tov
Good evening.	ערב טוב.	_erev_ tov
Hello.	שלום.	sha_lom_
Good-bye.	להתראות.	lehitra-_ot_
Excuse me.	סליחה.	sli_kha_
Excuse me? [Pardon?]	סליחה?	sli_kha_
Sorry!	סליחה!	sli_kha_
Please.	בבקשה.	bevaka_sha_
Thank you.	תודה.	to_da_
Do you speak English?	אתה דובר אנגלית?	_ata_ do_ver_ anglit
I don't understand.	אני לא מבין.	_ani_ lo me_vin_
Where is …?	איפה ...?	_eyfo_
Where are the bathrooms [toilets]?	איפה השרותים?	_eyfo_ hasheru_tim_

Emergency   חרום

Help!	הצילו!	ha_tzilu_
Go away!	לך מפה!	lekh mipo
Leave me alone!	עזוב אותי!	a_zov_ oti
Call the police!	הזעק משטרה!	haz-_ek_ mishtara
Stop thief!	גנב!	ga_nav_
Get a doctor!	קרא לרופא!	kra lero_fe_
Fire!	שריפה!	sre_fa_
I'm ill.	אני חולה.	_ani_ kho_le_
I'm lost.	תעיתי בדרך.	ta-_iti_ ba_derekh_
Can you help me?	תוכל לעזור לי?	tu_khal_ la-a_zor_ li

Police ☎ 100	**Ambulance ☎ 101**	**Fire ☎ 102**

Embassies/Consulates

U.K.	Embassy:	(03) 524 9171
	Consulates:	(02) 582 8281, (03) 510 0166
U.S.A.	Embassy:	(03) 519 7575
	Consulate:	(02) 628 2452/2231
Canada	Embassy:	(03) 527 2929
	Consulate:	(03) 544 2878
Australia	Embassy:	(03) 695 0451
South Africa	Embassy:	(03) 525 2566
Ireland (Eire)	Embassy:	(03) 696 4166/7/8